Economic Sociodynamics

Ruslan Grinberg
Alexander Rubinstein

Economic Sociodynamics

With 4 Figures
and 4 Tables

 Springer

Professor Dr. Ruslan Grinberg

Russian Academy of Sciences
Institute for International Economic
and Political Studies
Novocheryomushkinskaya 46
117418 Moscow
Russian Federation
E-mail: grinberg@transecon.ru

Professor Dr. Alexander Rubinstein

Russian Academy of Sciences
Institute for Social Economy
and State Institute of Arts
Kozitsky per. 5
103099 Moscow
Russian Federation
E-mail: aleshon@transecon.ru

Library of Congress Control Number: 2004116522

ISBN 3-540-23754-2   Springer Berlin Heidelberg New York

Springer is a part of Springer Science+Business Media
springeronline.com

© Springer-Verlag Berlin Heidelberg 2005
Printed in Germany

Cover design: Erich Kirchner
Production: Helmut Petri
Printing: Strauss Offsetdruck

SPIN 11342762   Printed on acid-free paper – 43/3130 – 5 4 3 2 1 0

Contents

Introduction 1

1 To the Reducibility Hypothesis 11
   1.1 Origins 14
   1.2 The Reducibility of Needs in Theories of Well-Being 17
   1.3 Reducibility in the Context of Realization of Social Interest 21
   1.4 Three Fundamental Negations 27

2 Meritorics and Social Interest 33
   2.1 The Pathological Case 34
   2.2 The Weak Will of Odysseus 38
   2.3 The Irrationality of the Indigent 42
   2.4 The Reducibility of Needs in Constitutional Economics 45
   2.5 The Quasi-Irreducibility of Social Needs 50

3 The Autonomous Interest of Society 53
   3.1 The Historical Landscape 53
   3.2 Holism and Teleology 57
   3.3 Meritorics Redux 63
   3.4 The Public Interests and the State 67

4 The Principles of Economic Sociodynamics 73
   4.1 The Postulates of Economic Socio-Dynamics 74
   4.2 Equilibrium and Evolution in Economic Sociodynamics 80
   4.3 Characteristics of the Realization of Autonomous Social Interest 84
   4.4 The Sociodynamic Multiplier of Economic Growth 88

5 The Realization of Social Interest 97
   5.1 The Traditional Model of State Intervention 98
   5.2 A Neo-Pareto Analysis of the Realization of Social Interest 102
   5.3 The State and its Interests in Economic Sociodynamics 108

6 The Individual, the State and Society 117
   6.1 Between an Ideal State and the 'Hand of Providence' 120
   6.2 From an Institutional Utopia to a Realistic Model of the State 127
   6.3 The State and Social Immunity 132

7 The Rational Behavior of the State **137**
  7.1 The Principle of Minority Support 138
  7.2 Realization of State Powers and the Principle of Correspondence 145
  7.3 The State in Market Exchange 153

8 Instead of a Conclusion… **159**

9 Economic Sociodynamics: Variations on a Given Theme **161**

References **181**

About the Authors **187**

Introduction

Economics has changed considerably over the past decades. Our main goal is to challenge the mainstream economic theory by removing the principle of individualism from its foundation, at least in that version which fails to recognize the existence of the interests of society as such, and does thus exclude the role of the state as an independent market player, which seeks to realize these interests. We fully recognize the difficulty of our task and the ways in which our effort challenges an analytical tradition that canonizes this postulate as a principle of methodological individualism.

Adherence to this principle transformed into an ideological directive gave birth to a dualistic attitude towards the state. On the one hand one cannot do without it; on the other hand, any activity of the state contradicts the postulate of individualism. In trying to find a solution to this paradox, economists engage in a permanent search for the possibility of 'harnessing' the state, and James Buchanan even brings it down to 'a set of techniques, machine and artefact'[1]. Being a passionate proponent of methodological individualism, this student of Frank Night and stalwart of Knut Wicksell is pleased to repeat the tirade of the famous Swede: 'If for an individual citizen utility is equal to zero, the aggregate utility for all members of society will be also equal to zero only and to nothing else but zero'[2]. The given formula seems so perfect to Buchanan, that he uses these actually one-hundred-year-old words of Wicksell as an epigraph to one of the sections of his Nobel lecture.

But is the real world so simple? According to the authors of a new version of the report to the Club of Rome, researchers from the Santa Fe Institute, engaged in the study of a mathematical theory of chaotic systems, have coined an elegant proverb: 'In theory, theory and practice are one and the same, but in practice, they are different'[3]. Actually, in traditional theory the utility of any good is determined by its utility to individuals. In practice, we also find goods which are of use to society as such but absolutely useless to an individual. In our book we cite numerous examples to confirm this thesis. Economic science 'doesn't want' to notice this so-

---

[1] Buchanan J.M., Tullock G. The Calculus of Consent: Logical Foundations of Constitutional Democracy. Ann Arbor Paperbacks, 1962 (Russian Edition: Nobel Prize Winners in Economics. James Buchanan. – Moscow, 1997, p. 49).

[2] Buchanan, J.M. The Constitution of Economic Policy. In J.D. Gwartney & R.E. Wagner (eds.). Public Choice and Constitutional Economics. Greenwich, Connecticut, 1988 (Russian Edition: Buchanan J.M. The Constitution of Economic Policy. // Nobel Prize Winners in Economics. James Buchanan. – Moscow, 1997, p. 210).

[3] E. Weizsaecker, A. Lovins and H. Lovins. New Report to the Club of Rome

cial utility as yet. The reason is the same: unconditional loyalty to the principle of methodological individualism.

The contradiction between the traditional theory and practice is revealed in the following parable, told however on another occasion: 'Once, an elderly economist was taking a walk with his small, well-mannered granddaughter. Suddenly the girl saw a 20-pound note lying on the road. "May I take it?" she asked her grandfather and he answered, "Leave it, darling. If it were genuine, somebody would already have taken it." '[4]. Economists refuse to accept the existence of a utility that the market itself doesn't manifest, and continue to insist that any utility must be reduced to individual preferences. The viciousness of methodological individualism proper, which makes both theory and practice '20 pounds' poorer, is reflected precisely in the conceptual narrow-mindedness of the above 'economic grandfather'.

The original premise of the traditional market theory saying that interests of society as such cannot exist, is just a statement and nothing more. The common thesis on the conventional nature of assumption seems to be a rather lame argument here. No agreement on basic theoretical assumptions can be eternal, since both the real world and the idea of it change. The phenomenon of the canonization of the theory always threatens to transform the science into religion.

This happened not only to Marxism. Such disease also threatens modern economic concepts. We witnessed how neoliberal theory became a purely ideological doctrine hostile to any state interference. As for the postulate of individualism, it was absolutized only in the 20th century. Earlier it was a subject of discussions, current results of which formed a pattern resembling a swing of the pendulum.

Up to the middle of the 18th century – during the era sometimes called the 'Big-Men-Society, where an individual with outstanding capabilities, kindness, and intellect became an outstanding person carrying out a fair trial and fair reallocation'[5], — the idea of 'enlightened despotism' or 'paternal monarchy' dominated: a wise and fair monarch was believed to use his power to serve the public benefit. Under such conditions, no interaction of an individual and state could exist. Since all rights were usurped by the state, an individual had not a single one. Therefore the question of harmony of public and individual interests could arise only when individual rights appeared.

Tough protectionist barriers in combination with severe governmental directions and regulations of economic activities doomed the European countries of that time to the continuous economic stagnation. An urgent need for economic growth conditioned the demand for and prompt success of ideas of economic liberalism, which were first expressed and systematized by Adam Smith in his system of natural freedom.

We would like to emphasize two essential circumstances. First, due to Adam Smith, an individual interest as a foundation for the mentioned system has been legitimated in economic theory. This is where an everlasting conflict between theoretical approaches to the economic interaction of an individual and state has

---

[4] Ibid., p. 207.
[5] Koslowski P. Gesellschaft und Staat. Ein unvermeidlicher Dualismus. Stuttgart: Klett-Cotta Verlag, 1982 (Russian Edition – Moscow, 1998, p. 272).

come from. Second, according to Adam Smith, an individual and state are not inherently hostile. It is only later that the notion of their everlasting antagonism was established, any weakening of one of them meaning strengthening of the other and vice versa. According to Smith's theory, the state was – without any ideological pressure – objectively forced out to the edge of social structure, since unimpeded realization of self-interest was considered sufficient for socium's normal functioning.

A social idea historian once noted precisely that philosophers of the 18th century, including Smith, 'in their concept of individualism didn't separate the demand for individual freedom from the striving, even with the state support, for maximum possible development of most individuals'[6]. We would like to emphasize that Smith, unlike some of today's neoliberals, was not hostile to the state. After a long period of domination of mercantilism with its regulations binding any individual initiative, he gave government a more adequate role. What he meant was simplification of government tasks, not its abolition – the latter was suggested by Johann Gottlieb Fichte, individualist philosopher, Smith's contemporary, who designated a purpose of each government 'to make the government unnecessary'[7]. Lack of opposition of an individual and state in Smith's theoretical model came from his teleological belief in predetermined harmony of common and individual interests. Smith's belief in harmony gave rise to optimism penetrating his entire system of 'natural freedom'.

The 19th century swung the pendulum away from the triumph of individualism. Rapid development of bourgeois relations provided a kind of renaissance for comprehensive theoretical paternalism, giving rise not only to the liberation of individual initiative, but also to mass poverty, this time in the form of 'organic state', 'Utopian' and 'scientific' versions of socialism. The main rebuke of socialists to adherents of the natural freedom system with its self-regulatory market mechanism was its indifference to the suffering of masses. As a result, various collectivist projects came into fashion, intending to relieve peoples from poverty and inequity with the help of total supremacy of social interest, which – voluntarily or involuntarily – denied individual interests.

Since then, a long period of continuous ideological conflict between individual and public interests started. Due to approximately equal spread of individualistic (Say, Rossi, Bastiat, Menger, Walras, Marshall, etc.) and collectivistic (Hegel, Saint-Simon, Fourier, Marx, Schaffle, etc.) orthodoxy, the main stream of economic thought could not take a distinct shape at the end of the 19th century; it was split into two parallel streams of opposite social and economic views.

---

[6] Michel H. L'idée de l'état. Essai critiquesur l'histoire des theories sociales eu politiques en France depuis la révolution. – Moscow: Tipografia Tovarishestva Sytina, 1909, p. 383.

[7] Fichte J. Einige Vorlesungen über die Bestimmung des Gelehrten. In: Michel H. L'idée de l'état. Essai critique sur l'histoire des theories sociales et politiques en France depuis la révolution. – Moscow: Tipografia Tovarishestva Sytina, 1909, p. 68.

Under the severe economic depression of 1930s, their conflict reached its apogee in the first half of the 20th century, as the scale started to incline to collectivistic structures embodied in Russia (total socialization of property) and Germany (total socialization of people). Due to John Maynard Keynes, however, the theoretical tradition of economic liberalism laid by Smith began to revive. Having ascertained the chronic deficiency of effective demand, which no one could make up but the state, Keynes urged the latter to fight with a 'bias towards saving' inherent in individuals and stimulate consumption and investment using the targeted budget and monetary policy.

Keynes put forward a completely heretical thesis of necessity to 'establish centralized control in spheres mainly under private initiative. A state should control inclination to consumption partially by creating a proper tax system, partially by fixing an interest rate, and perhaps by other means'[8]. For all that, he did not doubt the viability of market economy in general and private property in particular. He wrote, 'Establishment of the centralized control necessary for ensuring full employment will certainly call for considerable expansion of traditional government functions. But opportunities for private initiative and responsibility will remain ample'[9].

Thus at a new historical stage, Keynesianism turned out to be a concept that first confirmed the viability of a market as an economic mechanism, and, second, brought 'peaceful' (à la Smith) interaction of individual and social interests back into market theory. This aspect of Keynesianism should be emphasized, since at the end of the 20th century, some researchers were close to reckoning Keynes among socialists[10]. Actually, the essence of the Keynesian revolution was limited to complementation of a market's 'invisible hand' by a state's 'visible hand'. But still in the last quarter of the 20th century, the individualistic paradigm took the upper hand and again pushed the state to the edge of the social system.

We should stress that contemporary proponents of liberal economic doctrine didn't significantly advance in their perception of the role of government in a market economy. Adam Smith's thesis is at best reproduced today, i.e. two hundred years later, in saying that 'the economy needs no more of the state than is necessary.' At worst, we are faced with another slogan, 'The less state, the better for the economy.' In both cases a theoretical explanation for the criteria of interventionism is missing. However, if there was no obvious need for such substantiation in Smith's system of "natural freedom," today – when the powerful and systematic intervention of the state is firmly integrated into reproductive processes of any developed market economy – it seems absurd to limit oneself to the total critique of

---

[8] Keynes J..M. The General Theory of Employment, Interest and Money. London, Macmillan, 1936 (Russian Edition – Moscow, 1993), p. 428.

[9] Ibid., p. 430.

[10] See, for example, Howard K., Zhuravlyova G. Principles of Economics of Free Market System. — Moscow, 1995, p. 278.

the state, based on the purely ideological statement that 'any governmental activity is an evil imposed by some persons on other persons.'[11]

Antistatism, established in the mainstream under the motto 'Back to Smith,' is rightfully associated with the names of Friedrich Von Hayek and Milton Friedman, who expressively described imaginary and real horrors of state interventionism. It is due to their works that the thesis of inherent stability of the market mechanism of self-regulation (malfunctioning due to state interference alone) returned to neoclassical theory. This 'Manichaean' approach to the state (its treatment only in categories of good and evil) leaves no chance for an adequate interpretation of agents of contemporary economy.

Expansion of state activity, being an indisputable fact, requires an explanation 'without anger and prejudice,' regardless of whether it is excessive or not. However, the neoliberal doctrine seems to ignore this requirement, limiting itself to antistatist philippics of a normative nature. In this sense, neither numerous examples given by Friedman, nor severe Von Hayek's warning of dangers for liberty add to this explanation. The next attempt to resolve the 'damned' issue and settle a conflict between reality and its theoretical image was made by representatives of the institutional stream of economic thought.

Here, we should single out James Buchanan, one of the founders of the constitutional economic theory, in which the growing state influence still remains a strong allergen, but not every case of governmental interference arise protest. Buchanan considers theoretical grounds for 'correct' intervention from purely individualistic positions. According to the principle of methodological individualism, he allows any positive action of the state only if it corresponds to a unanimous decision of individuals regarding the goals which can be reached by them within a group.

It is hardly necessary to prove that such an approach to valuing real (not desirable) collective (state) decisions in the majority of cases does not correspond to reality. To present a variety of state activities as a result of consensus among all society's members means neither more nor less than to create another Utopian model.

It seems that the prolonged opposition of the state and individual in the economic theory has ended, and Francis Fukuyama's dream has come true. The pendulum stopped at the point of 'complete' triumph of individualism, proclaimed a gospel truth.

This is what became the main irritant for us, this is why we feel discomfort. Of course, one should feel greatly obliged to Ludwig Von Mises, Friedrich Von Hayek and James Buchanan, who (like Adam Smith in his time) used their powerful intellectual and moral potential to serve individual liberty, opposing any oppression of an individual by society. But still, aversion to state tyranny must not impede the development of the theoretical notion of socium, including its economic system.

---

[11] Mises L. von, Liberalism in the Classical Tradition. – Irvington on Hudson, New York, 1985, p. 57.

We clearly see the demand for and necessity of modernizing the postulate of individualism, particularly where the interests of society as a whole cannot be reduced to those of its individual members. We are in fact faced with a blatant contradiction between the general declaration that a modern market economy is 'mixed,' and a jealous and suspicious response to any attempts to limit methodological individualism as a governing principle. This contradiction cannot be solved within the framework of existing theoretical models. We are convinced that a 'mixed economy' is a practical projection of an as yet undeveloped economic theory of the 'third way.'

As James Buchanan put it, '...two "great alternatives," *laissez-faire* and socialism, are dying, and we can hardly expect their revival.'[12] On the threshold of the 21st century the need for an economic theory of the 'third way" became a categorical imperative. We hold that the concept of economic sociodynamics presented here constitutes the core of this theory. Having studied the evolution of the last three centuries of economic theory and modern economic practice, we have established the following pre-requisites for the above concept, the formulation of which is of the utmost importance.

First, we find many situations in which the market obviously does not function and the state must correct its 'failures.' After analyzing these cases, we conclude that they cannot in every case be motivated by individual interests. Other reasons also exist that induce the authorities to take action independently and even in spite of the interests of individuals. It is precisely these reasons that attract our attention.

Second, in observing the expansion of the zone of state involvement, we fail to sufficiently find convincing explanations of how these actions are related to the preferences of individuals. Despite sophisticated analytical contributions (such as the 'free rider problem', 'prisoner's dilemma', 'veil of ignorance', 'obedience paradox', etc.), this problem is not solved by those trying to identify an individualistic source of state intervention. In fact, the contradiction between the dominant trend in economic science toward minimizing governmental activities and increasing the role of the state in economic life even within developed market economies is becoming more acute. We believe that the specific interest of society, which differs from any aggregate of individual preferences, lies behind it.

Third, previous attempts to define and include this social interest in market models have obviously been insufficient. The social welfare function (A. Bergson, P. Samuelson), two utility functions (H. Margolis) and other similar constructions are nothing more than attempts to fit social interest into a 'Procrustean bed' of the postulate of individualism. By using this approach, everything is reduced to individual preferences, which supposedly embrace any social interest. That is why these models are unsuited for the analysis of society's specific needs.

Fourth, Richard Musgrave's attempts to integrate the concept of 'merit goods' into traditional market theory added doubt as to the universality of the postulate of

---

[12] Buchanan J. The Limits of Liberty: Between Anarchy and Leviathan. Chicago: The University of Chicago Press, 1975 (Russian Edition: Nobel Prize Winners in Economics. James Buchanan. – Moscow, 1997, p. 430).

individualism. The more than forty-year old discussion of the goods and services 'deserving' governmental support has produced two regularly reproducing points. On the one hand, society's specific needs (*merit wants*), which differ fundamentally from individual interests, are the object of analysis. On the other hand, we witness endless attempts to level this specificity with the aid of an individualistic argument for their existence. By analogy with biblical topic, we can say that during the same forty years the people of Israel managed to learn freedom again, modern economists managed neither to find meritorics' place nor to reject this theory. Evidently, everything is not as simple as some authors, trying to explain any phenomenon exclusively from the individualistic standing, believe. A thorough study of the critical sources on meritorics merely testifies to the assumption that the interests of society as such do exist.

Fifth, after reading a number of books on economics and related disciplines we have come to the conclusion that economic theory itself is unable to provide an answer to the question we are interested in. Almost every attempt to prove or disprove the assumption that any public interest is reduced to individual preferences ends up with a discussion of basic postulates, raising philosophical issues and transgressing the boundaries of economic theory. We mean the basic notions of socium, multitude of individuals forming it, and its structure. There is also a vivid contradiction between the modern understanding of socium and the postulate of individualism. We believe that canonization of this postulate is similar to an attempt to solve this contradiction, 'squeezing' the society structure into a strictly limited individualistic room. Therefore, the view from the point of social philosophy strengthens confidence in the necessity of modernizing the postulate of individualism.

Having formulated five major reasons that encourage us to carry out the theoretical research, we should mention one other. We could be reproached for superficiality or even worse for ingratitude, if in this introduction we said nothing about the philosophical foundation for the concept of economic sociodynamics and did not mention in this regard the influence of Ilya Prigogine's works on our understanding of socium. His postmodernist vision of the universe has altered our own picture of the world. We have realized that the growth of entropy and a system's tendency towards equilibrium are not the only trend. The real intrigue in the dynamics of all physical and social systems consists in the counterpoint of NECESSITY and CHANCE. Determinism in the equilibrium formation exists parallel to stochastic processes of its destruction. The dominance of equilibrium is only one more assumption of traditional economic theory.

We proceed from more universal notions of society seeing it as a multitude of individuals in constant change and fluctuation, who act independently and in various groups. Here all sociodynamic processes reflect both negative and positive reverse interdependences and are described on the basis of an original analogue of Prigogine's theorem: if obstacles appear in the way of an equilibrium, the stationary state of the socium corresponds to minimal entropy, and the energy of disturbance is transformed into interest inherent to the social system as a whole; the latter thus adopts a new qualitative level.

In other words, any disruptive impetus observed in society on a daily and hourly basis (such as changes in the environmental situation, an increased need for education, science, culture, growing differentiation in the population's incomes, a decline in the competitiveness of a branch which is important for a country, simply the development of a new product or technology, etc.) generates two consequences. In the first case, fluctuation is suppressed, a new equilibrium emerges and the disruptive energy is absorbed by the dynamics of individual preferences. In the second case, the fluctuation energy does not dissipate in new individual biases; it, instead, is preserved, even encouraging the formation of societal interest as such.

The first situation obviously is merely a specific case of economic sociodynamics. If a negative reverse interdependence is observed (the mechanism of the 'invisible hand' is attributed to it alone), then entropy increases, the energy of disruption decreases, fluctuations become less intense and disappear. Under conditions of a competitive market and the reducibility of needs, changing demand generates a corresponding supply reaction, and a new market equilibrium arises. If the phenomenon of positive reverse interdependence gives birth to increased fluctuation and their energy rises, new qualities arise in a social system, and an interest of society as such is formed which fails to be reflected in individual preferences. It is clear that this aspect of the dynamics of the socium, as well as its transposition to new levels of complexity, fundamentally contradicts with the postulate of individualism.

Doubting that this basic assumption, customary for economic theory, is well-grounded, we want to express our active disagreement with canonization of the principle of methodological individualism whether by Ludwig Von Mises, Viennese patriarch, or James Buchanan, our contemporary from Virginia. No eternal truths exist in science. And we believe that the time has come to revise the postulate of individualism. It is here that we find additional opportunities for development of economic theory. One of these opportunities is reflected in the concept developed by the authors of this book, which aspires to become the core of a 'third way' economic theory.

* * *

Work on this book started in 1997–99, during our training in Marburg (FRG). This opportunity was given to us by Marion Countess Doenhoff Fund. We express our gratitude to this outstanding woman, who conspired against Hitler and now owns *Die Zeit* publishing agency. We are also grateful to the Adenauer Fund, having enabled the next stage of our work in Munich and Innsbruck. This book would not have been published without the support of the Russian Fund for Fundamental Research – its grant made it possible for us to complete our theoretical research, if it is possible to speak about any completion here.

Aspiring to establish a 'third way' economic theory[13], we discussed our first results with Professors V.N. Lifshits and V.M. Polterovich, Academicians D.S. Lvov and A.D. Nekipelov, whose friendly criticism and comments considerably influenced our further speculations. We recall those conversations with gratitude. Our research paper *Unknown Economy*, which we presented in February 1998 at the seminar of the Department of Economics of the Russian Academy of Sciences, became a specific stage in the formation of our views. The discussion that followed it proved to be very useful and urged us to take further steps in research. In light of this, we'd like to express our gratitude to Professors V.G. Grebennikov, R.N. Evstigneev, G.B. Kleiner and Academician V.L. Makarov, whose advice enabled us to verify some theses of our theory.

We are also thankful to our foreign colleagues. Unprejudiced discussion of our works in Marburg University with Professor Alfred Schüller, Doctor Karl von Dalhaes and Doctor Reinhard Peterhoff allowed us to discover many pitfalls, to go into the root of the matter in which we are interested, and to see it in the context of contemporary economic theory. We'd like to express our special gratitude to Professor Helmut Leipold, who was the first to draw our attention to the closeness of out views to Musgrave's meritorics.

We should specially mention discussions of the basic theses of economic sociodynamics with Professor Bernhard Felderer, Director of the Vienna Institute of Top Research, and Vienna University Economics Professor Peter Rosner. Their objective analysis and careful attitude to our developments allowed us to avoid a number of inaccuracies in interpretation of the categories of public needs and social utility. We highly appreciate our friendship with Doctor Roland Götz (the Federal Institute for Eastern European and International Research (Cologne)) and feel genuine gratitude for his editorship of the German translation of our brochure *Economic Sociodynamics and Rational Behaviour of the State.*[14]

We believe that the present publication will cause response from our colleagues. We also hope that we'll be able to take into account any comments and criticism of our concept.

---

[13] Grinberg R., Rubinstein A. Social Economics: Introduction to New A Economic Journal, 1997, No. 1; Grinberg R. Rubinstein A. Problems o of Social Economics // Economic Science of Modern Russia, 1998, No. 29.

[14] Grinberg R., Rubinstein A. Ökonomische Soziodynamik und rationales Verhalten des Staates. — Köln, 1999.

1 To the Reducibility Hypothesis

After rereading many old books and reconsidering modern theories, we find that two hundred years of economic thought were spent in the environment of the opposition of individualistic philosophy, defending individuals' economic freedom and sovereignty, to the concepts of social interests, their realization requiring interference of the state and restriction of economic agents' activities. Repeating the pendulum swing from the concept of 'organic state' to its individualistic interpretation, economists of different eras and schools gave various answers to the question: what for and in what degree should the state be involved in the economic life? Due to 'vaccination' in the form of totalitarian regimes, the twentieth century made its choice. The mainstream preserved only one – individualistic – concept of the state, to which individuals delegate a part of their powers in accordance with a constitution.

Everything seemed to be fine: who dare oppose individual freedom and democracy? Friedrich Von Hayek's imperatives really sound like a song of a 'fruity bird'. However, everything is far from being as simple as it seems. It proved to be very difficult to explain many present-day economic phenomena proceeding from such notions of state functions. And the theoretical model itself is full of contradictions, the main thing being that it is based on numerous assumptions, many of which are of purely speculative nature. Consider just one example – *'homo economicus'*. Even without referring to a famous definition given by Thorstein Veblen, it is easy to understand that the behaviour of real people has a broader and more diverse motivation than 'self-interest' attributed to them. In this regard, the institutional model with its socialization paradigm, value orientation, customs and norms often allows explaining the things which the neoclassical theory fails to explain.

This might be a reason for the renaissance of institutional theory in the end of the 20th century. Unlike the founders of institutionalism, contemporary institutionalists do not reject neoclassicism – vice versa, they are searching for the ways to improve it by involving a rather developed methodology of analyzing interpersonal relations and principles of the socium's functioning. It became clear that they succeeded in it after works by James Buchanan and Douglas North were published. The hope revived for reconciliation of individualistic interpretation of the state with its social orientation interfering with individual sovereignty. We believe that the institutional approach competes with game models and in some cases replaces them completely. To say the least, economists today have the same great expectations for institutional models as they once had for game theory which showed the possibility of individuals' effective cooperation.

We'd like to emphasize contemporary economists' adherence to the theoretical scheme suggested by Vilfredo Pareto in the beginning of the 20th century. Today, his philosophical understanding of optimum is present in almost every concept aspiring to combine neoclassicism and institutionalism. This is probably due to the conceptual potential of Pareto's system of axioms. The postulates formulated by him make individualism and private law an indefeasible law, and on the other hand allow the determination of 'what is good and bad' for an aggregation of individuals as a whole[15].

We'll return to this subject essential for us later, and now we want to pay attention to other aspects of Pareto's doctrine. To this end, we'd like to turn to traditional criticism of his system of axioms, which, according to Seligman, has an excessively tough structure[16]. Pareto considers it inadmissible to carry out interpersonal comparison and to reallocate resources to the loss of any individual, even if the total benefit exceeds the total loss[17], thus creating the restrictions which cannot always be overcome. That is why when expanding the zone of application of Pareto scheme, it is often impossible to do so without placing value judgements, which neoclassical theory traditionally tries to avoid. Not regarding such judgements as 'original sin', let us consider another impediment for building up a generalized optimum scheme. We mean Pareto's axiom determining the society's well-being solely in terms of well-beings of individuals.

This is the axiom which sets barriers to the introduction of socialized market agents into a market model, thus creating the main difficulties for us. Actually, if the society's well-being is only a function of individual well-being, if any societal need can be reduced to its members' needs, then in the market there is no place left for socialized agents, since, according to this axiom, their interests are completely dissolved in individual preferences. In this regard, Pareto stuck to the classical outlook, implicitly based on the reducibility hypothesis, which can be formulated so: *in a society, any can be reduced to a function of individual needs.*

We believe that the universality of the reducibility hypothesis naturally comes from an old doctrine of psychologism being applied to the whole market area. It is the psychological phenomenon of striving for wealth, which John Stuart Mill used

---

[15] It can be considered that Pareto-improvements provide a sufficiently effective solution to an ancient individualistic paradox known as 'fallacy of composition': on the one hand everything beneficial for every single person within a group is beneficial for a group; on the other hand if everybody is striving for his own benefit, then all together individuals can come to a result unfavourable for society as a whole (see, for instance, Koslowski P. Gesellschaft und Staat. Ein unvermeidlicher Dualismus. Stuttgart: Klett-Cotta Verlag, 1982 (Russian Edition – Moscow, 1998, p. 284)). In this sense Pareto pointed out the limits within which a person can act as a '*homo oeconomicus*', and outside – as a member of socium, subjecting himself to established restrictions.

[16] Seligman B. Mainstreams of Contemporary Economic Thought. - Moscow, 1968, p. 258.

[17] We mean the compensation principle by Kaldor-Hicks, according to which the society's well-being is considered to be improved, if at the expense of those individuals whose well-being improved losses of other can be compensated, the formers' well-beings being maintained at least at the initial level.

in order to explain the market itself[18]. 'Laws of social events are nothing else but laws of people's actions and passions. When united in a society, people don't turn into anything different'[19]. This is how the English economist of the 19th century saw the world. A hundred years later, supporting the ideological opposition to holism, the Austrian philosopher Karl Popper found methodological individualism[20] in psychologism: 'In psychologism it is only possible to accept what can be called "methodological individualism" contrary to "methodological collectivism". Psychologism is right to insist that "behaviour" and "actions" of such collectives as social groups and state *should be reduced* to behaviour and actions of individuals'[21].

We have italicized a part of Popper's statement in order to demonstrate a direct connection of both old psychologism and relatively new methodological individualism with the reducibility hypothesis. Its universality seems to become common for the economic theory based on the unconditional recognition of applicability of this hypothesis to the whole society and market. In the part of a market where isolated players are acting, having opportunities to improve their status without paying attention to each other, any interest of their aggregation can be really considered in terms of individual preferences. This is actually a starting point and a basic assumption of a traditional market model.

However, the situation changes radically when socialized agents (members of different social groups and society as a whole) join the game. Under such circumstances, the universality of the reducibility hypothesis causes serious doubts. In other words, we are facing a theoretical option: either 'methodological individualism' with its traditional reducibility of public needs, or socialized market agents and a different interpretation of the essence of social interest, which cannot be presented as a combination of individual preferences.

Therefore, it is evident that any attempts at a theoretical synthesis involving the expansion of the neoclassical model as a result of its integration into the institutional environment where socialized market agents are acting are connected with rejection of the *universality* of the reducibility hypothesis. In other words, one should assume that this hypothesis is untrue and an interest represented in neither

[18] Mill J.S. A system of logic, ratiocinative and inductive; being a connected view of the principles of evidence, and the methods of scientific investigation. New York and London: Harper & Brothers, 1900 (Russian Edition – Moscow, 1914, p. 819).

[19] Ibid., p. 798.

[20] The principle of methodological individualism was known before. It was advocated by Von Hayek (Hayek F.A. Scientism and the Study of Society. Part ', Section VII // Economica, 1943, p.1) and his teacher Von Mises (Mises L. von The Human Action. Contemporary Books. – Chicago, 1966, pp. 41-43). This approach is still a key thesis of a number of modern concepts. (Buchanan J., Tullock G. The Calculus of Consent: Logical Foundations of Constitutional Democracy. Ann Arbor Paperbacks, 1962 (Russian Edition: Nobel Prize Winners in Economics. James Buchanan. – Moscow, 1997, pp. 35, 47-41)).

[21] Popper K. Open Society and Its Enemies. V. 2. Princeton: Princeton University Press, 1971 (Russian Edition – Moscow, 1992, V. 2, p. 109).

any of individual utility functions nor their aggregate function exists. But the whole history of economic thought demonstrates quite the opposite – the universality of the reducibility hypothesis has been a 'sacred cow' for both classical and neoclassical theories. This statement requires special comments, since the reducibility hypothesis has never been formulated explicitly.

1.1 Origins

We believe that this hypothesis belongs to the most general assumptions in the economic theory. We also mean a more general context connected with basic assumptions concerning interrelations between individuals' and societal needs, between individual preferences and social choice. The absolute belief in the impossibility of an autonomous social interest not reflected in individual preferences threads almost every concept. There are many confirmations to that. In this connection let us consider a number of the most famous theoretical constructions.

Let us start with Adam Smith. In his famous *The Wealth of Nations* he wrote, 'No individual... will think about social interests... he will strive only for his personal benefit, and in this case like in many others he will be guided by an invisible hand which will take him to the goal having nothing in common with his intentions'. Considering this thesis from different standpoints, we'd like to draw attention to the implicit assumption present there that any goal of society is reached through individuals seeking to realize their own interests.

By charging the 'invisible hand' with society's well-being, Adam Smith excluded any possibility of defining this well-being aside from realization of individual interests. Moreover, he associated the category of public well-being only with a result of market players striving to maximize their own utility functions. According to Smith, a market mechanism reduces any socially beneficial result to individual benefits. Therefore, without any risk of making a mistake, we can state that Adam Smith implicitly assumed the universality of the reducibility hypothesis.

The same hypothesis is implicitly present in one of the most significant results of modern economic theory — the conceptual theorems of the theory of well-being. The first of them says that every competitive equilibrium is Pareto-optimal, the second – that 'every Pareto-optimal allocation can be achieved as a competitive equilibrium after a suitable redistribution of initial endowments'[22].

We'd like to pay attention to the traditional interpretation of the above theorems in connection with the issue of 'efficiency and equity' and quote Kenneth Arrow. In particular, he writes, 'If the current wealth allocation is estimated as unfair, it is

---

[22] Arrow K.J. The Potentials and Limits of the Market in Resource Allocation, in Feiwel, ed., Issues in Contemporary Microeconomics and Welfare, 1985 (Russian Edition: THESIS: Theory and History of Economic and Social Institutions. – Moscow, 1993, V1, No. 2), p. 57. See also Stiglitz J. Economics of the Public Sector. London, New York: WW Norton & Co., 1988 (Russian Edition – Moscow, 1997, pp. 68-70).

necessary, first of all, to reallocate the available resources (by a one-stroke free transfer of respective quotas) and then to allow the market free function; no direct interference into its functioning, for example, price regulation or fixing, is required in this case[23].

This theoretical achievement set economists' minds at rest, since under certain conditions[24] the way to reconcile individual and social interests without any state interference was found. However, we believe that the said conditions are not sufficient to provide the traditional degree of adequacy of the neoclassical model to the reality[25]. An assumption of the universality of the reducibility hypothesis should be without doubt added to these conditions. This hypothesis underlies the second theorem of the theory of well-being, which is easy to show reasoning by contraries.

Let us assume that the hypothesis in question is unfair, and there is a social need for 'justice' that cannot be reduced to individual interests. This means that on the 'frontier of satisfaction options'[26] not a single point exists that would correspond to this autonomous interest. Under such circumstances, no variant of resource reallocation, ensuring the Pareto optimality for different combinations of individual preferences, can realize the irreducible social interest. Thus, the assumption of the existence of the 'fair' Pareto optimality, i.e. an efficient resource allocation which satisfies both individuals and society as a whole is, as a matter of fact, another version of the same basic assumption of the universality of the reducibility hypothesis; since, if the 'wealth allocation is estimated as unfair' (we should remember Arrow), such estimation is possible only from the standpoint of a reducible social interest.

Two more examples refer to the cases when the basic pre-conditions of the neoclassical model are not met, and the market faces so-called externalities. Public goods are to be considered here; demand for them cannot be revealed in individual preferences, and the respective social interest cannot be reduced to individual interests. In this case vulnerability of the reducibility hypothesis seems evident. Nevertheless, belief in its universality is boundless: even in cases of market failures (externalities), to maintain the universality of this hypothesis, neoclassical theory is ready to sacrifice even the comprehensiveness of its market model and allow contraction of the market area. Dominating economic concepts of the 20th century show the following alternatives: either the market failure zone is simply excluded from the market area (public goods becoming an object of the state concern), or some specific way to 'correct' such failures is found within the reducibility hypothesis.

---

[23] Arrow K.J. Op. cit., p. 57.

[24] We mean the basic assumptions of the neoclassical market model – about the conditions of perfect competition, absence of external effects and many other things, which have been many times discussed in the specialized literature.

[25] Here we do not consider other basic assumptions – of zero transaction costs and perfect information.

[26] Samuelson P.A., Nordhaus W.D. Economics. New York: McGraw-Hill, 1992 (Russian Edition – Moscow, 1997, p. 311).

One such way is explained by Ronald Coase. Analyzing the problems of state interventionism in connection with market failures, he concludes that correction of these failures does not always require state interference. Moreover, according to Coase's theorem, whenever externalities appear, the parties concerned can come together and under certain conditions work out an agreement, according to which externalities turn into internal factors, and resource allocation becomes efficient[27].

According to Coase, these conditions include quite developed ownership rights and local nature of externalities. Admitting (under such conditions) the possibility of reaching the respective agreement, Coase actually suggests that in this case the state is only interested in correction of market failures. In other words, he proceeds from the assumption that any other social interest is completely realized in individual preferences of the negotiating parties. Thus, though implicitly and in another version, the same basic assumption is present here – that under certain conditions an aggregate consumer effect (including externalities exceeding a private market deal) can be *reduced* to satisfaction of individual needs.

And the last example we are going to give here is also connected with one of the ways to correct market failures through internalization of externalities. It is the well-known 'prisoner's dilemma'. We would like to summarize its conditions and arising collision. An investigator describes two prisoners, suspected of breaking the law, their unenviable position as follows: if *both* of them admit committing the crime, the sentence will not be as severe as if *both* do not confess. But if only *one* of them confesses, he will be punished, and the other one will be set free. In such situation, the corporate behaviour, implying that each prisoner admits guilt, is known to be more beneficial[28].

Having applied this collision to the production of public goods, we could suppose that there are conditions under which the respective social interest may agree with individual interests. Then for each free rider it is beneficial to pay for personal consumption of a public good. Only in such cases does the internalization of externalities take place. External effects are 'dissolved' in individual benefits, that is in differences between advantages and costs of consumption of a specific good.

However, in the case of 'game' correction of market failures, it is necessary to adhere to quite tough conditions, such as situation repetition, limited number of consumers of public goods, and perfect information about each other at their disposal[29]. Any violation of these conditions, which are difficult to observe, resumes

---

[27] Coase R.H. The Problem of Social Cost // Journal of Law and Economics, 3, 1960, pp. 1-44; also see: Coase R.H. The Firm, the Market and the Law. — Chicago, IL: University of Chicago Press, 1988.

[28] This is one of the general results of game theory. Actually the 'prisoner's dilemma' is an elegant variation on a theme of 'efficient strategy of cooperation'.

[29] We would like to point out a rather curious similarity of the pre-conditions of Coase's theorem and the 'prisoner's dilemma'. The only difference between them is that in the first case the information on property rights is required, and in the second case – that on individuals' intentions and behaviour. Moreover, this difference disappears as well, since according to Coase's theorem the information on property rights actually turns into that on possible intentions and behaviour of the parties to the deal.

all consequences of market failures and actually forces public goods outside the market area.

So, in the model of corporate behaviour ('prisoner's dilemma') we also face reduction of the market 'pebble-leather' to a narrow area where special conditions exist. But compliance with game model conditions and availability of an efficient corporate strategy mean the admittance of the reducibility hypothesis. Actually, the possibility of cooperation, ensuring realization of the social interest, means the reducibility of this interest to individual needs.

All the above examples lead to the conclusion that the philosophical basis of classical and neoclassical theories has always been the universality of the reducibility hypothesis, which contradicts our views. Giving rise to serious doubts, it forces us to turn to a detailed analysis of the concepts where the interrelation between individual and social interests the specifically examined.

1.2 The Reducibility of Needs in Theories of Well-Being

A special place in the analysis of interrelation of economic interests in a socium is occupied by one of the fundamental concepts of the 20th century – the theory of well-being[30]. Not limited to the individualistic motivation for economic behaviour, this theory, unlike that developed by A.Smith, considers defining the public well-being as its priority task. Both old and new versions of this theory try to answer three questions: WHAT is the public well-being, HOW can the social interest be defined, and WHAT should be the mechanism for its realization? What plays the main role in all theoretical constructions is the search for the so-called integral (or aggregate) function of the social well-being, linking individual preferences of market agents with interests of society as a whole.

Before the theory of well-being appeared, such function, though in a simplified form, had been suggested by Marshall. Later Pareto modified and expanded Marshall's model considerably.[31] Analyzing the Pareto scheme, we'd like to emphasize once again that among the axioms he suggested there is a postulate according to which social well-being depends exclusively upon individual judgements of societal members, which is usual for Smith's concept.

Having doubts that the assumption of the universality of the reducibility hypothesis is well-founded, we still have to admit that Pareto made a step forward as

---

[30] In 1924, Arthur Pigou, Marshall's successor in Cambridge, published *Economic theory of well-being*. 60 years later this book was translated into Russian (Pigou A.C. The economics of Welfare. London: Macmillan, 1962 (Russian Edition – Moscow, 1985, p. 30)). Not dealing with general issues of this theory, we'll consider only those aspects that are directly associated with building the functions of public well-being.

[31] Utilitarian and Rawlsian functions of well-being should be mentioned here, too (without paying attention to chronology, though). They represent two different ways of aggregating individual preferences. According to the *utilitarian* concept, the function of public well-being is the sum of all individual utilities, and the *Rawlsian* function determines the society's well-being through the utility of the less well-to-do individual.

to understanding the social interest. While Smith meant any *a posteriori* result of maximization of market agents' individual interests by the public well-being, Pareto determined this well-being *a priori* [32]. For us the main point for discussion is that Pareto (unlike Smith and his orthodox progeny) did recognize the category of public interest as such. We'd like to point out that Pareto's research made the basis for the 'new theory of well-being', which almost fully included his axioms.

Radical theoretical innovations are associated with the names of Adam Bergson and Paul Samuelson. Proceeding from Pareto's axioms, they suggested an absolutely new approach. According to it, social well-being is defined as an aggregate of *individual functions of preferences for different states of society*[33]. Strictly speaking, interpretation of the social well-being in this concept transgresses Smith's theory, since it evidently assumes that each individual will think about the public interest[34]. Bergson and Samuelson believe that every market agent should have not only a function of preference for goods and services but also the function of preference for alternative states of society. They suppose that using some mechanism of collective decision-making, it is possible to build an aggregate function of individual preferences, which actually determines the social interest. Like Smith, they charge the 'invisible hand' with its realization.

However, a search for a collective decision-making procedure is an 'everlasting issue' of concordance of each person's interests with those of society. This search is impeded by the incompatibility of the paternalistic nature of the concept of public well-being and the postulates of rational behaviour. Studying the mechanisms for 'aggregating individual functions of preferences for alternative states of society'[35] and trying to evaluate the possibility of making correct collective decisions, Kenneth Arrow proved the well-known theorem 'On Impossibility'. Having built a model for three participants with two alternative preferences, he showed that in a general case it is impossible to identify the social function of preferences taking into account opinions of all market agents[36]. This fundamental result made the hope for building a correct aggregate function of well-being even less realistic.

Returning to the discussion of the reducibility hypothesis we should state that in the Bergson-Samuelson concept, the public interest is identified only through

---

[32] We mean Pareto-optimum, according to which the maximum social well-being is reached in the situation when it is impossible to improve the well-being of one individual without infringing that of another one.

[33] Bergson A. A Reformulation of Certain Aspects of Well-being Economics // Quarterly Journal of Economics, February 1938. See also: Samuelson P. Reaffirming the Existence of 'Reasonable' Bergson-Samuelson Social Well-being Functions// Economics, 1978, No. 173. Inclusion of prices, capital, state services, etc. in the social well-being function has led to a variety of theoretical results. We'll stick to the part of this concept which directly deals with the problem of interrelation of individual and public interests.

[34] According to Smith, 'no individual ...will think about public interests'. He will be guided by the self-interest and the invisible hand.

[35] Arrow K.J. Values and Collective Decision-Making. Philosophy and Economic Theory. –Oxford, 1979, p. 118.

[36] Arrow K.J. Social Choice and Individual Values, 2nd Ed. – New York: Wiley, 1963.

individual functions of preferences for society's alternative states. In this respect it is not important what individuals evaluate – goods' utility or society's state. It does not matter whether they have one individual preference function (Pareto) or two (Bergson, Samuelson). What really matters is that in both cases any public interest can be reduced to individual preferences. In other words, the assumption of the universality of the reducibility hypothesis is present in both concepts.

Remaining within the limits of reducibility hypothesis, the theory of well-being has evolved considerably. While according to Smith, the public well-being is just of *a posteriori* nature and exists only as an indefinite result of the realization of individual self-interests, upon this theory's emergence, societal well-being turns into a concrete notion. Though the Pareto scheme still does not consider social interest explicitly, the public well-being itself is completely determined by Pareto optimality *(Table 1.1)*.

Table 1.1. Evolution of Notions of Interaction of Social and Individual Interests

	Social well-being	Social well-being is determined through:		Mechanism for realization of social interest
		Individual interests of market agents	Individual preferences for society's states	
Smith	Not defined	–	–	The 'invisible hand'
Pareto	Defined	Function of individual interests	–	Pareto optimality
Bergson-Samuelson	Defined	–	Aggregate function of individual preferences for society's states	Pareto optimality & maximization of an aggregate function

Another version of the theory in question already contains a formally expressed social interest in the form of a respective aggregate of individual functions of preference for alternative states of society. In Bergson-Samuelson concept, the bearers of this society's interest are still individuals, and in a mechanism for realization of this interest the Pareto scheme is completed by maximization of an aggregate function of social well-being.

Analyzing the reducibility hypothesis in the context of the theory of well-being, we'd like to point out that along with the development of this theory, the basic notions of utility have been changing. As a result, a common individual utility was supplemented by individual evaluations of social states. From our point of view, this means that economic theory actually recognized the existence of specific interests of an individual, which are characteristic of him not only as an individual but also as a member of society. Though in the latent form, a more complicated system of needs was developed, making it necessary to regard participants in market relations not only as individuals but also as members of respective social groups and society as a whole. In this sense, it looks as though the theory of well-being 'wandered' into the field of institutionalism with its paradigm of individuals' socialization.

It should be noted that modern institutionalists more and more often involve categories of neoclassical theories[37] in their analysis, and it is wholly applicable to the key notions of the theory of well-being. In this regard, we'd like to pay attention to an extremely important work by Howard Margolis, who in the early 1980s suggested the double utility model, which, in our opinion, has not gained proper recognition yet. According to Margolis, individuals have two utility functions. But unlike Bergson-Samuelson concept, Margolis model includes individual interests supplemented by *individual preferences of purely social character (orientation towards group interests)*[38].

Combination of neoclassical analysis and institutional outlook allowed Margolis to make an important theoretical step. In his model, analysis of the public well-being was supplemented not by a mere opportunity of an individual to evaluate alternative states of society (Bergson-Samuelson concept) but by utility function characteristic of an aggregation of individuals as a whole. Though he still 'transfers' this autonomously-existing public interest to individual market agents, theoretical significance of his model is great. Maybe without even knowing it, Margolis was the first to give rise to doubts as to the universality of the reducibility hypothesis. We'd like to comment on this statement in greater detail.

In Margolis model, we first meet the assumption that there is a *group interest as such*[39], existing independently along with traditionally-considered individual preferences. It is in the projection of this autonomous interest, i.e. in the value orientations and behavioural norms adopted by members of a group, that Margolis sees (in terms of the theory of well-being) individual functions of preferences for society's alternative states. While the authors of the theory of well-being define the social interest on the basis of individual utility functions, Margolis, figuratively speaking, turns this pyramid of interaction of individual and public interests upside-down. In his model the public interest is not an aggregate of individual preferences – vice versa, it exists as an independent interest of an aggregation of individuals as a whole, being projected to market agents and attributed to them in the form of specific individual preferences.

The main thing about Margolis' scheme is that recognition of an autonomously-existing public interest – regardless of whether institutional norms or needs are

---

[37] See, for instance, North D.C. Institutionen, institutioneller Wandel und Wirtschafts-leistungen, Tuebingen: Mohr, 1992 (Russian Edition – Moscow, 1997). It seems to us that after publication (in 1990) of this book by Douglas North, it became possible to optimistically evaluate the chances to unite all these 'irreconcilable' branches of economic thought.

[38] Margolis H. Selfishness, Altruism and Rationality: A Theory of Social Choice. — Cambridge: Cambridge University Press, 1982.

[39] Strictly speaking, 'collective needs', considered by the German financial economics (Finanzwissenschaft), and 'common values', introduced by Richard Musgrave, should be also mentioned here. We'll return to them in analysis of the concept of 'merit goods'.

mentioned – sheds doubt on the universality of the reducibility hypothesis. While in the theory of well-being an aggregate utility function is always derived from individual ones – thus actually transforming this hypothesis into an axiom –, the presence of an autonomously existing public interest in Margolis' model indicates the possibility of its incomplete 'dissolving' in individual preferences. The 'residue' actually testifies to the limitedness of the reducibility hypothesis.

Margolis himself did not seem to notice this possibility, having considered only a particular case when public interest is reduced to individual preferences. Having suggested the second utility function and attributing definite weights to personal and group interests of an individual, he started to aggregate them according to the neoclassical tradition, thereby reducing both utilities to one function. Thus Margolis first went beyond the limits of the reducibility hypothesis but then, having 'transferred' the public interest to individuals and summed utilities, actually returned to these limits. Moreover, we hold that it is incorrect to aggregate personal and group interests.

In this connection we'd like to point out fundamental differences in the nature of two types of utility, making it unacceptable to aggregate them in the form of a weight function. Any compromise (weighting) of individual and group interests (adjusting an individual utility function) distorts group preferences and autonomous social interest. And the rational behaviour of individuals, even having fully recognized the respective group values, may (remember Smith!) bring about a 'result having nothing in common with their intentions'. An individually-adopted social norm would almost always differ from an interest of society as such. Karl Popper wrote, 'Why does it happen so? Why do the results differ so much from intentions? It happens so because the social life is not just an arena where antagonistic groups try their strength against each other; it is an activity within a more or less flexible but often fragile structure of institutes and traditions, and it gives rise – in addition to different forms of conscious counteraction – to a great number of unforeseen reactions in this structure'[40].

Criticizing Mill, Popper directly indicates the impossibility of reducing all social situations to outcomes of individual urges[41]. Though we see an evident contradiction in Popper's rather scholastic reasoning, it seems right to ask a general question: is it possible to correct the said distortions? And if yes, then how? We would like to note that we are now considering the issue formulated above. What should be the mechanism for realization of social interest?

1.3 Reducibility in the Context of Realization of Social Interest

This question is in the focus of attention for many economists, including institutionalists. Analyzing the chances for this issue to be resolved, Michael Taylor in

---

[40] Popper K. Op. cit., pp. 113-114.
[41] Ibid., pp. 106-118.

particular, states that to harmonize public and individual interests, the most important principle of a community should be the sharing of respective beliefs and norms by its members[42]. Having a pessimistic view of this recipe, we can only agree with North, who regards this condition as absolutely inapplicable to large groups of people and especially to society as a whole[43].

Robert Sugden, another typical proponent of institutionalism, believes that coincidence of individual and social interests can be assured by institutions, i.e. some customs, traditions, formal and informal rules, adherence to which is a recognized behavioural norm. However, according to Sugden, this coincidence is possible only in a few cases when the so-called cooperation morale appears, 'when almost all members of society adhere to customs'[44]. Actually, Sugden just repeats Arrow's conclusion. According to the theorem 'On Impossibility', the social preference function, which into consideration opinions of all market agents, can be built only for a degenerate case when opinions of all individuals are identical (the case of dictatorship). It is easy to notice that Sugden's 'almost all' refers to the phenomenon of 'mass consciousness' (*Vermassung*), in the limit coinciding with Arrow's 'dictatorship'.

Besides extreme options (dictatorship and complete standardization of people's consciousness), the problem of social choice can be solved by ensuring cooperation between market agents. One of the key theses of game theory says that individuals, striving for maximization of their own utility functions, gain additional benefit in cooperating with others. This conclusion, similar to the fundamental thesis about trade benefits, has given rise to many research works devoted to developing corporate strategies of individual market agents' behaviour, which ensure opportunity for efficient coordination of individual and group interests[45]. The above 'prisoner's dilemma' – many economists' favourite illustration – can be used as an example here.

Despite this theory's success and development of numerous models of economic behaviour on its basis, an understanding of its very limited applicability has evolved. Here we'd like to refer to the analysis from the second chapter of the above-mentioned book by Douglas North. Summarizing the capabilities of game theory, he writes in particular that self-sustaining corporate solutions exist only 'under very simplified conditions, that is in cases in which both parties have full information at their disposal, the game will last indefinitely into the future, and the cast of players remain invariable... It is hardly worth saying that these conditions

---

[42] The issues of individuals' interaction within a community and the problems of social order were considered by M.Taylor in two books. See: Taylor M. Community, Anarchy and Liberty. – Cambridge: Cambridge University Press, 1982; Taylor M. The Possibility of Co-operation. – Cambridge: Cambridge University Press, 1987.

[43] North D.C. Op. cit., p. 31.

[44] Sugden R. The Economics of Rights, Co-operation, and Well-being. — Oxford: Blackwell, 1986, p. 173.

[45] We would like to mention the classical work: Von Neumann J., Morgenstern O. Theory of Games and Economic Behavior. Princeton: Princeton University Press, 1944 (Russian Edition – Moscow, 1970).

are not only excessively strict but simply rarely existent[46]. Sharing this view, we can state that hopes placed in game theory as a means of harmonization of public and individual interests have shown themselves to be illusory.

What is the conclusion? Using the traditional mechanism of the invisible hand to realize the public interest (Margolis' scheme) may, as we have already proved, produce results having nothing in common with original intentions. Coordinating social and individual interests through adoption of common behavioural norms acording to Taylor, phenomenon of 'mass consciousness' according to Sugden and dictatorship according to Arrow turns out to be possible, but obviously insufficient theoretically. All these are evidently degenerate cases. Unlike them, game models are quite able to provide a general solution. But the use of these models calls for meeting obviously unrealistic conditions *(Table 1.2)*.

Conditions we find in institutional models, social choice procedures and game theory are so unrealistic that the area where the use of the reducibility hypothesis can be substantiated seems to be extremely narrow. In a general case we can evidently speak about the existence of the interests of socium which cannot be reduced to individual preferences. In particular, they can often be observed in the circumstances which traditional theory usually associates with market failures.

---

[46] North D.C. Op. cit., p. 79.

Table 1.2. Evolution of the Understanding of the Social Interest and Mechanisms for its Realization

	Definition of social interest	Market agents	Mechanism for realization of social interest
SMITH		Individuals	The 'invisible hand'
UTILITARIANISM	Sum of individual interests	Individuals	The 'invisible hand'
MARSHALL	Function of individual interests	Individuals	The 'invisible hand'
RAWLSIANISM	Improvement in the less well-to-do individual's status	Individuals	Maximization of the less well-to-do individual's utility
PARETO	Function of individual interests	Individuals	Pareto optimality
BERGSON-SAMUELSON	Aggregate function of individual preferences for society's states	Individuals	Pareto optimality & maximization of weight function
MARGOLIS	Weighted sum of individual and group preferences	Individuals	Adoption of community's norms by individuals
TAYLOR	Beliefs and standards of a community	Individuals	Mass adoption of customs
SUGDEN	Social customs	Individuals	Mass adoption of customs
ARROW	Harmonizing individual interests	Individuals	Dictatorship
GAME MODELS	Harmonizing individual and social interests	Individuals	Corporate strategy

Without repeating well-known arguments, we'd like to express our doubts as to an answer to the question: who is to 'blame' – market or economic theory? Is the thesis about correct theory detecting market failures indisputable? Or vice versa, alleged imperfection of the market is conditioned by failures of the theory with its unrealistic basic assumptions? Not to answer these questions but to illustrate the current situation, we'd like to give the following example.

Example 1.1. Market imperfection and Professor William Nordhaus' mistake. For this purpose we have chosen an abstract from the book written by famous ecologists E.U. von Weizsäcker, A.B. Lovins and L.H Lovins, the authors of the Report to the Club of Rome (1995). It is so expressive and persuasive that we cite it almost completely[47].

'In the era of Reagan-Bush, Yale University economics professor William Nordhaus published estimates (1990) according to which, if the USA tried to stabilize CO_2 emission at the level established by the international group in Toronto and regarded by most climatologists as the first modest step towards stabilizing the climate on the Earth, this would have reduced the gross domestic product by about USD 200 billion per year (according to the mass media, this would have been the stabilization 'cost'). This astronomical cost of just preliminary measures meant to stabilize the climate startled John Sununu, the Head of the Presidential Administration, and paralyzed the politics in that area. The method of computation suggested by Nordhaus is simple.

First, he assumes that more efficient use of power should not be connected to reduction of costs at current prices, since, if it were so, people would have already implemented it. Any market failures are considered insignificant and *nobody believes that twenty-pound notes are waiting to be found (we italicized – R.G. and A.R.[48]).* Empiric data available to those actually selling energy-saving technologies and those spending their time fighting with numerous facts of market mechanism's inefficiency, is ignored.

Nordhaus further assumes that the only way to make people buy more energy-saving technologies is to increase the price for power through taxation. Since the market is not believed to make significant failures, their correction along with keeping the prices for power at a constant level seems unreasonable.

Then Nordhaus supposes that revenues from tax on electric power are not invested but returned to taxpayers so that they could buy anything they want (which means reduction of GDP, while reinvestment could increase it).

Nordhaus studies previous research works to find out how much the consumption of electric power fell when its price increased. (This price elasticity of demand is just a stenographic record of millions of inadequate decisions made under conditions far from the real ones. One of the goals of energy policy is often to confuse people.)

Finally, he turns to a computer model to see how much the energy tax should be increased to reduce power consumption to the amount complying with the recommendations regarding CO_2 emission adopted in Toronto, and how this tax level would affect the economic activity in general to find out that this would result in a decrease in GDP by USD200 billion. The figure is probably exact, but the sign should be changed from minus to plus. To reach

---

[47] Weizsaecker E.U. von, Lovins A.B., Lovins L.H. Factor Four: Doubling Wealth — Halving Resource Use. The New Report to the Club of Rome. London: Earthscan Publ., 1998 (Russian Edition – Moscow, 2000, pp. 208-209).

[48] We would like to refer the reader to the parable about an elderly economist and his grand-daughter, who found money while they were walking. We cited this story in the introduction to our monograph.

the CO_2 emission value set in Toronto would mean not to lose but save about USD200 billion per year, since fuel saving would be cheaper than its burning.

Bewildered by this potential difference of USD400 billion per year, one of the authors visited a scientific conference where Nordhaus' report was presented and during the discussion asked Professor Nordhaus why in his computations he had not used abundant empirical documentation showing the actual cost of power saving, measured and documented by thousands of firms tackling it on a daily basis. Professor answered, "I've just used a thesis of economic theory. Mr. Lovins, your hypothesis that many power-saving measures at current prices make it possible to reduce costs, which is not realized due to inefficient market mechanism, is interesting. Using this assumption instead of mine, you have come to an absolutely different conclusion".

However, he refused to take the responsibility for the fact that his hypothesis has deadlocked the global attempts to approach the climate issues based on the principle: minimal costs, purchased at the most competitive price. Nordhaus is so fond of his *theory* that he simply doesn't want to consider *facts* and seems not to see any difference between the former and the latter'.

Commenting on the quoted abstract, we are not going to make a point of how much Professor William Nordhaus, a co-author of a famous textbook, is 'fond of his theory', or whether he sees any difference between theory and practice. We believe that Nordhaus' mistake was programmed by the theory itself. This is what Nordhaus says, 'I've just used a thesis of economic theory'. It does not matter how Amory Lovins, physicist and ecologist from the Rocky Mountain Institute, reasons, and what a wonderful collection of practical cases he demonstrates – William Nordhaus, economist, cannot 'see' the things that the market ignores. According to traditional theory, 'efficient' means 'beneficial for individuals', and only the market can reveal individual preferences. This universal neoclassical formula shows the limitedness of the reducibility hypothesis. Therefore, Professor Nordhaus' mistake was quite predictable.

Let us make some more remarks on the fundamental character. All attempts, inspired by practice, to transgress an atomistic market model without considering its basic postulates have only resulted in an artificial withdrawal of some activities from the sphere of market relations. It is easy to understand. An exclusively individualistic (according to classical axioms) nature of utility should have inevitably contradicted this category's application to a multitude of individuals living in a society.

That is why the theory of well-being gave rise to a family of methodological mutants like 'individual preferences for societal states', 'aggregate preference function' or weight function summing utilities of different nature. All these categories inherit the said contradiction. Efforts to solve this problem by including groups of people and society as a whole in the analysis, at the same time regarding an individual as the only market agent, have resulted in construction of degenerate cases

– description of individual behaviour in a 'community', *Vermassung* and dictatorship.

Finally, without any risk of simplification, it is possible to state that a contradiction generated by the socialization of individual utility is being transformed into opposition of the market and state. That is why we indisputably regard Hayek's imperatives, let alone all sorts of imitative incantations concerning a 'harmonious' state and withdrawal of the state from the economic life in general, as attempts to cure an illness by fighting its symptoms. We are sure that the problems of economic growth and social equity should be solved not by pushing the state out of the market sphere, but by resolving the basic contradiction between individual utility and socialization. In this regard, the theory of public goods confirms our conclusion.

1.4 Three Fundamental Negations

As we started to discuss irreducible social needs, it became clear that goods and services able to meet such needs somehow relate to public and merit goods.[49] There is no doubt that a more detailed consideration of these relations will bring about a better understanding of social interest, thus presenting the reducibility hypothesis in a broader context. But first, we'd like to make a preliminary remark on public and merit goods.

Having read recent publications – from standard textbooks on economics to special monographs –, one will hardly see any difference between public and merit goods. Many authors 'ignore' merit goods, not differentiating them from public goods[50]. Even those dividing the goods in question into separate groups fail to clearly establish this boundary. For instance, the well-known standard textbook by Fischer, Dornbusch and Schmalensee [51] and the popular special textbook by Atkinson and Stiglitz[52] devote only half a page to merit goods.

This is hardly by accident. The thing is that contemporary theory bases its explanation of merit and public goods on the same assumption that some 'correct' or *true* individual preferences exist, the main difference between merit and public

---

[49] Taking into account the importance of meritorics for our concept, we'll devote a special chapter of this book to its consideration.

[50] We would like to note that even the most popular *Economics* (for example Samuelson P.A., Nordhaus W.D. or McConnell C.R. Brue S.L. Economics : principles, problems, and policies. Boston, Mass.: McGraw-Hill, 2002) don't even mention merit goods. The same can be said about many special monographs (for example Jacobson L.I. Economics of the Public Sector Basics of the State Finances Theory – Moscow, 1996; Stiglitz J. Economics of the Public Sector. London, New York: WW Norton & Co., 1988 (Russian Edition – Moscow, 1997)).

[51] Fischer S., Dornbusch R., Schmalensee R. Economics, 2nd Ed. New York: McGraw-Hill, 1988. (Russian Edition – Moscow, 1997).

[52] Atkinson A., Stiglitz J. Lectures in Public Economics. New York: McGraw-Hill, 1980 (Russian Edition – Moscow, 1995).

goods being the motivation for consumers' behaviour. In the case of merit goods, consumers cannot actually 'see' their own true preferences and therefore show only false demand[53]. As for the case of public goods, individuals, acting as free riders, disguise their true preferences consciously and do not show any demand for the said goods[54]. Such explanations may bring one to the conclusion that consumers of public and merit goods are nothing else but a group of 'weak-sighted free riders'.

Introduction of a double standard, legalizing the existence of some individual utilities different from actual individual preferences, corresponds to the above-mentioned attempts to reduce societal needs to its members' needs, which is impossible. Trying to resolve this unsolvable problem, traditional theory has actually designed a 'new historic community of people', who either pathologically do not understand 'their luck' or prefer not to confess that they do.

Meanwhile, stopping to absolutize the reducibility hypothesis and recognizing interests of society as such make all these recherché constructions unnecessary. Having recovered their 'sight and consciousness', individuals will stop suffering from split personality, each of them finding his or her sole and true utility function. Along with them, a state should become a market agent also maximizing its (social) utility. If we consider merit and public goods from this point of view, it becomes clear that they do differ, and considerably. Moreover, usual goods divisible in consumption, having nothing to do with public goods, may belong to merit goods[55].

Anyway, a connection between meritoric actions and social needs is evident. We are going to prove that these actions are always conditioned by the interest of society as such. Therefore, any merit good has its social utility. But since this utility is nothing but a good's ability to meet irreducible needs, it inevitably manifests itself in specific features of the good.

For convenience, we'd like to introduce the following definition. We'll say that *irreducibility* is characteristic of goods and services, if a social need for them cannot be reduced to individual needs. Using this characteristic, it is possible to make

---

[53] This issue will be examined in detail in the next chapter.

[54] In particular, Samuelson pointed out the egoistic interest of an individual in giving a false signal of lack of demand for public good (Samuelson P.A. The Pure Theory of Public Expenditure //Review of Economics and Statistics, 1954; Samuelson P.A. The Pure Theory of Public Expenditures and taxation. Public Economics, J.Margolis and H.Guitton (Eds). — London: Macmillan, 1969). See also Stiglitz J.E. Op. cit., p. 121; Fischer S., Dornbusch, P., Schmalensee, P. Op. cit., p. 64; McConnell C.R. Brue S.L. Op. cit., p. 100. As a matter of fact, the 'free rider' phenomenon can be observed not only in the sphere of public goods (Atkinson A.B., Stiglitz J.E., Op. cit., p. 692), but this is another topic.

[55] This is confirmed by well-known critics of meritorics: 'Properties of a public good (positive externalities) are not a constituting feature, so pure private goods as well as public goods can be supplied as merit ones' (Tietzel, M., Müller, C. Noch mehr zur Meritorik. // Zeitschrift für Wirtschafts- und Sozialwissenschaften. 118. Jahrgang, 1998, Heft 1. – Berlin, p. 92).

the following statement: while not every merit good is a public good, every merit good can meet some irreducible societal need, thus incorporating the irreducibility.

As for a connection between irreducible social interests and public goods, it is more complicated. Usually public goods include the national defence, public order protection, fundamental research, etc. There are several definitions of these rather specific goods. According to Samuelson, 'public good is a good which is equally included in two or more individual utility functions'[56]. Proceeding from a study by Ugo Mazzola, the Italian economist of the 19th century, Mark Blaug, the English expert of economic studies, gives another definition. He writes, 'Specific nature of public goods is manifested in the fact that their consumption can be only collective and equal: the more one household gets of these goods, the more gets any other household'[57].

This definition is connected with two fundamental characteristics of public goods. First, if they are available to someone, they should be available to everyone – this means *non-excludability* in consumption. The second feature is *non-rivalness* – the consumption of these goods by anyone does not hamper consumption by others. These are specific features that single out public goods from all other goods and services and have a great theoretical potential[58].

Nevertheless, regardless of the said clear characteristics, the notion of public goods is rather vague. The definition is not precise because of the lack of exact limits of these features' spread in the sphere of goods and services. This vagueness generated so broad and ambiguous interpretations that any demarcation of boundaries between public and usual goods becomes almost impossible. As a result, along with classical public goods we often come across 'goods, whose consumption is beneficial for society', so-called quasi-public goods – those which are only partially public – and even less clear, mixed public goods[59].

We consider it surprising and even paradoxical to include in the group of public goods all goods produced as a result of the fulfillment of the state's traditional tasks. We mean national defence, public order protection, support for fundamental

---

[56] Samuelson P.A. Op.cit., 1969, p. 108.

[57] Blaug M. Economic Theory in Retrospect. Fifth English edition. Cambridge: Cambridge University Press, 1997 (Russian Edition – Moscow, 1994, p. 549).

[58] In this context, M. Olson's ideas are of great interest, which he set forth during a famous discussion with Rudolf Penner, Richard Musgrave and Gordon Tullock (Olson, M. Toward a More Theory of Governmental Structure. Budget Reform and of Theory of Fiscal Federalism //AEA Papers and Proceedings, May 1986, vol. 76, No.2, pp. 120-125).

[59] In particular, dividing the public goods into social goods and *goods whose consumption is useful for society*, L. Khodov defines the latter as goods 'located somewhere between the consumership services and social goods' (Khodov L.G. Grounds of State Economic Policy – Moscow, 1997, p. 37). In his textbook, L. Jacobson writes that *mixed public goods* are goods having 'at least one characteristic of public goods manifested moderately'. (Jacobson L.I. Op. cit., p. 42). In his fundamental work *Economic Theory in Retrospect*, M.Blaug writes about *quasi-public goods* as goods which 'at least partially have public nature' (Blaug M. Op. cit., p. 550). It seems hardly possible to speak about the strictness of these concepts.

research, etc. Having failed to find a place for them in the market sphere, the neo-classical theory transferred them to the group of pubic goods. It has become so customary that similar features of, say, the national defence and the lighthouse have become a commonplace found almost in every standard *Economics*[60]. However, it is here that we can see inaccuracy in using well-known notions.

In this connection let us return to the definition of public goods and pay attention to the fact that two specific features of *individual consumption* are mentioned in it: impossibility of excluding any individuals from consumption of this good and an absence of their rivalry for it. After Blaug, we'd like to stress the fact of a good's consumption by individuals in this definition. This is what is meant by the above Samuelson's definition, according to which a public good must come into two or more individual utility functions.

It is clear that a lighthouse is a public good consumed by individuals. But the situation with national defence is obscure: goods like strategic missiles, bacterio-logical and other types of weapons are not consumed by any individual directly, and these goods are not included in any individual utility function. The same applies to fundamental research, since it is difficult to imagine how individuals can consume, for example, Pontryagin-Kuratowski theorem from graph theory, Arrow-Debreu and McKenzie models from mathematical economics or the concept of economic sociodynamics, or how these can be included in individual utility functions.

The arising 'mess' shows traces of the same reducibility hypothesis, according to which any social need is reduced to individual needs. In the case of traditional absolutization of this hypothesis, the state's needs for armed forces and fundamental research are at the same time individual needs. However, having given up the universality of the reducibility hypothesis and recognizing the phenomenon of irreducible social needs, we should clearly understand that there exist goods consumed exclusively by the state. Such goods are not included in any individual utility function and are *not designed* for individual consumption. We believe that national defence and fundamental research belong to these goods.

As for non-excludability and non-rivalness, they are manifested only in the *results of these goods' consumption by the state*. The social effect of national defence and fundamental research is therefore characterized by these properties: it is

---

[60] We would like to quote popular textbooks. 'The best example of a public good is national defense. When a country defends its liberty... it does the same for its people regardless of whether they want it or not' (Samuelson P.A., Nordhaus W.D. Op. cit., p.76). 'A good is a public good, if, even used by one person; it is available for consumption by others. Clean air is a public good, like national defense or social security. If the armed forces protect a country, then maintenance of your safety does not in anyway impede maintenance of anybody's safety'. (Fischer S., Dornbusch, R., Schmalensee R. Op. cit., p. 64). 'National defense is one of the few pure public goods meeting both requirements, i.e. impossibility and undesirability of exclusion from their consumption. Lighthouse is another example of almost pure public goods: it is difficult (but not impossible) to exclude those not making any contribution to its maintenance from using the services provided by it' (Stiglitz J. Op. cit., p. 124).

available for all members of society, and nobody can be limited in its consumption. Achievements of fundamental research, as well as bacteriological weapons technology as it is, do not have such properties, since they are not involved in individual consumption. Therefore, these specific goods can be not included in either public or merit goods. However, not having individual utility, the said goods can meet society's irreducible needs; that is they have social utility. Taking this fact into consideration, we will call them *'social goods'*.

Probably, it would have been not worth speculating on this topic here, if it were not for three specific *negations* - *irreducibility* of needs, *non-excludability* and *non-rivalness* in consumption. These three social characteristics of goods *DO NOT* allow the regarding of the neoclassical market model as the ultimate truth and actually mark the boundary of the reducibility hypothesis' universality. Therefore, having introduced the category of social utility in theoretical use, it is necessary to see the difference between goods and services having this utility and hence the irreducibility feature, and public goods characterized by non-excludability and non-rivalness.

Pay attention to another remarkable fact. It is easy to notice that both merit and social goods can meet irreducible public needs. In other words, both of them have a fundamental irreducibility feature. But the existence of one common characteristic, however important it might be, does not make these goods identical. Any merit good has social utility, but not any good having social utility is merit. We would like to emphasize that merit goods, as well as the public goods considered above, are mostly consumed by individuals. As for social goods, they are consumed only by a state. Now, let us analyze meritorics in greater detail.

2 Meritorics and Social Interest

We have analyzed the problem of the reducibility of social needs (and indirectly the place of the state in a market economy) from the standpoint of the standard theory of well-being; now it makes sense to consider this problem through the prism of a special concept. We mean Richard Musgrave's meritorics, which, just as it is, can be incorporated neither in the theory of well-being nor in concepts of collective decisions and constitutional economics. Staying apart from the mainstream and even being in a sort of information blockade, this concept remains topical, being a significant theoretical result.

Quite striking things happen to this concept. Meritorics has already been under discussion for forty years and all these years Anglo-Saxons have hushed it up. Even the critique of this concept from the standpoint of extreme liberalism comes only from German economists. This is why in addition to Musgrave's works[61], we will use materials of discussions which were mostly published in German journals (*Zeitschrift für Wirtschafts- und Sozialwissenschaften* and *Finanzarchiv*) and some special works published in Tübingen. We wish to pay attention to the latest study on meritorics – the critical analysis by Manfred Tietzel and Christian Müller, published in Berlin in 1998.

Speaking about meritorics, we would like to single out the key definition of this concept. Merit goods are goods individuals demand which falls behind the one which is 'socially desired' and is therefore stimulated by the state; demerit goods are those goods whose consumption the state tries to reduce. Thus the concept of meritorics comes directly out of public interests not manifested in individual preferences. We consider this aspect of Musgrave's concept particularly important; it is here that we see its genetic relationship with our theory. Despite numerous differences, the comparative analysis of these two concepts show that Musgrave's meritorics and our sociodynamics have the same basic element (a kind of DNA) — the *existence of public needs not revealed in individual preferences.*

Our theory deals with irreducible social interests, and Musgrave's concept – with society's merit wants. Musgrave singles out three specific types of such

---

[61] Musgrave R.A. Principles of Budget Determination //Joint Economic Committee, Federal Expenditure Policy for Economic Growth and Stability. — Washington, 1957, pp. 108-115; Musgrave R.A. A Multiple Theory of Budget Determination. //Finanzarchiv, 17, 1957, pp. 333-343; Musgrave R.A. Finanztheorie.— Tübingen, 1974; Musgrave R.A. Merit Goods. //Eatwell J., Milgate M., Newman P. (Hrsg.). The New Palgrave. — London-Basingstoke, 1987, pp. 452-453; Musgrave R.A, Musgrave P.B, Kullmer L. Die öffentlichen Finanzen in Theorie und Praxis, Bd. 1, 6. Aufl. — Tübingen, 1994.

wants[62]. First, *pathological cases*, when a society 'wants' to protect inadequately informed or retarded people from their possible incorrect decisions. Second, the interest in resolution of the collision known as *'weak will of Odysseus'*, when the state has to hinder incorrect individual decisions[63]. Third, the demand for *reallocation of goods in kind* aimed to provide assistance to indigent members of society. Let us analyze each type of society's merit wants of and respective cases of government interference.

2.1 The Pathological Case

Considering 'pathological cases' as the first type of motivation for state interference, most authors, like Musgrave himself, single out two basic situations – *irrationality* of individual's behaviour and his *unawareness* of goods' real properties. A typical example is the preferential status of retarded people or children, for whose choice 'accuracy' the society is responsible. Not considering other reasons for irrational behaviour[64], we wish to mention that in this case the legitimacy of the trustee state is recognized only when an economic agent fails to learn to act rationally in order to improve his well-being even if the situation is repeated. In this situation, like in others, meritoric actions should ensure adjustment of individual preferences. However, being concerned about individual sovereignty, Musgrave indicates the temporary nature of 'a thrust choice as assistance in the process of learning'[65].

Admitting the possibility of irrational behaviour of market agents and trying to justify state interference from exclusively individualistic positions, some critics of meritorics reduce this case to implementation of unanimous individual decisions under Rawls' 'veil of ignorance'. Rawls himself insists that the intuitive idea of the 'veil of ignorance' was implicitly present in Kant's ethics[66]. Not completely sharing

---

[62] Musgrave R.A. Op.cit., 1987, p. 452. Musgrave also singles out the fourth type of merit wants, which we will analyze further.

[63] The same collision is studied by the so-called *'egonomics'* – Economics of Temptation (Koboldt, C. Ökonomie der Versuchung; Drogenverbot und Sozialvertragstheorie. – Tübingen, 1995, p. 9-15; See also: Elster J. Ulysses and Sirens. – Cambridge, 1979).

[64] See Head J.G. On Merit Goods // Finanzarchiv 25, 1966, p. 5; Andel N. Zum Konzept der meritorischen Güter // Finanzarchiv, 42, 1984, p. 646.

[65] Musgrave R.A. Provision for Social Goods // J. Margolis, H. Guitton (eds.). Public Economics. — London-Basingstoke, 1969, p. 143; Musgrave R.A. Fiscal Systems. — New Haven, 1969, p. 12.

[66] Rawls J. Op. cit., pp. 130, 223-229. Commenting on the notion of 'veil of ignorance', Rawls directly indicates that 'the formulation introduced in the book is implicitly contained in Kant's doctrine of categorical imperative, regarding both determination of the procedural criterion and the way it was used by Kant. When Kant advises us to verify our maxims by considering the case when they become a universal law of the nature, he must suggest that we don't know our place in this imaginary system of the Nature' (Ibid., p. 171).

this rather disputable thesis, we would like to consider only the original concept by Rawls and his definition of the 'veil of ignorance'.

Defining this category, he writes, 'We must reduce to zero those specific chances that put people at a disadvantage and tempt them to use social and natural circumstances in order to gain advantages for themselves. To do this, I'd suggest that the parties are under the veil of ignorance. They don't know how different alternatives will impact their own case and undertake to evaluate all principles based on general consideration... Nobody knows his place in society, class or social status. Nobody knows his fortune as for allocation of natural gifts, mental faculties, strength, etc.'. In other words, nobody knows the 'economic and social situation in the society or the level of civilization and culture'[67].

Such broad digression to the topic not directly associated with meritorics is easy to explain: the method 'discovered' by Rawls has been in demand by economists, especially by those for whom the contractual process is the basic element of any social organization[68]. Musgrave's critics, who persist in their attempts to prove that the 'merit concept does not transcend the individualistic one', also found this method convenient[69]. According to them, adjustment of irrational preferences of market agents and fulfillment of respective meritoric functions by the state can be explained from purely individualistic positions. Suppose individuals are under a 'veil of ignorance' and know nothing about their future economic and social status; then, insuring their own welfare, they would voluntarily agree to state interference.

Continuing to study a society's response to the irrational behaviour of individuals in the 'pathological case', we would like to give the most common example of children's right to paternalism, including the right to education. In connection with this, we should recall Musgrave's argument. He considers the possibility of irrational individual decisions regarding children and the state's responsibility to provide children with free schools[70]. Agreeing with Musgrave for compulsory elementary and secondary education, Tietzel and Müller believe that 'under the "veil of ignorance" individuals will insure themselves against the case when those having the right to bring up children decide that these individuals' children don't have to study at school by voting for compulsory school education introduced by the state'[71].

In this way, using Rawls' artificial scheme, a merit interest, interpreted by Tietzel and Müller, becomes reducible and dissolves under the 'veil of ignorance' in individuals' unanimity. The imperative of undesirability of state interference remains the main thing for the mentioned authors. Permanent adherence to this ideo-

---

[67] Rawls J. Op. cit., p. 127.

[68] Here, it is enough to mention James Buchanan, who used the 'veil of ignorance' to ground the rule of unanimity (Buchanan J. The Limits of Liberty: Between Anarchy and Leviathan. Chicago: The University of Chicago Press, 1975 (Russian Edition: Nobel Prize Winners in Economics. James Buchanan. – Moscow, 1997, pp. 431-432)).

[69] Tietzel M., Müller C. Op. cit., p. 106.

[70] Musgrave R.A. Op. cit., 1974, p. 16.

[71] Tietzel M., Müller C. Op. cit., p. 107.

logical principle forces the tolerance of the state only in areas in which it is impossible to avoid it. Then to restore the customary picture of the world, only one thing is needed – to find the individualistic substantiation for legitimacy of state activity, i.e. to prove the reducibility of its specific interest to individual preferences[72].

We shall further discuss this fundamental issue, and now, analyzing the 'pathological case', we wish to pay attention to another aspect of meritorics. Even recognizing the legitimacy of the state meritoric actions aimed at correcting irrational individual decisions, some authors (first of all, Tietzel and Müller) express their doubts about the form of interference suggested by Musgrave. Like faithful liberals, they strongly object to subsidies (in our example to schools) and defend the neoclassical principle, according to which budget transfers to consumers are always more efficient than financial support for producers. Proceeding from the famous individualistic principle of minimum compulsion, Tietzel and Müller consider that only those state actions are admissible, as a result of which 'parents, upon receiving the financial support, may freely choose among various educational institutions, including private, and not depend on a quasi-monopolistic supply in this area'[73].

Without dwelling upon a rather complex issue of relative efficiency of transfers and subsidies, we purport that no sole decision is possible in this case. Choice of any means of meritoric interference should have no underlying ideological reasons, whether it is the individualistic principle of minimum compulsion or total paternalism. Our studies showed that the form of state support essentially depends on the size of supported social groups: 'small marginal groups require the use of direct subsides to consumers, while support for socially significant marginal groups require an appropriate restrictive price policy based on subventions to producers'[74].

Now, let us consider the case of unawareness, in which an individual is not aware of or incorrectly assesses a good's qualities. In this situation a social interest in correction of the distorted individual preferences also springs up. As for the boundary separating awareness from unawareness, it is quite subtle, which makes opportunities for meritoric interference too wide. But even when state actions are recognized as legitimate due to informational failure of the market, both supporters and critics of meritorics try to justify them solely from individualistic positions. In other words, here we also see a search for any possibility of reducing a social interest to individual preferences, the state being allowed to interfere only within the limits meeting the basic principle of minimum compulsion. Hence the basic form of meritoric interference in the case of individual unawareness is compulsory information.

---

[72] Strictly speaking, it is this theme that is developed in both works written in the 1960s — by Schmidt (1964), Head (1966) and McLure (1968), — and recent works — by Brennan and Lomasky (1983), Andel (1984), Head (1988), Schmidt (1988), Priddat (1992), Tietzel and Müller (1998).

[73] Tietzel M., Müller C. Op. cit., p. 107.

[74] Grinberg R. Rubinstein A. Difficulties of Market Adaptation, Income, Social Welfare // Social Sciences and the Present, 1992, No. 5, pp. 43-44.

Here we wish to direct special attention to a rather essential point. State expenditures on informing the population or directly forcing the producers of goods and services to inform consumers about their true qualities often cannot make up for the chronic deficit of information. Musgrave wrote, 'Uneducated people cannot appreciate all benefits of education'. Therefore, any source of information – even that regularly reproducing the same situation – may fail to teach an individual to act correctly. In this sense unawareness is always fraught with irrationality. And the state has no choice but to stimulate individuals to act appropriately using the tried and true method of reducing prices for merit goods by subsidizing their producers. In some cases this conditions the introduction of a 'zero tariff', that is the provision of free services.

Analysis of various standpoints shows that most economists see no way to justify meritoric interference. It is easy to understand. To agree with meritorics means to indirectly doubt the universality of the reducibility hypothesis. Meanwhile, Tietzel and Müller insist on the opposite conclusion: 'Strictly speaking, the basic characteristic of the state meritoric interference – infringement of the basic individualistic norm – can be seen neither in the case of irrationality, nor in the case of unawareness'[75]. As a matter of fact, they reiterate doubts of Musgrave, who thinks that this case relates to 'defects in realization of consumers' sovereignty rather than its repudiation as a norm'[76]. This position is shared by Andel[77] and Head[78].

Taking into account the state's rather vague idea of true individual preferences and meritorics' lacking any solution as to the form of state interference, some authors insist on the complete inapplicability of this concept in the 'pathological case'. Their verdict looks rather categorical: 'In the case of individual irrationality, the concept of merit goods is evidently inapplicable: it is of no use for deciding on necessity of the state interference, since it leads to the same results as the individualistic approach; in considering the subject of interference, it is even less definite than this approach and in some cases it doesn't even exclude the interference which can be perceived as totalitarian by those affected by it'[79]. As we see, it is the chronic nihilism in regard to the state and an inherent fear of totalitarianism that impede perception of meritorics and prevent the majority of its critics to see its essence – the evidence of the existence of society's interests not reflected in individual preferences.

Meanwhile, the real world around us, at least in 'pathological cases', does not allow for the discounting of state interference and requires, from our standpoint, recognition of the autonomous social interest not revealed in individual preferences. Nevertheless, adherence to normative individualism, learned at the mother's knees, forces economists in the opposite direction. Then the 'veil of ignorance' and 'hypothetical consensus' appear, which consider social interest solely from the

---

[75] Tietzel M., Müller C. Op. cit,, p. 109.

[76] Musgrave R.A. Op. cit., 1987, p. 452.

[77] Andel N. Op. cit. p. 109.

[78] Head J.G. On Merit Wants //Finanzarchiv, 46, 1988, p. 17.

[79] Tietzel M., Müller C. Op. cit., p. 107.

standpoint of the universalism of the reducibility hypothesis. Meritorics itself 'perishes' in a vicious circle: to be recognized, it must show its adherence to normative individualism, and having succeeded in this, meritorics turns out to be unnecessary. Let us consider other cases that, according to Musgrave, help us to understand the concept of merit goods best.

2.2 The Weak Will of Odysseus

When sailing past one of the islands of the Aegean Sea, Odysseus ordered all his sailors to stuff their ears with wax and to tie him to the mast to hear the mellifluous sirens sing without being able to make wrong decisions. The well-known plot by Homer is probably the first description of the situation when a person is not strong enough to make a correct decision and therefore deliberately agrees to someone else's interference. The same type of meritoric actions is demonstrated by the traditional example regarding narcotics, when people taking them, not relying on their own will, want to be helped to give up the noxious dependence.

Describing this case, Musgrave proceeded from the unrealistic assumption that state actions coincide with some true interests of individuals. Thus, the father of meritorics failed to find a general case, in which the state is interested in limiting or prohibiting some goods and services' consumption regardless of or even contrary to individual preferences. The basic reason for this 'failure' of Musgrave is his conviction of reducibility of social interest.

Trying to exclude any possibility of infringing on the principles of normative individualism, Tietzel and Müller went further along this path. They interpret the case of the 'weak will of Odysseus' proceeding from an even more radical hypothesis that 'a man can simultaneously have several preferential systems, i.e. evaluation standards, and under certain conditions these systems can exclude each other so that completely different, even opposite actions are evaluated as optimal'[80]. This interpretation usually supposes that there are strategically correct and distorted individual preferences, the latter arising under the pressure of current conditions which hinder a 'weak-willed' person from making correct decisions. Therefore, in this case the state meritoric assistance should be aimed at overcoming individual weakness; that is, it should aid in realizing true individual preferences, not a social interest.

Nothing new in this regard seems to be added by R. Thaler and H. Shefrin, postulating the 'split personality' – simultaneously acting as a weak-willed victim of a tempter (*I-doer*) and its rational antipode and 'pride of the creator' (*I-planner*). If a 'doer' prefers shortsighted egoistic actions, a 'planner' strives to realize long-term enlightened interests[81]. Under such circumstances, there arises a problem of self-

---

[80] Tietzel M., Müller C. Op. cit., p. 116. See also: Tietzel M. Zur Theorie der Präferenzen //Jahrbuch für Neue Politische Ökonomie, 1988, p. 38-71.

[81] Thaler R.H., Shefrin H.M. An Economic Theory of Self-Control //Journal of Political Economy, 89, 1981, pp. 392-406.

control, consisting in the fact that in a concrete situation, a person would act differently compared to his deep and comprehensive evaluation of consequences for the decisions he makes[82].

R. Thaler and H. Shefrin suppose that 'I-planner' can agree to the state meritoric actions restricting 'I-doer'. The general position is formulated by Tietzel and Müller as 'self-paternalism' of an individual – his desire to create institutions which, according to the preferences of a 'planner', limit and adjust a 'doer's' behaviour[83]. This is the source of many examples, which have started to live their own lives: a biker who does not wish to wear a helmet but agrees to the introduction of regulations prescribing compulsory wearing of a helmet; a young man who believes other expenses are more efficient but agrees that the state provides for him in his old age; a drug addict who gives in to his pernicious dependence but dreams of giving it up. All these examples serve the same end – to prove that any meritoric interference, even in the case of the 'weak will of Odysseus', can be justified solely by individualistic motives.

Head considers the case of 'weak will' and the relevant problem of self-control from another standpoint. He reduces this type of meritoric interference to the 'pathological case' analyzed above, in which a lack of information makes individual behaviour irrational. For this reason, Head substantiates state interference with the requirement of improving an individual's awareness. According to Head, meritoric actions should be aimed at 'stimulating the information-based choice and excluding false or misleading information'[84]. Head considers the tactical preferences of a weak-willed 'doer' only in the context of his 'unawareness' or lack of understanding of true consequences of his consumer choice. It is clear that Head's interpretation is also connected with the individualistic scheme. Accordingly, every person can have false and true preferences, and the state's role is reduced only to creating conditions under which an individual desires (or has) to abandon erroneous decisions and choose correct estimations.

In this seemingly clear case, which mainly deals with restrictions and prohibitions (this is how Musgrave[85] sees the way to tackle manifestations of weak will), Tietzel and Müller again pay special attention to the form of meritoric interference. And again, defending the individualistic principle of minimum compulsion makes them actually call into question all state actions. In particular, they write, 'In this case, to remedy the weak will, the informative or even non-governmental solution should also be preferred to the meritoric compulsion to use safety belts or motor cycle helmets. If a biker yields to no persuasion of his friends and relatives and doesn't put on a helmet, he must have his own reasons for this, which should be respected from the individualistic standpoint'[86].

Even recognizing that the state meritoric interference is legitimate, these authors try to make it so 'unnoticeable' that they agree to discard the basic motive for

---

[82] Koboldt C. Op. cit., p. 13.
[83] Tietzel M., Müller C. Op. cit., p. I 17.
[84] Head J.G. Op. cit., 1988, p. 17.
[85] Musgrave R.A. Op. cit., 1987, p. 453.
[86] Tietzel M., Müller C. Op cit, p. 119.

it. Not challenging the requirement with respect to personal preferences, we still must note that if an intervention is recognized as necessary, it should be efficient. In this sense, the principle of minimum compulsion should be interpreted as the principle of reasonable adequacy. In other words, unless government measures are sufficient to achieve their purpose – even the most faultless – from the individualistic point of view, this form of interference should be repudiated as inadequate.

Though Tietzel and Müller go so far in their adherence to the principle of minimum compulsion that interference often loses reasonable adequacy (so, money transfers to the indigent aimed at increasing the consumption of certain goods may result in an increased demand for some other goods), they still must admit to the inadequacy of a liberal scheme in the case of drug addiction control using the excise duty. This measure will inevitably fail. Inveterate drug addicts will hardly give up (and will be able to give up) drugs as a result of the state interference. For this consumer group, taxes or expected costs connected with penalties always remain low. Crime can rise as an undesirable by-effect, which will cost much for society. The demonstrative examples are drug trafficking and bootlegging during the period of prohibition in the USA[87]. Excise taxes in the case of demerit goods are as inefficient as money transfers to consumers of merit goods[88].

Pensions should be especially considered. They are traditionally included in merit wants connected with the necessity to correct decisions made by weak-willed young people who often prefer to spend money for quite different momentary goals. The practice of compulsory insurance and provision of pensions, which is common for many countries throughout the world, is actually an example of state meritoric interference. Everything seems clear and even commonplace. But in this case, the critics of meritorics cannot put up with the infringement of the principle of minimum compulsion, many of them insisting on maintaining the sovereignty of the individual, including his right to make decisions regarding his old age welfare. But even if state interference is recognized as necessary, they try to find a justification different from that given by meritorics.

---

[87] Tietzel M., Müller C. Op. cit., p. 121; See also: Pommerehne W.W., Hart A. Drogenpolitik aus Ökonomischer Sicht // G. Grozinger (Hrsg.) Recht auf Sucht. – Berlin, 1991, p. 66-96.

[88] We would like to note the extremely low elasticity characteristic of such goods as alcohol and tobacco. Expectation of high tax revenues makes them especially attractive for the fiscal authorities. For this reason, meritoric arguments are often used as an 'ideological screen' for budget repletion. We could see this in Russia – where in the second half of the 1990s excise tax rates were increased – and in developed market economies. We would like to refer to some German economists: 'Raising taxes on cognac and tobacco in the Federal Republic of Germany in recent years was not actually aimed at improvement in the citizens' health as a result of a decrease in consumption of these goods, which would become more expensive. An unstated goal – to gain additional budget revenues – was always in the foreground'. (Hansmeyer K.-H., Caesar R., Koths D., Siedenberg A. Steuern auf spezielle Güter. // Andel N., Haller H., Neumark F. (Hrsg.) Handbuch der Finanzwissenschaft. Bd. 2, 3 Aufl. – Tübingen, 1980, p. 734.

Tietzel and Müller succeeded in it. The skill of their substantiation can be only compared with artificiality of their construction and their absolute reluctance to recognize any other reason for state interference but the realization of a hypothetical consensus. They write in this regard, 'A plausible ground for the state interference in the sphere of old age welfare could be, for instance, the fact that each citizen can expect that his fellow citizens won't leave him to die of hunger if he himself misses an opportunity to take adequate measures to provide for his old age. Here, since everyone has an equal incentive to become a "social and political free rider" for account of other members of society, the state interference (for example, in the form of general insurance obligation), could be justified by the existence of externalities, not by the problem of weak will'[89].

One has to think out different arguments just to avoid recognition of meritorics. Fine writings from proponents for the theory of social contract are based on the non-trivial assumption that 'each citizen can expect that his fellow citizens won't leave him to die of hunger if he himself misses an opportunity to take adequate measures to provide for his old age'. It is interesting how far Tietzel and Müller are ready to go within this logic. Their master key seems to open any door. Since any action or inaction of a person can be presented as a result of expectation that the society 'won't leave him to die of hunger', then, in accordance with the designed scheme, any state interference can be justified from the individualistic standpoint (by internalization of externalities).

We think that the justification of state interference using purely logical constructions of hypothetical consensus depends solely upon the interpreter's talent. The command of such universal methodological means as the 'free rider phenomenon', 'prisoner's dilemma' and 'veil of ignorance' allows one to design perfectly fine but absolutely unrealistic schemes for achievement of unanimity[90]. And the main thing is that in the heat of the fight for an individual's liberty and sovereignty it is easy to justify even a dictator, since for his every decision there is always an adequate scheme of reaching that hypothetical consensus. All are equal under the 'veil of ignorance', and the hypothetical consensus becomes actual unanimity and the thing which Arrow considered absolutely impossible becomes possible.

---

[89] Tietzel M., Müller C. Op. cit., p. 122. It is curious that Kant gave the same argument when considering 'others' happiness as a goal and a duty at the same time' (Kant I. Foundations of the Metaphysics of Morals. Chicago: University of Chicago Press, 1950 (Russian Edition: Collected Works. – Moscow, 1965, V. 4(2), pp. 328-329)). But according to Kant, any person who finds himself in difficulties and relies on others' assistance must provide assistance to them in a similar situation. (The same, p. 328). Replacing this moral maxim with the 'free rider' phenomenon, Tietzel and Müller use Kant's argument to reach the opposite conclusion. They believe that the state can have 'others' happiness' as its legitimate goal, but only because it is not everybody's 'duty at the same time'.

[90] Peter Koslowski, the German philosopher and economist, pointed out the artificiality of such structures. In particular, he wrote that 'Rawls' rules are inapplicable to an actual consensus, they are valid only within his ideal model' (Koslowski P. Op. cit., p. 273).

2.3 The Irrationality of the Indigent

Musgrave considers the case when the state provides the in-kind assistance to the indigent a typical example of meritorics. However, he justifies this governmental activity from purely individualistic positions, linking it with specific interests of taxpayers. According to Musgrave and his co-authors, the situation is possible when 'an individual donator provides the in-kind support instead of financial one, since he believes that it is necessary for its recipient. Taxpayers may prefer social programs providing for such subsidies in kind as foodstuffs, coupons for clothes or warrants for flats to money assistance'[91].

It is known that initial market resource allocation can not only be modified using taxes and transfers. The world experience is also evidence of the provision of the vital minimum in the form of in-kind relief for the poor. In connection to this, one cannot but agree with Musgrave who stresses that any 'goods subjected to non-market allocation can be considered merit goods'[92]. In such a situation, the state actually comes up with an additional demand for these goods (different from the 'distorted' individual preferences) in order to allocate them (on a free or beneficial basis) among the indigent. Correcting their preferences, meritoric interference realizes 'insurance interests' of taxpayers, thus not contradicting the theory of social contract.

Considering the in-kind relief for the indigent and finding state interference possible (why not if it can be explained from the standpoint of the constitutional theory with its 'veil of ignorance'), Tietzel and Müller question the form of state involvement in solving this problem[93]. Just as in treating Musgrave's first example regarding individual irrationality or unawareness, these authors categorically insist on only one possible form of government interference, money transfers. In particular, they write that 'in-kind and monetary forms of relief are not equal options; in this case, the optimal "insurance" against poverty (costs being equal for a donator) would be money transfer. Thus, the "meritoric" change from monetary support to the in-kind one cannot be legitimated'[94]. The same principle of minimum interference is used as an argument. According to this principle, whenever it is necessary to interfere, it should only be done in the form of taxes and transfers. It is clear there is nothing else here but ideological considerations.

In this connection we'd like to consider a famous example involving the provision of subsidies to the opera. Tietzel and Müller write, 'Here, the illegitimacy of the state interference, is even more evident, since this merit good doesn't meet

---

[91] Musgrave R.A., Musgrave P.B., Kullmer L. Op. cit., p. 90.

[92] Musgrave R.A. Op. cit., 1987, p. 453.

[93] We wish to note that with respect to this point, these authors not only disagree with Musgrave but also with Head, who justifies the material reallocation on the basis of 'multiple preferences' suggested by him (Head J.G. Op. cit., 1988, p. 36). Neither are convinced by Andel's arguments, which point out the fact that a recipient maintains his liberty and can remain in his current position having rejected the suggested assistance (Andel N. Op. cit., p. 644).

[94] Tietzel M., Müller C. Op. cit., p. 111.

even the requirements of the theory of social contract... Nobody will want to include a visit to the opera in vital necessities which can be legitimate only under the "veil of ignorance". But if we wanted to go as far as to assume that all individuals have a constitutional interest in the opera, then subsidizing musical theatres would have contradicted the principle of inadmissibility of compulsion, since there is an option with a higher degree of freedom – direct money transfer to potential opera goers[95].

What can we say? Only living behind some special 'veil of ignorance' can one be unaware or reluctant to be aware of the fact that, for example, four-fifths of all expenses of musical theatres in Germany are covered by budget subsidies. The situation is similar thoughout the world[96]. It is nearly religious devotion to the individualistic orthodoxy that makes these authors ignore the real state of affairs; It keeps them in the trap of doublethink[97] and continuously generates nihilism regarding financial support for the opera. No other explanation exists for doubts about the 'consistency of justification' of state interference.

Strictly speaking, without budget subsidies theatres cannot survive at all[98]. Unless a theory recognizes this fact, it can hardly claim to adequately understand the real world. As for an alternative to budget subsidies (transfers to potential theatre patrons), they haven't been used since the time of ancient Rome and Greece, and even then, the treasury provided free citizens not with money but with special *tabols* which could be spent only to purchase theatre tickets. Afterwards theatres exchanged these tabols for real money.

Such a scheme is now used for distributing food stamps among the indigent. But we want to repeat that this form of supporting the poor is efficient only when this marginal group comprises an insignificant part of the population. When transferring money to the indigent, one should take into consideration that a 'free choice – to go to the opera or spend money for some other kind of entertainment – may not meet desires of a paternalist (*here Tietzel and Müller are certainly right – R.G., A.R.*); but the principle of minimum compulsion doesn't allow any other

---

[95] Ibid, p. 112.

[96] To prove this thesis, we refer the reader to the statistical overview prepared by request of the European Council by F.-O.Hofecker, the Austrian specialist in the field of economy of culture (Hofecker F.-O. Current Trends in the Financing of Culture in Europe. European Task Force on Culture & Development. Circle-Round-Table. — Barcelona, 1995).

[97] In conclusion of their article, Tietzel and Müller themselves point out that 'subsidies account for more than 80% of the financing of opera performances in Germany' (Tietzel M., Müller C. Op. cit., p. 123).

[98] One of the first theoretical foundations for the state support for performing arts was given in the classical work of William Baumol and William Bowen (Baumol W.J., Bowen W.G. Performing Arts: The Economic Dilemma. The Twentieth Century Fund. — New York, 1966). Due to their study, economists know about 'Baumol's cost disease', its symptom being the fact that in performing arts production costs tend to grow faster than prices for the end product. We hereby wish to draw attention to the recent monograph where manifestations of 'Baumol's cost disease' in various sectors of the economics are analyzed (Baumol's Cost Disease: The Arts and other Victims. Ed. Ruth Towse. — London: University of Exeter, 1997).

resolution (*here they are right again – R.G., A.R.*)[99]. This is the reason why this form of interventionism gives rise to obvious aversion.

When defending any form of state interference (we do not think it possible to speak seriously about a one and only form), it is always necessary to compare the goals and expected results. An ideological striving to maintain freedom of individual choice at any cost even in case a decision is made on its limitation is like saying, 'We'll interfere but in a way as though we were not interfering; that is, as though individuals had made all decisions themselves'. Having to face all negative consequences of such interference (individual opportunity costs), the society risks gaining nothing in return.

Among the arguments against providing subsides to the opera, Tietzel and Müller give a rather funny thesis. They write, 'What will happen, if lovers of fine arts consider subsidies to museums as vital as opera-lovers – cheaper theatre tickets? What will happen if sportsmen consider that subsidizing opera and arts means their unfair preference and get satisfied only when their sports facilities and clubs receive equal subsides? And how about other hobbies, stamp-collecting or bird breeding?'[100]

This list can be made as long as one wishes. We suggest spreading it to the areas of activity where such questions *must* be asked. For instance, how about the 'military entertainment' in the Balkans and in Chechnya and the financing of bacteriological and chemical weapons? A lot of taxpayers' money is being spent for these government decisions? Does anyone really believe that individualism dominates here? Only under the 'veil of nightmare' is it possible to imagine unanimity of individuals regarding these absolutely 'unjust causes'.

We are not speaking about world imperfection here – that is another topic. We are not discussing politics; this also requires a special discussion. Rather we are talking about the extent to which a theory may disagree with the real world and the things that can be done about it. But let us return to the problems of meritorics. Agreeing with Bonus[101] regarding the reasons for the expansion of state involvement in the economy, Tietzel and Müller make the following surprising statement. 'There are solid grounds for supposing that continuously growing share of the state is the result of 'meriting' of technically private goods, this trend contradicting the individualistic principle of minimum compulsion'[102]. So, what should we do: require another globe to live on or revise the dogmas of normative individualism, which have become a subject of religious worship?

An answer should also be given to the question previously asked – about an expanding zone of the state meritoric interference and competition between different activities for public resources. There is nothing dramatic about it. It is wonderful if museums and arts receive the public support. Actually, this is what happens in many countries of the world, including Germany, where considerable budget

---

[99] Tietzel M., Müller C. Op. cit., p. I 12.

[100]Ibid.

[101]Bonus H. Verzauberte Dörfer, oder: Solidarität, Ungleichheit und Zwang // ORDO 29, 1978, p. 77.

[102]Tietzel M., Müller C. Op. cit., p. 112.

funds are allocated to art museums and galleries[103]. There is also nothing wrong with the fact that the state supports collectors who preserve cultural heritage, whether it is an ancient manuscript or a rare stamp. Subsidizing sports is quite legitimate; look at the USA and Great Britain, let alone France and Germany[104].

We do not believe that the root of this practice should be looked for in some hypothetical consensus, developed behind some skillfully designed 'veil of ignorance'. Such theoretical approach is unpromising. We should not speak about a way to coordinate individual interests but about societal needs that fail to be reflected in individual preferences. Besides, there is competition between different public interests requiring the respective mechanisms for the development of priorities. We shall deal with this issue later, and now let us consider another aspect of meritorics.

2.4 The Reducibility of Needs in Constitutional Economics

'What is right and wrong?' When still a child, a human being does not know the answer to this fundamental question. Only upbringing, education and experience allow people to make more or less correct decisions, i.e. behave efficiently. But, first, it happens only in course of time, and second, not all individuals are able to make correct choices due to unequal distribution of *knowledge, will* and *resources* among them. Some people do not have and cannot have enough knowledge about goods' true qualities. Others who do possess the necessary knowledge lack enough will to make a decision beneficial for them. Preferences of a third group of people are distorted due to the lack of resources necessary for consumption of goods essential for society and strategically useful for individuals.

Meanwhile, the neoclassical model is based on the postulate of a person's rational behaviour. Ignoring the problem of knowledge and will, it 'worries' only about the material provision of market agents. If initial resource allocation does not provide a fair solution, then, according to a fundamental theorem of wellbeing, the situation can be corrected through wealth reallocation. Here we wish to quote again, 'Every Pareto-optimal allocation can be achieved as a competitive equilibrium after a suitable redistribution of initial endowments'[105].

---

[103]The artistic life of the modern society. The arts in the context of the social economy (Ed. Rubinstein A.). – Moscow, 1998. V.3, pp. 311-329.

[104]So called non-profit organizations are functioning successfully in many countries of the world in sports, as well as in arts, education, public health and other branches of the social sphere. The state provides such organizations with tax benefits being a legitimate form of their budget support. Direct budget allocations used to fund major sports events – the Olympic Games, World and European Championships, etc. – should also be mentioned here.

[105]Arrow K. C. Op. cit., p. 57.

In fact, everything is absolutely different. When a person does not know 'what is right and wrong' or when he knows but does not have enough will to make correct decisions, then even wealth reallocation will not achieve the optimal outcome. Some people will continue to proceed under false preferences. It is hardly possible to reallocate knowledge and will as one would economic resources. At least, present theory knows of no respective procedures similar to fundamental theorems of well-being.[106] Therefore, it is absolutely clear that the 'invisible hand' alone is not enough. Quite real ('visible') actions aimed at adjusting individual preferences are necessary[107].

To ensure the rational behaviour of all people (this is what the classical model took for its basic postulate), Musgrave thought out his meritorics. In three situations (the pathological case, weak will and material assistance), a 'father' (the state taking meritoric actions) has to create certain conditions encouraging a 'kid' to make the right choice. These are the cases of state interference which do not fit in with the traditional market model for quite understandable reasons.

Being 'scared' first by pre-Smith feudal despotic power and then even more by totalitarian economies of nazism and communism – in which state interference formed the essence of economic system –, liberal economists made individualism a gospel truth. Every theoretical concept started to be obligatorily tested for correspondence with the individualistic theory. Among them, in the very centre of examination for 'blood purity', is Musgrave's meritorics, suggesting state interference and a correction of individual preferences. It is enough to look at the discussion raised by this concept to notice that one question has always been essential: to what extent can meritoric interference be justified from an individualistic standpoint?

In connection with this, a semi-centennial debate over Musgrave's concept looks like a code of attempts to resolve a contradiction between the declaratively individualistic image of the state and its obviously non-individualistic meritoric actions. Among them there are endeavours of direct combination of meritorics

---

[106]The gap which appeared in the neoclassical model due to lacking procedures for redistribution of knowledge and will is evidently covered by Rawls' institutional model, the 'veil of ignorance'. This construction realizes the required redistribution of these human qualities, since under the 'veil of ignorance' all people are equal. Therefore, it is possible to regard the 'veil of ignorance' as a kind of virtual analogue of the mentioned theorems of well-being.

[107]The following remark should be made. If it is impossible to expect knowledge and will to actually be redistributed, it is still possible to replenish the deficit of 'human resources' with the help of an institutional 'substitute'. Informal rules adopted by society (group) as value orientations and behavioural norms, can substitute the knowledge of true qualities of some goods and services. The system of formal rules, fixed in respective legislative acts, civil and criminal codes, can make up for people's weak will to a certain extent. In this sense, the requirement for equal distribution of 'knowledge, will and resources' can be replaced by the requirement for the *adequate institutional environment,* i.e. a system of public institutions that forces all members of socium to behave economically efficiently. However, we wish to emphasize that this is a similarly strong assumption, so it cannot be considered as a matter of fact.

with normative individualism[108]. In this case its general understanding is applied, according to which meritorics is based on the so-called individual 'reflexive preferences'. In certain situations individuals may regard these preferences as more adequate. Therefore, as long as state actions are aimed at realizing these 'reflexive preferences', they are compatible with the principle of consumers' sovereignty. As many authors believe, this is a special case of a more general concept of constitutional economics.

Without considering this theory in detail[109], we wish to direct attention to its basic assumption. According to it, if not real then at least efficiently acting individuals would come to a unanimous decision when choosing common rules (a constitution). We would like to stress that the difference between actual people's behaviour and efficient behaviour is connected with the initial distribution of 'knowledge, will and resources' between them. Unanimous decision on a constitution is possible only if all people have the same knowledge concerning qualities of goods and services, and none of them lack will and resources necessary to make correct decisions.[110]

The critics of meritorics interpret this 'contract paradigm' in a peculiar way. Analyzing the problems of meritoric interference, Tietzel and Müller claim, 'A rule can be generally adopted only if according to this rule uncompensated costs that can be avoided cannot be imposed on anyone'[111]. Here we can see an evident logical loop; the thesis that is absolutely clear in the context of Pareto's theory cannot help contradicting meritorics. We would like to explain our conclusion.

The thing is that unlike Pareto's axioms, considering each person a single judge of his own well-being, meritorics assumes the existence of the goods which cannot be adequately evaluated by an individual since he does not have enough knowledge, will and resources. It is in connection with this that meritorics introduces the rules which should be adopted even in the case when – according to the 'false' opinion of an individual – he is burdened by uncompensated costs, which, from the 'correct' standpoint of society, are the expenses eventually ensuring individual benefits. This is the situation that Brennan and Lomasky associate with the existence of people's 'reflexive preferences' being different from those displayed on the market[112].

---

[108]Brennan G., Lomasky L. Institutional Aspects of 'Merit Goods' Analysis// Finanzarchiv, 41, 1983, S. 183-206; Head J.G. Op. cit., 1988, pp. 1-37; Priddat B.P. Zur Ökonomie der Gemeinschaftsbedülrfnisse: Neuere Versuche einer ethischen Begründung der Theorie meritorischer Güter //Zeitschrift für Wirtschafts- und Sozialwissenschaften, 112, 1992, S. 239-259; Koboldt C. Op. cit., p. 153.

[109]See, for example: Buchanan J.M. The Domain of Constitutional Economics //Constitutional Political Economy, 1, 1990, pp. 1–18; The Calculus of Consent; The Limits of Liberty.

[110]It is clear that the conditions of individuals' actions under the 'veil of ignorance' meet this requirement best.

[111]Tietzel M., Müller C. Op. cit., p. 98.

[112]We would like to point out the closeness in the positions of Brennan and Lomasky to our understanding of the public interests not reflected in individual preferences.

The most important aspect distinguishing constitutional economics from other interpretations of state meritoric interference concerns the specific conditions for the formation of consensus. Among them, a possibility for the universalization of individual behaviour is usually mentioned, meaning that in conflict situations to which the prisoner's dilemma is applicable, all individuals affected by interference can improve their position by 'abandoning their interests (even the use of a free rider strategy) to sign a contract by which everyone forbears from causing damage to others'[113].

Rawls' 'veil of ignorance' is also seen as a universal norm. It is a hypothetical construction within which at the moment of signing a constitutional agreement, individuals know all general facts about the post-constitutional society but are not aware of their social status and preferences in this society. The 'veil of ignorance' should make all rational individuals choose the same constitutional principles. According to this theory, meritorics can be justified only within the constitutional agreement. It is clear that such an approach allows meritorics to be applied only in a very narrow area within which a number of artificial conditions necessary to form the consensus are met.

At the same time, some economists consider that the interpretation of state actions based on social contract is better than meritorics with respect to the legitimation of interference in individual preferences. A more general conclusion is implied: in the sphere in which the legitimation on the basis of social contract is applicable, meritorics is superfluous. Despite such confidence, we still have doubts regarding compatibility of meritorics and constitutional economics. There are no answers to the basic question: is it possible to legitimate any meritoric action from the individualistic standpoint?

Here, three viewpoints can be singled out. First, Brennan and Lomasky consider meritoric interference as the one based on the above 'reflexive preferences' of individuals[114]. In this sense, the constitutional unanimity justifying the meritoric interference is always possible. Second, Head states that analysis based on social contract can justify any meritoric actions, since the idea of multiple preferences applies to the 'whole set of problems connected with both merit and aggregate public needs'[115]. Third, Tietzel and Müller express their contrary opinion regarding the constitutional theory as a factor restricting state interference. They claim that 'rational individuals under Rawls' "veil of ignorance" will come to unanimity only regarding the transfer of certain "insurance functions" to the state'[116].

We wish to consider another aspect of meritorics, which we have mentioned before. It deals with the 'scale' of state interference as well as the problem of 'adherence' to the principles of normative individualism. Sticking to the basic individualistic norm, Tietzel and Müller use the aforementioned principle of minimum

---

[113]Tietzel M., Müller C. Op. cit., p. 99.

[114]Brennan G., Lomasky L. Op. cit., p. 187.

[115]Head J.G. Op. cit., 1988, p. 30.

[116]Tietzel M., Müller C. Op. cit., p. 102. We wish to add that they believe that only the old theory of insurance with its 'minimum norms', suggested by Hobbes, can legitimate Musgrave's merit goods.

compulsion – 'as much compulsion as necessary, but as little as possible!'[117]. It should be noted that this purely emotional motto is a projection of the famous principle of subsidiarity. On its basis, Walter Eucken, one of the founders of ORDO-liberalism, describes the general scheme of interaction of individuals and the state, 'The society should be built bottom-up. The things that can be done by individuals or their groups, should be done on their own initiative with maximum efficiency. The state should interfere only in the cases when it is impossible to do without its assistance'[118].

But the point is that there is no clear notion of what individuals can actually 'do on their initiative with maximum efficiency' in the market environment. The neo-classical model, with its individualistic dogma, states that they can do absolutely everything except for coping with the cases of 'market failures'. And various liberal economists repeat this purely ideological statement like 'Our Father', not getting tired of reproducing it in superfine models of the virtual economic reality.

But practice testifies to quite the opposite. Any modern state actions go far beyond the zone of market failures. Furthermore, any researcher dealing with concrete figures knows that even in the most liberal countries the budget share in GDP in the course of the 20th century grew five to sevenfold. Any attempts to explain this contradiction, for instance, by marking out the group of merit goods, meet head on with the dead wall of individualistic orthodoxy. This is how Musgrave's meritorics was 'condemned' according to the criteria whose universality it questions.

In addition to incorrectness of both the substantiation and criticism of meritorics from the standpoints of absolutely different basic postulates, we would like to mention a number of other important circumstances. First, we would emphasize that any attempts to interpret state meritoric interference using the theory of social contract are based on the belief in the universality of the reducibility hypothesis. In other words, according to this theory, state interference requires not only unanimity of all individuals but also, primarily and basically, reducibility of every social interest to individual preferences. We have already mentioned the limitedness of this assumption.

Second, a realization of any irreducible want of society always generates false assessment of 'uncompensated' individual costs, since individuals cannot see all benefits of the state meritoric interference. Actually, it is irreducibility that makes a connection between positive results of this interference and individual benefits 'invisible'. Therefore, adoption of only unanimously approved rules, often based on the false evaluation of the costs and benefits by individual market agents, will always result in the inefficient use of resources available to the aggregation of market agents.

Third, non-interference of the state (the principle of minimum compulsion is a purely ideological lexical element) inevitably results in the inefficient use of resources which the market itself is unable to improve. Thus sooner or later, economic, social, cultural or any other outcomes of the state's detachment will force it

---

[117]Tietzel M., Müller C. Op. cit., p. 103.
[118]Eucken W. Grundsätze der Wirtschaftspolitik, 6. Aufl. – Tübingen, 1990, p. 348.

to interfere. Speaking about non-interference, hypothetical consensus, unanimous decisions and absence of compulsion, we therefore find ourselves in a virtual reality, in which artificial basic postulates give rise to artificial notions of real market environment, collective decisions and the state's role.

With this in mind, special attention should be paid to the fourth type of merit wants which Musgrave singled out not long ago. Analyzing this specific case of meritorics, Musgrave approaches a more general understanding of the motives for state interference. This is where he actually assumes the possibility of repudiation of the universality of the reducibility hypothesis and the existence of the 'interest of society as such, the interest that can be attributed to society as a whole'[119].

2.5 The Quasi-Irreducibility of Social Needs

This section deals with the so-called *common needs* (reflecting the interests of an aggregation of individuals), realization of which may have priority over purely individual preferences. Marking out this case, Musgrave assumes that in the case of some goods and services, *common norms* can replace individual norms[120]. Musgrave conditions the existence of the former by the possibility of individual adoption of some 'common values or preferences, even though individual preferences may not coincide with them'. In his opinion, such common values include 'preservation of historic monuments, respect for national holidays, nature, erudition and arts'[121].

Strictly speaking, this case differs too little from the above Bergson-Samuelson model and Margolis' two utility functions, which oblige an individual to 'agree' to the notions of his personal and society's well-being on his own. Thus, instead of abandoning the universality of the reducibility hypothesis we can see only half measure – the emergence of *quasi-irreducible* public preferences; that is social needs which may be presented as common values, but only as those adopted by all or nearly all individuals[122]. Again we see Musgrave's reluctance or lack of preparedness in giving up individualistic fundamentalism, which – in our opinion – does not allow him to make a necessary step towards transforming the meritoric state into a normal market player.

---

[119]Musgrave R.A., Musgrave P.B., Kullmer L. Op. cit., p. 88.

[120]Musgrave R.A. Op. cit., 1987, pp. 452-453.

[121]Ibid., p. 452.

[122]We direct attention to a rather old article by Kurt Schmidt that contains a detailed historical review of the problems of common needs (Schmidt K. Zur Geschichte der Lehre von den Kollektivbedürfnissen // Kloten N. u.a. (Hrsg.). Systeme und Methoden in den Wirtschafts- und Sozialwissenschaften, Erwin von Beckerath zum 75. Geburtstag. – Tübingen, 1964, p. 335-362). The author proceeds from the assumption that common needs are always interests of individuals who recognized them as private. We would like to mention that we have already considered this situation. In particular, according to Sugden, it is rigidly associated with emergence of 'cooperation morale' (Sugden R. Op. cit., p. 173).

Musgrave's point of view is shared by Head, who assumes only limited legitimacy of common needs, which are hypostatized only when they are projected to the individual. In particular, Head also believes that in certain situations common values or preferences can be formed, which make individuals 'nearly unanimously back up the policy determining the essential aspects of the common culture or warning of unwise short-sighted behaviour of contemporary generation, including decisions made by the majority'[123].

As for Tietzel and Müller, they do not agree even to *quasi*-irreducibility. While in the previous cases these critics of meritorics – rejecting Musgrave's concept – were looking for an individualistic justification of state interference, the case of 'common needs' is rejected by them from the very start. All Musgrave's examples demonstrating an 'alternative norm' are interpreted by them using other concepts or the first three types of merit wants, which have already been interpreted from the individualistic standpoint. We associate this criticism with the famous techniques of military strategist Karl von Clausewitz – 'divide the enemy's army into parts, block them and destroy every separate part'.

It is the splitting of common needs and separating of individual cases which Musgrave gives only as examples that makes the base for criticizing common needs in the work of Tietzel and Müller. So, they consider 'preservation of historic monuments' and 'respect for nature' from the viewpoint of the theory of public goods, and 'respect for arts' from the viewpoint of reallocation of resources in the form of material assistance[124]. It is difficult to call this approach correct. The main thing about meritorics is that it has 'managed' to see the common motivation for state interference in different abnormal (in the context of the neoclassical market model) phenomena.

Therefore, any other explanation of, say, the social need to preserve historic monuments – whether on the basis of the 'prisoner's dilemma', theory of public goods or 'veil of ignorance'[125] – separately from other examples given by Musgrave does not deny meritorics itself. It is also impossible to regard the chosen method of critique as appropriate if methodology is considered. It makes it possible 'to overlook' people's common biological need in the foodstuff, only recognizing as legitimate the encouraging of the consumption of fruits possessing the necessary vitamins (Scandinavian countries, the last quarter of the 20th century) or a ban on the sale of Belgian chicken-meat containing harmful dioxin (European countries, 1999).

We even disagree more strongly with the viewpoints of Tietzel and Müller regarding state support for arts and education, which is also explained by Musgrave from the standpoint of 'common values'. In this case these authors do not assume

---

[123]Head J.G. Op. cit., 1988, p. 27.

[124]Besides, Tietzel and Müller single out the examples of demerit goods given by Musgrave, prostitution and drugs (Tietzel M., Müller C. Op. cit., S. 115). However, they prefer not to consider education ('respect for erudition'). This is probably due to the fact that the legitimacy of interference in this case is recognized even by those under the 'veil of dogmatic individualism'.

[125]Tietzel M., Müller C. Op. cit., p. 114.

any common needs and try to reduce everything to 'reallocation in the form of material assistance', the only legitimate method of interference, in their opinion, being money transfers, for instance, to the needy opera goers. We cannot accept such a view, even in a case in which opponents do not want to 'go as far as to assume that all citizens have the constitutional interest in operas'[126]. Confirming our previous doubts about correctness of considering only one form of state interference, we draw attention to an absolutely different aspect of support for arts.

The point is that in addition to ensuring access of individuals to the values of classical art – Bach, Mozart, Verdi, Rafael, Rembrandt, Picasso, Shakespeare, Moliere, Chekhov, – support should be provided for innovation like that of Bekket, Gratovski, Stockhausen, Boulez, Gubaydulina and other representatives of the avant-garde, which becomes traditional only in the course of time but makes it possible for arts to develop. So, if in the first case – though conditionally – it is possible to speak about support for consumers, in the second case support is required for 'art creators ', to be more precise, for their professional activity. We are referring to something usually called 'seeking and striving': new artistic ideas, 'lab' projects which do not have any consumer demand for the time being. It would be a mistake to think that support for art innovation can be reduced to support for the indigent, that is to the maintenance of the subsistence level of 'poor artists'. In this case, according to Musgrave, we face absolutely different interests of society, which do not relate to its interest in support for the indigent and which 'may be regarded as a result of historical process of individuals' interaction, leading to the creation of common values or preferences'[127].

Without considering too deeply the institutional nature of 'common values' and mechanisms of their formation (we shall address this core topic later), we wish to once again point out Musgrave's recognition of the category of 'common needs' characteristic for an aggregation of people as a whole. This is the fact that gives rise to most incomprehension and aversion among critics. But we consider this motive for state meritoric interference the most adequate and therefore especially valuable in Musgrave's concept.

---

[126]Though Tietzel and Müller consider this an absolute nonsense (Tietzel M., Müller C. Op. cit., p. 112), our friend Professor Bernhard Felderer, Director of the Institute for Advanced Studies, Vienna, mentioned such a possibility. He regards state support for music theatres a direct reflection of national consensus existing in the Austrian society regarding music.

[127]Musgrave R.A. Op. cit., 1987, p. 452.

3 The Autonomous Interest of Society

Let us now examine in greater detail and in broader context the category of 'common needs', which has had many supporters and opponents throughout its long history. Despite its rich bibliographic background, one can hardly find a work devoted to the theory of needs without referring to the fundamental research of Kurt Schmidt. This well-known historical survey – accompanied by the author's critical remarks – 'closed' the topic concerning common needs for nearly forty years; a conclusion about the uselessness, if not falseness, of this category commanded widespread agreement in the world of economics with its ideological adherence to individualistic canons.

Having carefully studied this historical survey and examined most of the works analyzed there, we'd like to return to common needs, since we do not consider Schmidt's arguments convincing enough. Besides, the purpose of analysis seems rather limited. Having actually reduced the most important theoretical problem to one question (how the doctrine of common needs helps resolve the problem of forms and scale of government activity), he himself answers it. 'Common needs are an unreliable starting point for deciding on respective state expenditures'[128]. Setting aside this final conclusion, let us to return to the 'filling' of Schmidt's study and examine the category of common or collective needs in the context of society's autonomous interests.

3.1 The Historical Landscape

Casting a retrospective glance at economists' attitude to the category of common needs, we single out three types of bearers of such needs (according to Schmidt). First, is the community as a whole; second, members of community; and third, just individuals[129]. This classification allowed Schmidt to systematize a variety of opinions regarding the collective needs scattered all over the field of economics during the past hundred years. Schmidt includes Herman, Schaffle and Menger (economists of the end of the 19th century and the beginning of the 20th century) in the first group of authors who regard a group of people or their community as a bearer of the said needs[130].

---

[128]Schmidt K. Op. cit., p. 359.

[129]Ibid., p. 335.

[130]Herman F.B.W. Staatswirtschaftliche Untersuchungen, 2. Aufl. — München, 1870; Schaffle A.E.F. Das gesellschaftliche System der menschlichen Wirtschaft, 3. Aufl., 1.

Despite well-known differences in these authors' views, the commonality amongst them is the assumption of some autonomous interest of an aggregation of people as a whole. According to Menger, for example, common needs felt by members of a group should be differentiated from the group's common needs. Menger wrote, 'Not only individuals, making up communities, but also these communities have their own nature and thus the necessity to maintain their essence and develop – these are common needs *(Gemeinbedürfnisse)* which should not be confused with individual interests and even with interests of all individuals taken together'[131]. In other words, any community of people can have and pursue its own specific purposes differently from the interests of individuals making up this community.

This thesis, seeming so clear and evident, has been confirmed by different philosophical principles many times, showing that the whole can have its own qualities other than qualities of its parts. And the economists themselves appear to warn of applying to the whole that which is true for its parts[132]. Nevertheless the main critique of common needs deals mainly with the relation of the whole to its parts. H. Jecht writes, 'The bearer of common need is always an individual and never a social community as a whole, which, unlike an individual, has no live centre capable of emotions'[133]. Even thirty years later Musgrave is reluctant to transcend the following commonplace statement: 'Since a group of people as it is cannot speak, the question arises: *who* can express this group's feelings?'[134]. And Schmidt, who rejects existence of needs inherent to society as such, remarks ironically that 'a community (collective) feeling needs is a mystical body'[135].

We wish to repeat, yet without any comments, Jecht's statement (especially as it fits into one of the cases singled out in Schmidt's classification) that a 'bearer of common needs is always an individual'. Analyzing this viewpoint, Schmidt refers to the works by Sax, Cuhel, Ritschl and Seligman[136]– also written in the end of the 19th century through the beginning of the 20th century – whose theoretical developments are all based on a quite simple thesis: the goals of a community of people give rise to objective common needs which are felt not by society but by individuals to the extent they possess the 'sense of community'. It is important not to overlook the accents Schmidt made analyzing the said works; they seem to draw atten-

---

Bd. — Tübingen, 1873; Menger C. Grundsätze der Volkswirtschaftslehre, 2. Aufl.— Wien-Leipzig, 1923.

[131]Menger C. Op.cit., p. 8.

[132]Samuelson P.A., Nordhaus W.D. Economics. New York: McGraw-Hill, 1992 (Russian Edition – Moscow, 1992, V.1, p. 13).

[133]Jecht H. Wesen und Formen der Finanzwirtschaft. – Jena, 1928, p. 62.

[134]Musgrave R.A. The Theory of Public Finance. – N.Y -London, 1959, p. 87.

[135]Schmidt K. Op. cit., p. 337.

[136]Sax E. Grundlegung der theoretischen Staatswirtschaft. – Wien, 1987; Cuhel F. Zur Lehre von den Bedürfnissen. – Innsbruck, 1907; Ritschl H. Theorie der Staatswirtschaft und Besteuerung. – Bonn-Leipzig, 1925; Seligman E.R.A. Die gesellschaftliche Theorie der Finanzwirtschaft // Die Wirtschaftstheorie der Gegenwart, 4 Bd. – Wien, 1928.

tion from collective needs to their bearer. We think that this approach simplifies the problem.

We are sure that analysis of common needs cannot be reduced to the issue of their bearer. The fact of the sheer existence of such needs is of primary importance. The thesis about collective needs being 'felt' only by individuals, – not by their aggregation which 'has no mentality of its own'[137]– is not enough to substantiate the rejection of these needs as specific interests inherent to a community of people as a whole. Meanwhile, some authors, including Schmidt, use this premise. This is the reason why the discussion of collective needs has been reduced mainly to one question: who can feel them?

Commenting on the views of the said authors, Schmidt himself digresses from the essence and reduces everything to mechanisms for the identification of common needs and people capable of 'detecting' them. In particular, he makes the following conclusion, 'Groundlessness of views of Sax, Cuhel, Ritschl and Seligman becomes especially vivid if we remember that in case of any disagreement with otherwise-minded persons regarding themselves as bearers of collective needs collective's bodies have compulsion as a legal means at their disposal'[138].

This aspect of the problem – mechanisms for the formation and actualization of common needs – is essential for us, and we are sure to return to it. Even keeping in mind that Ritschl's position is closer to ours[139] and that we disagree with Schmidt, we emphasize once again that another question essential here, that pertaining to the existence of collective needs. Schmidt does not seem to answer it. As for Sax, Cuhel, Ritschl and Seligman, their viewpoints in this respect do not differ too much from those of Herman, Schaffle and Menger. They all recognize common needs. The temptation to include these authors in one group is impeded only by the classification criterion selected by them, public interest bearer.

Quite surprisingly, Schmidt singles out one more group of researchers including Wagner, Kaizl, De Viti and Lindahl[140]– who actually represent the same historical period of the end of the 19th century and the beginning of the 20th century – and Musgrave, who is a key person in this debate. Strictly speaking, the views of Wagner, Kaizl and De Viti differ from those of the above groups of authors so

---

[137]Ritschl H. Op. cit., p. 55.

[138]Schmidt K. Op. cit. p. 345.

[139]Ritschl is sure that a community of people will not put up with the bodies which do not act according to the collectivistic approach for long, and that 'according to the sense and purpose of such bodies' existence, the trend to serve common interests will dominate in their actions and decisions' (Ritschl H. Op. cit., p. 55). If we avoid a barefaced approach and take into consideration the duration of time and currently recognized factor of 'social groups' interests', we can probably agree that the teleological approach to the formation of public interests is possible. We think that the predetermination present here should result in 'spontaneous order' concerning common interests.

[140]Wagner A. Grundlegung der politischen Ökonomie, 3. Aufl., 1. Theil, 2. Halbband.— Leipzig, 1893; Kaizl J. Finanzwissenschaft, l.Teil. – Wien, 1900; De Viti de Marco A. Grundlehren der Finanzwirtschaft. – Tübingen, 1932; Lindahl E. Die Gerechtigkeit der Besteuerung. – Lund, 1919.

negligibly that even a sophisticated reader can hardly detect any difference. As an example, we refer to the definition of common needs suggested by Wagner: these are the 'needs, which individuals feel as members of human collectives to which they belong voluntarily or involuntarily; without meeting these needs communal life and economic interaction of individuals, possessing their own will, are impossible'[141]. If this understanding of collective needs is compared with views of Sax and Ritschl, it is easy to notice that they coincide. Lindahl's approach is quite different.

In his theory, collective needs are determined by an exclusively collective form of goods consumption[142]. Moreover, Lindahl actually regards only the needs that individuals have for public goods as public needs. He writes, 'Public needs are collective *(gemeinsam)* in the sense that the collective component should refer to the goods towards which these needs are directed'[143]. The same approach allowed other researchers to interpret state activity as measures having sole purpose, to meet collective needs for public goods.

Disagreeing with such judgements, we wish to note that the process of meeting a demand for public goods and state activity may not coincide. To prove this thesis, let us refer to De Viti, who is confident that collective need and state activity should not correlate, 'since sometimes the state produces goods designed to meet individual needs, and sometimes private firms produce goods designed to meet collective needs'[144]. For us it is absolutely clear that interrelation between common needs and behaviour of the state exists, but it has an absolutely different nature. And of course, it is not limited to the interpretation traditionally given by the theory of public goods[145]. In this sense, inclusion of Lindahl in the group of authors examining common needs looks a bit artificial to the extent at which the issue of collective needs can be reduced to the need for public goods.

As for Musgrave, his concept is the last link in a chain. We started with a consideration of his views, speaking in the previous chapter about collective needs as a special type of merit wants. His definition (formulated in the end of the 20th century) of collective needs as an 'interest of society as such, an interest that can be attributed to society as a whole'[146] best corresponds to the German tradition, marking the return – at a new level – to the notions we find in the works of Herman, Schaffle and Menger. But it is this interpretation of common needs that Schmidt regards as mystical and rejects completely.

---

[141]Wagner A. Op. cit., p. 830.

[142]Lindahl E. Op. cit., p. 53. Lindahl uses another term – 'public' *(öffentlich)* needs – instead of collective needs.

[143]Lindahl E. Op. cit., p. 57.

[144]De Viti de Marco A. Op. cit., p. 11.

[145]See, for instance, Atkinson A.B. and Stiglitz J.E, Lectures on public economics. – Moscow, 1995, pp. 651-681, 703-710.

[146]Musgrave R.A., Musgrave P.B., Kullmer L. Op. cit., p. 88.

3.2 Holism and Teleology

But mystique has nothing to do with this. To examine collective needs, it is not necessary to imagine the community of people as a talking organism with a live centre capable of emotions. As usual, the reality is not that simple and that complex at the same time.

We would like to repeat that the whole can possess specific qualities other than those of its parts. This thesis, which has become generally accepted, is currently used in the form of the terms 'system', 'integrity' or 'holism' as habitually as, for example, the term 'gene' is used in biology. Moreover, it can be stated with confidence that in the second half of the 20th century, the outlook of many researchers vividly transformed in favour of the approach which Simon Ramo called a 'general, not fragmented view of things'[147], and Alvin Toffler associated with the Third Wave of Culture, having 'attributed special importance to the contexts, interrelations, etc.'[148].

To give an emotional touch to a methodological attack on the 'conceit with which separate phenomena are studied', Toffler used the warning words of Ervin Laszlo, who wrote, 'We are a part of interdependent system of nature, and since the cultural "unitors" don't do their job as for development of the theory of system schemes of interrelations, our short-term projects and limited capabilities of managing the processes may lead to our destruction'[149]. Maybe it is not worth sharing such a gloomy prophecy, but it is certainly worth reflecting upon the fact that fragmentariness and analyticity do not allow us to explain and especially foresee many phenomena without a general view of the whole.

In this sense, economic theory with its individualistic canon finds itself among the humanities determined by the spirit of reductionism. That is why in any general system, the economists usually see only its components and perceive collective needs based solely on a projection of individual interests. This is how common needs became somewhat mystical (according to Schmidt), and the real world found itself in the gripe of the absolutized reducibility hypothesis. Outside this narrow area, the 'terrifying' organic concept looms.

Even modern institutionalists, who attribute great importance to holistic thinking[150], are still cautious of applying these views to society as a whole, confining themselves to the consideration of groups of people or other limited communities. Absolute aversion of the organic concept of society seems to impede the spreading of the Third Wave outlook (according to Toffler) in economic theory. This is the only way we can explain the categorical repudiation of common needs or societal needs by the mainstream.

---

[147]Ramo S. Cure for Chaos: Fresh Solutions to Social Problems through the Systems Approach. – New York, 1969, p. 6.

[148]Toffler A. The Third Wave. New York: Morrow, 1980 (Russian Edition – Moscow, 1999, p. 484).

[149]Ibid., p. 488.

[150]Nesterenko A.N. Present-Day Status and Basic Problems of Institutional and Evolution Theory // Voprosy Ekonomiki (Economic Issues) 1997, No.3, pp. 45- 47.

We see the simplification and even wrong interpretation of the holistic version of society as the main hindrance to the natural course of events. Considering an aggregation of people as a whole is not equal to identifying a society with an organism[151]. That is why – sharing the views of Popper, Buchanan and other social philosophers and economists rejecting the organic concept – we cannot agree to anathematize every concept regarding society as a whole[152]. Thus, we cannot recognize the existing criticism of common needs.

Taking into account the teleological principle[153], saying that it is possible to reach predetermined harmony, we can approach the issue of collective needs quite differently. Proceeding from the assumption that everything in nature is rational, it is possible to assume the existence of social analogues of physical laws. We mean a kind of social homeostasis – the *law of self-preservation of socium*. The above words of Menger (all communities of people 'have their own nature and thus the necessity to maintain their essence') should be treated in the context of this universal law.

We emphasize that it is a matter of modern interpretation of the teleological mechanism accumulating the energy of negative and positive reverse interdependences. In this respect, attention should be paid to the role played in the formation of new views of the world by the famous theorem of thermodynamics of non-equilibrium processes proved by Ilya Prigogine, the Belgian scientist of the Russian origin, in 1947[154]. Bringing forward a philosophical interpretation of this theorem, Toffler writes, 'Prigogine emphasizes that in any complex system, from molecules in a solution, to neurons in the nerve tissue or a city transportation system, its parts are continuously changing. The internal frame of any system quivers and suffers fluctuations. In case of a negative reverse interdependence, these fluctuations become less intense and disappear; the system's equilibrium is maintained. But due to a positive reverse interdependence, some of these fluctuations may increase to the extent threatening the equilibrium of the whole system... The

---

[151]Please, remember that Hegel and Marx, who accepted the organic concept of society, based this structure on nations and classes. That is why a collective interest, according to Hegel, is the 'spirit of nation', and a public need, according to Marx, is the interest of a certain class.

[152]Only the 'child's complex' can explain the aversion for a holistic approach to the intermediate level – a society within a state. Meanwhile, at the micro-level (social groups) and macro-level (complex of states) this type of thinking is already widespread. Effectively it is adopted within the sphere of international relations, where market globalization has become the most fashionable topic for economists and politicians.

[153]The most vivid example for the use of the teleological approach in economics is Smith's market theory. He was the first to notice the potential of rationality in the self-interest. Actually, the 'invisible hand', which, according to Smith, must bring about wealth for everyone, represents the said teleological principle. This idea of Smith enables Kant to build the first model of constitutional state. Kant's theory of law also uses teleology in the form of the 'invisible hand' or, according to Kant's terminology, in the form of 'secret plan of the nature'.

[154]It is often formulated as follows: if obstacles appear in the way of equilibrium, the stationary state of the socium corresponds to minimal entropy.

works by Prigogine not only combine chance and necessity but postulate their interconnection. In short, he insists that at the moment when the system "leaps" onto a new level of complexity, it is impossible to predict what shape it will take. But if the route has been chosen and a new structure has appeared, the determinism comes into force as before[155]. We keep this understanding of an aggregation of elements as a whole and this interpretation of its inclination for equilibrium and 'leaps onto new levels of complexity' in mind when we speak about teleology supplementing the holistic view of socium. We would like to explain this important thesis, characterizing the philosophical basis of economic sociodynamics.

Let us use a physical analogy and present an aggregation of individuals, making up a society in the form of a multitude of market agents undergoing continuous changes, i.e. 'quivering' and experiencing various 'fluctuations' connected with dynamics of their position, changes in personal preferences and capabilities. If a negative reverse interdependence is observed (the mechanism of the 'invisible hand' is attributed to it alone), then entropy increases, the energy of disruption decreases, fluctuations become less intense and disappear; under conditions of a competitive market and the reducibility of needs, changing demand generates a corresponding supply reaction, and a new market equilibrium arises. But the general situation is not limited to this process.

If new qualities arise in a social system and an interest of society that fails to be reflected in individual preferences as such is formed, the phenomenon of positive reverse interdependence gives birth to increased fluctuations, and their energy rises. It is clear that this aspect of the dynamics of the socium as well as its transposition to new levels of complexity cannot be explained on the basis of the mechanism of the invisible hand, which corresponds only to the negative reverse interdependence and the system's tendency to equilibrium. With this in mind, we wish to repeat some propositions concerning the philosophical basis of economic sociodynamics.

We proceed from more universal notions of society, seeing it as multitude of individuals in constant change and fluctuation, who act independently and in various groups. Here all sociodynamic processes reflect both negative and positive reverse interdependences and are described on the basis of an original analogue of Prigogine's theorem: *if obstacles appear in the way of an equilibrium, the stationary state of the socium corresponds to minimal entropy and the energy of disturbance is transformed into interest inherent to the social system as a whole; the latter thus adopts a new qualitative level.*

In other words, any disruptive impetus is observed in society on a daily and hourly basis (such as changes in the environmental situation, an increased need for education, science, culture, growing differentiation in the population's incomes, a decline in the competitiveness of a branch which is important for a country, simply the development of a new product or technology, etc.) generates two consequences. First, fluctuation is suppressed, a new equilibrium emerges and the disruptive energy is absorbed by the dynamics of individual preferences. In the second case, the fluctuation energy does not dissipate in new individual biases; it,

---

[155]Toffler E. Op. cit., pp. 495–497.

instead, is preserved, it even encourages the formation of an interest of society as such. It is not necessary to say that the first situation is only a particular case. Therefore, we wish to reiterate that we proceed from more universal notions of society which always faces both situations in the process of its development.

Various external impulses and different communities' striving for self-preservation may generate the socium's interests which, according to Menger, 'should not be confused with individual interests and even with interests of all individuals taken together'. Thus, recognition of the legitimacy of public needs is just an extension of the teleological principle, valid in the physics, to the socium. However, teleological justification of collective needs certainly does not entail resolution of the issue of their bearer.

It is essential to understand that before a common need becomes actualized and determines a specific goal of a society, recognized by the majority of its members or represented on behalf of society by a group of people authorized for that, the said need evolves and exists in latent form as a *teleological response* to external disturbance and non-equilibrium. This is how, regardless of individual desires of people, the natural balance of male and female birth rate is maintained, and the male birth rate increases in the post-war years. Due to the same kind of mechanism, societal goals concerning the preservation of the environment deemed unthinkable not long ago were set.

No doubt, only people can feel and express their feelings. But not all people are able to 'detect' society's needs, to become as such its medium, a 'nature recipient'. Only a few passionaries[156] are 'pregnant' with a collective need; perceiving it, they determine the social purposes, 'persuade' others in their urgency, and make them the state's purposes. It is clear that along this way – from the emergence of a common need to its transformation into a governmental aim – many hindrances and distortions emerge. Nevertheless, however long this course of action may be, the time comes when the collective need starts to dominate in the minds of those making decisions on behalf of the whole society.

The more developed its institutional structure, the shorter this way, the easier its leap onto a new level of complexity, and the more adequate the chosen goals to the actual public needs. This is how the social need to preserve the environment evolved: from timid appeals of separate persons to the broad activities of Greenpeace and the formation of influential political parties.

Returning to the category of common needs, we would like to indicate three points. First, the existence of the interests of society as such undermines the universality of the hypothesis of reducibility of all needs to individual preferences. Second, the process of evolution of collective needs includes several stages, from a teleological response and its perception by separate individuals to the formation of value judgements and behavioural norms adopted by society and manifested in

---

[156]It was the great Russian cultural geographer Lev N. Gumilev who introduced the concept of 'passionarity' – a genetic sign which determines people's activity and thanks to which big social systems rise and develop. 'Passionarity' is the sign which starts up because of mutation (passionarity hit) and creates some quantity of people inside population who possess increased craving for action. These people are called 'passionaries'.

individual preferences of the dominating majority of people. And last but not least is the final phase of the dynamic process of negative and positive reverse interdependences, in which individuals start to accept collective needs as their own interests, i.e. when public needs become reducible and completely dissolve in individual preferences.

It is evident that critics of the category of common needs, implicitly defending the universality of the reducibility hypothesis, 'notice' only the final phase, when there is no need to consider this category. At this stage, an individual bears a collective interest, always being revealed in the market, where individual preference functions are 'melted' into some averaged aggregate – a reducible public need.

But the situation is absolutely different at the previous stages of the evolution of a collective interest. There are also some individual bearers of this interest who adopted the society's needs. But they are so few that the market fails to notice their preferences, which are therefore not reflected in an aggregate utility function. In other words, at this stage, the market mechanism is unable to reveal the collective interest.

The intermediate phase with the positive reverse interdependence is the most important for our reasoning. As a result of the teleological response, the number of individuals having adopted a public need increases at this stage to such an extent that this need gets adopted by the group of people authorized to set the state goals and make decisions on behalf of the whole society. In the meantime, the public need remains irreducible, and the market still cannot detect it. Thus in addition to the market aggregate of individual preferences, an explicit public interest irreducible to individual needs emerges.

This stage of the process of public interest formation is ignored by the critics of collective interests, who try to prove that it does not differ from the final stage. Actually, Musgrave himself more or less purports this view, as does Head. They substitute the irreducible need for the quasi-irreducible one and recognize the interest of society as such only in the form of the norm 'almost unanimously accepted by individuals'. The same technique is used by representatives of constitutional economics, who present the common need only in the form of a consensus of individual interests[157].

This way seems to be unpromising as fails to explain many phenomena. It is certainly possible to isolate oneself from the real world and, sticking to the position of *normative negativism*, stubbornly repeat that our world is imperfect and that it would be much better if – according to the liberal doctrine – the state did not interfere at all or its functions were limited to those of a 'night watchman', and everything were decided by the free choice of individuals.

This is the way radical liberals treat Keynesianism, believing that in the previous period the excessive interference and erroneous monetary policy of the state resulted in the crisis, which Keynesian recipes for the state regulation are meant to overcome. But such 'blindness of science' always entails a double standard. It is easy to prove it, comparing theoretical doctrines with real policy.

---

[157]See the already cited works of Musgrave (1987, p. 452), Head (1988, p. 27), Buchanan (1990, pp. 1–18) and other authors.

Liberals, for instance, claim that Roosevelt's team, even before Keynes, obtained the desired results staying within the former limits of market theory. In reality, regardless of whether there was any connection between Keynes' ideas and the US policy of that time, it is clear that Roosevelt's methods were far from fitting into traditional market theory. Thus Keynes' restoration in some respect of a theoretical image of the world should certainly be regarded as a merit. We have to admit that this is one of few episodes in the history of economic theory, and as for double standards, they are uncountable. Liberal theory is one thing, and real life is another; ideological postulates and recipes 'for export' are one thing, and internal policy is another. Some concrete examples follow.

> Example 3.1. *The policy of state interventionism in the USA in the first half of the 19th century.* Below is a quotation from a monograph by A. M. Schlesinger, a famous American historian, who describes the US economic policy under John Quincy Adams, the sixth President (1825–29). 'The state interference in the economy has become unprecedented. Only the degree of the expediency of some measures of the state regulation of economy or the respective excessive expenditures were criticized. The business world approved of the government support... Abbot Lawrence, a manufacturer from Massachusetts, expressed common opinion by characterizing the unrestricted freedom of enterprise as an "ephemeral philosophy, which would hardly be accepted by any government"'[158]. This was half a century after publication of *The Wealth of Nations* by Smith, a book so popular in the USA! 'Even those who like Jefferson supported the ideas of liberalism, in practice had to act according to the real conditions. So, it was not unawareness of the liberal ideas or aversion for them, but understanding of their non-applicability to the society with scarce resources'[159]. The double standard was caused by the usual American pragmatism. And nowadays it forced the US government to resort to state interference, absolutely rejected in theory, when a threat of severe crisis in the automobile industry emerged.

> Example 3.2. *The system of support for the arts accepted in the USA.* Its basic thesis is the rejection of state subsidies as not fitting in the liberal doctrine, which firmly turns down any paternalism. The motto 'individual choice instead of the state interference' is implemented here in the form of charity provided by corporations and individuals. They account, for instance, for about 90% of the financial resources of non-profit theatres. The liberal ideas appear to triumph, if it were not for one rather essential 'but'. The point is that charity is accompanied by substantial tax benefits, i.e. the state voluntarily gives up a part of budget revenues, which could reduce the total tax bur-

---

[158]Schlesinger A.M. The Cycles of American History. Boston: Mifflin, 1986. (Russian Edition – Moscow, 1992, pp. 322-323).

[159]Golitsyn G.A. From Collectivism to Individualism // Cultural Notes, Ed. 2 – M. 1997, p. 290. It is necessary to pay special attention to this work. Its author upheld a simple thesis: only a rich society can afford economic liberalism.

den. So, the 'free choice' turns out to be free only with respect to money allocation within the sphere of arts, but it is not free in forming the necessary resources as a result of re-allocation of imposed taxes. State interference here is evident; it is simply in another form: subsidies are substituted for tax benefits, which also fail to conform to normative individualism. Moreover, in consideration of the total tax benefits offered, the USA can be regarded as one of the greatest state interventionists in the sphere of culture and education.

Turning again to the criticism of common needs from the standpoint of individualistic canons, we would like to note that it often conceals weak points of the existing theory. Unwillingness to recognize the interests of society as such and attempts to reduce them to various arithmetical combinations and hypothetical consensus of individual interests can result in a loss in the positive potential of economic theory. It is clear that acceptance of the idea of collective needs, i.e. actually of the interests of community as a whole, signals a rejection of the customary universality of the reducibility hypothesis – one of the cornerstones of modern market theory. Let us now look at meritorics from this standpoint.

3.3 Meritorics Redux

Returning to an essential topic for us, we wish to quote the epigraph to the famous article by Kurt Schmidt *Mehr zur Meritorik*, 'Be careful, Philipe, you have thought about happiness of the mankind' (Alfred de Musset, *Lorensaccio*).

This epigraph precisely expresses the mood of most neoliberals. In a harmonious chorus of singers of freedom, who are not free from individualistic dogmas, one can hardly hear a voice supporting the concept threatening the basic individualistic norm. But still a forty-year discussion of meritorics has shown it impossible to ignore the practice of state interference. Ideas of Musgrave, who tried to explain state interference and sometimes reconcile it with liberal economic theory, are not yet disproved.

Thinking about 'happiness of the mankind', he understood the main thing: it is impossible to leave everything to the 'invisible hand'. The state should do something as well, regardless of individual desires. This is the point explained by Musgrave's meritorics. According to him, the society should give everyone the opportunity to become happy, including those who do not have true ideas about happiness, those who lack resources to make their dreams come true or will to make right decisions, and those belonging to future generations.

But the warning 'Be careful' is still urgent. Meritorics' good intentions, being used by unscrupulous politicians, can pave the road to hell. But one should search for safety not in refutation of the theory trying to explain the phenomenon of society, but in democratization of society, establishment of efficient institutions ensuring detection, actualization and realization of the actual interests of the majority of its members. Individualistic fundamentalism, being remote from real life, fails to prevent the most appalling infringements of liberty. Moreover, an overzealous adherence to unconditional individualism and oblivion of others result in violation of personal sovereignty. We believe that even sticklers for individualism understand this well.

Now let us turn to the real drawbacks of meritorics. One of the main arguments against Musgrave's concept is the state's unawareness of true preferences of market agents. We think it to be Achilles' heel of this theory, making it too vulnerable to any critique. In this respect we agree more with McLure – who already pointed out this drawback thirty years ago – than with Tietzel and Müller, who claim that the state does not have to know the 'true' preferences of individuals[160]. The loyalty of these authors in this particular issue is caused by their absolutely firm position regarding the reducibility of all public interests. Staying adherent to normative individualism, they implicitly proceed from the universality of the reducibility hypothesis.

At the same time, we agree with neither Buchanan – who believes that individuals should be regarded as the 'sole source of evaluations'[161]– nor his fanatic followers, who find absolutely incredible possibilities to reduce any other 'source of evaluations' to a consensus of individual interests. Tenacious efforts to defend the 'one true' individualistic doctrine should have inevitably resulted in the multiplicity of preferences of individuals themselves. Examples are provided by both Head's endeavours to reconcile meritorics with normative individualism, and the analysis by Tietzel and Müller, who challenge Head's reasoning. We have already noted that meritorics itself is based on the assumption of the existence of at least two systems of individual preferences. Whoever tried to build their hierarchy[162], true and false preferences of individuals were always meant.

In other words, belief in the universality of the reducibility hypothesis or confidence that any public need can be represented as a compromise of individual assessments has led to the more 'sinful' assumption of the *multiplicity* of individual utility functions. In this situation, actual preferences are always false and true preferences are only of a 'reflexive character'[163], the state having 'only a vague idea'[164] of the latter. In this case we have to put up with the fact that individuals are not the 'sole source of evaluations', for, in order to understand which individual preferences are distorted, we should have another source of evaluations. It is a closed circle.

More than that, due to the state's 'vague idea' of the true interests of individuals, the probability of arbitrariness in determining the 'true' preferences increases. This creates a favourable environment for unscrupulous politicians, who use meritorics

---

[160]McLure C.E. Merit Wants: a Normatively Empty Box// Finanzarchiv, 27, 1968, p. 479.

[161]Buchanan J.M. Liberty, Market and State. — Brighton, 1986, p. 249.

[162]See, for instance, Thaler R.H., Shefrin H.M. Op. cit., pp. 392–406.

[163]Brennan G., Lomasky L. Op. cit., pp. 183-206.

[164]Schmidt K. Mehr zur Meritorik. Kritisches und Alternatives zu der Lehre von den öffentlichen Gütern // Zeitschrift für Wirtschafts- und Sozialwissenschaften, 108. Jahrgang, 1988, Heft 3, p. 384.

to reach the goals far from society's interests[165]. In addition, producers may 'exaggerate' the degree of distortion of individual preferences regarding specific goods, looking forward to meritoric assistance. The argument by Tietzel and Müller regarding the motivation for directors of museum and theatres in particular is fair[166]. This danger should be treated seriously, since 'nobody but the subsidies' addressees (who have no reason to protest in case they are subsidized) know the 'true' preferences'[167].

In our opinion, however, all these negative aspects of meritorics refer to a great extent not to the concept itself but to its interpretation, to the attempts of its individualistic justification, this tradition having been established by Musgrave himself. The basic dilemma worded by him – false and true preferences of individuals – is actually false. Repudiating Pareto's third axiom, according to which society's well-being is determined by individual well-beings, we share his first postulate (with an adjustment concerning the socialization of market agents). Every person is the best judge of his well-being. In this sense, individual preferences are always true. And according to one of the principles of the Rome private law, a desire cannot be recognized unfair, 'volenti non fit iniuria'.

In our view, the only reason for meritoric activities is the state's desire to realize its specific interests, corresponding to irreducible public needs. In the case of societal preferences that can be reduced to preferences of individuals, the statement of Tietzel and Müller must be correct, 'All that is valid in meritorics is already contained in other theories; all that is new in it is not valid from the individualistic viewpoint'[168]. In other words, there is indeed no place for meritorics in the 'zone of reducibility' of public needs.

Thus everyone who insists on the universality of the reducibility hypothesis automatically becomes an opponent of meritorics; nobody can sit on two chairs in this case. Thirty years after having put forward meritorics, this dilemma forced Musgrave to suggest its modernization based on the category of 'common needs'. According to our terminology, these are autonomous interests of society that cannot be reduced to individual preferences and form the goals of the state.

Unlike Musgrave, who regards 'common needs' as a special case, we believe however that all cases of meritoric interference are connected only with irreducible interests of society. In the 'pathological' case, in the case of 'weak will of Odysseus', and certainly in the case of 'providing material support', there is always an external 'source of evaluation', i.e. some notions of 'what is good and bad' dif-

---

[165]It is given that meritoric arguments can be used by politicians realizing the 'interests of special groups'. But this relates not only to meritoric interference. In particular, it is well known that public employees not always serve the 'lofty patriotic purpose to increase the national wealth and raise economic efficiency' (Silvestrov S.N. Politics Like Business' // Russian Economic Journal, 1995, No. 2, p. 84).

[166]The 'unverifiable' argument which is often used when applying for additional subsidies is as follows: maintenance of interest in, say, theatres requires additional expenditures for raising the quality of their services (Tietzel M., Müller C. Op. cit., p. 123).

[167]Tietzel M., Müller C. Op. cit., p. 124.

[168]Ibid.

ferent from an individual's opinion. Therefore, in our concept there are also two systems of preferences, but one of them refers to individuals, the other to their aggregation as a whole – in general, one system of preferences not being reduced to the other. If an external source of evaluations can be represented in the form of individual preference function, we face a specific case in which societal interests are completely dissolved in individual judgements and both preference systems merge.

What fundamentally distinguishes our interpretation of meritorics from others is not a negation of the ambivalence inherent to the evaluation of goods and services, but a different understanding of the nature of this ambivalence. We believe that the ambivalent attitude of an individual towards a good is conditioned by the existence of two different sources of its evaluation which does not imply an individual's double-think. Therefore, a situation in which an individual does not know about his 'second thought', but others do know and stimulate it for his benefit, does not change anything substantially. This is still an 'external' viewpoint.

'The evaluations are supported upon whose learning an individual accepts them as his own evaluations; therefore, they should not be regarded as external...' Such logical structures are absolutely unconvincing. There is nothing in them except for an almost religious striving for the preservation of the individualistic picture of the world along with the universality of the reducibility hypothesis. We are sure that an ambivalent evaluation of goods and services means the existence of an external source of this evaluation.

We wish to emphasize the main point here. Until a theory proceeds from the purely individualistic canons, it is not necessary to speak about individual interests that differ from those manifested in the market, or about any societal needs other than the market aggregate of individual preferences. The hypothesis of the reducibility of public needs is another expression for the same individualistic notions of the world. But as soon as the economic outlook expands to recognition of the market agents' socialization, i.e. when a theory starts to consider their behaviour in socium, it becomes clear that to explain such behaviour, a category of individual preferences and their market aggregation are not enough.

This problem manifests itself in the aforementioned individualistic paradox known as 'fallacy of composition': on the one hand what is good for all is good for everyone; on the other hand if everyone acts for his own benefit, all together can come to a result unfavourable for society as a whole. The fallacy of notions formulated in the first part of this paradox is demonstrated by the following example, borrowed from the aforementioned monograph by Peter Koslowski.

> Example 3.3. *Manifestation of the 'individualistic paradox' in inflation.* Examining the dilemma of individualism in the market sphere, Koslowski considers a situation in which the market mechanism produces results contrary to the initial interests of its agents. Characterizing this situation, he writes in particular, 'Market failures may occur in the cases based on the said fallacious conclusion, for instance, in the case of a "wait-and-see" position on the market as the means of price level stabilizing, when everyone has a motivation to become a "free rider". If, trying to protect oneself from inflation, eve-

ryone thinks it can be achieved by buying the real estate, for all taken together this may bring about the opposite result – a galloping inflation due to
an increase in the price of land. The result achieved on the market proceeding from individual consumer decisions turns to be unreasonable and undesirable from the viewpoint of the society as a whole'[169].

To resolve the individualistic paradox according to Smith's theory, based on the
teleological mechanism of the invisible hand, it was necessary to meet a number
of special requirements, the central one being an atomistic concept of an aggregation of market agents – that is, their autonomous behaviour. All further attempts to
fit an aggregation of individuals into an atomistic market model, though having
resulted in the development of corporate strategies[170], did not allow the resolution
of all contradictions within a community of people with different interests. The
limitedness of the category of individual preferences, of their various combinations and their generalized functions provides no opportunity to take into consideration the interests of society as such. Adherence to normative individualism and
universality of the reducibility hypothesis does not allow an increase in the number of market agents by adding a bearer of public interests.

Another opportunity widely, though implicitly, used in different theoretical
concepts is the assumption that all people in a socium are able to make correct
choices due to equal distribution of *knowledge, will and resources* among them
and that all of them are equally endowed with *civic virtue*. Rejecting this evidently
artificial assumption, we would rather suggest that it is the existing variety of people that finally generates social interests different from the interests of individual
members of society. Thus the variety of individuals evidently refutes the requirement for the reducibility of all needs.

Firm repudiation of universality of this hypothesis along with recognition of a
category of societal needs is, in our opinion, one of the possible solutions to this
fundamental problem. Instead of trying to artificially integrate individuals into socium (from Pareto's concept to game theory) and transfer the responsibility for the
realization of public interest to them (the socialization of individual utility), it is
necessary to personify the bearer of this interest. In our paradigm, it is the state as
a normal market agent.

3.4 The Public Interests and the State

Analyzing theoretical notions of social interest and mechanisms for its realization,
we could not surpass the impression that an internal spring of inventing different
'mutant' categories, designing various degenerate cases, and absolutizing the re-

---

[169]Koslowski P. Op. cit., pp. 284-285.
[170]We mean the institutional 'discoveries' (the above Taylor's community behaviour, Sugden's *Vermassung*, Rawls' 'veil of ignorance', or Buchanan's constitutional agreement)
rather than the 'prisoner's dilemma' or achievements of game theory.

ducibility hypothesis has always been a desire to free the market from the state. Negative experiences of totalitarian systems have only strengthened this desire. Evidently, it is not by chance that in the second half of the 20th century, the theoretical models suggesting that social order exists without state involvement won popularity. Moreover, results of many research works not meant to resolve the issues of opposition of the market and state came to be used to justify the possibility of pushing the state out of the market sphere.

A typical example in this regard is the interpretation of Arrow's theorem 'On Impossibility' by Joseph Stiglitz, the famous expert in public economics. According to him, 'Arrow's theorem on impossibility states that as long as no individual possesses a dictator's power, we should not expect the state to act with the same consciousness and rationality as an individual can act...We don't aim at its personifying, regarding it as an individual, or attributing to it more wisdom than the individuals constituting it have'[171]. Indeed, 'desire is a father of thought', since Arrow's theorem only demonstrates the impossibility of correct social choice taking into consideration opinions of all market agents, and says nothing about involvement of the state in this procedure[172].

Unintentionally allowing the substitution of concepts by identifying the mechanism of 'social choice' with the state, Stiglitz simultaneously points out the undesirability of this step. It is this ambivalent attitude that conditioned the said 'adjustment' of Arrow's theorem to substantiate antistatism. Though it makes no sense to attribute more wisdom to the state than to its citizens, it does makes sense to think of it as having specific needs other than individual needs (its own wisdom!). It is easy to notice that the circle closes here again, and the same fundamental issue about the reducibility of public interests to individual preferences arises.

It should be emphasized that Arrow[173], Stiglitz and many other economic authorities agree over the universality of the reducibility hypothesis. Lack of any doubt as to this issue is also demonstrated by the Russian economist Victor Polterovich. Characterizing the rule of public choice (according to Arrow), he, in full accordance with neoclassical theory, writes, 'Of course, it should depend on individual preferences and, moreover, be universal, i.e. give a solution in case of any preferences of society's members'[174].

Why 'of course'? Why should a theoretical construction be that rigid? Why can some autonomous public interest not exist, the one that is irreducible to individual preferences? One has to be an extreme optimist and firmly believe in inspiring illusions of democracy to imagine a situation in which every state interest, even that concerning the computer model of molecules of prion protein or creation of the bacteriological weapon, is conditioned by individual needs for this fundamental

---

[171]Stiglitz J. Op. cit., p. 159.

[172]In any case, we think it incorrect to ascribe Arrow the simplified understanding of the state, according to which its role is reduced to coordinating individual interests.

[173]We emphasize that dependence of public preferences on individual ones is included in the initial conditions of Arrow's theorem 'On impossibility'.

[174]Polterovich V.M. Economic Theory Crisis // Economic Science of Modern Russia, 1998, No. 1, p. 54.

scientific research and these types of weapons. In our opinion, such a view has something in common with an instinctive wish to 'hide one's head under the wing' and isolate oneself from reality.

One can oppose us saying that the given examples relate to the general state's needs for fundamental research and the country's defensive capacity, being a reflection of individual interests. But even if we admit this, the state's interest in the bacteriological weapon as such cannot be expressed in the form of utilitarian, Rawlsian or any other function aggregating individual preferences. Such relation between public and individual needs is possible only in the case of *coincidence* of the views of those postulating goals and making decisions on behalf of a society with the ideas of its members[175].

At the same time one should keep in mind that all individuals are in some socium. And in this sense, there is really a certain connection between their needs and interests of society as such. Like a physical medium enabling electromagnetic waves to spread, the institutional structure of a society makes it possible for interrelations between individual and public interests to emerge, exist and disappear.

Absorbing all 'formal and informal restrictions' and responding to the tension between them[176], the institutional environment changes continuously and creates new restrictions and incentives. Some of them refer to individuals, others only to the whole society. In this regard there is probably always an institutional dependence of the whole society's needs on individual needs, and only some cases in which this dependence becomes functional (and only in these cases the reducibility hypothesis is true).

Here we note again that preferences of public officers, like any other individuals, are formed under the influence of national traditions, cultural stereotypes and value orientations, i.e. of the whole system of institutions existing in a society. Only in this context – depending on a degree of the society's democratization – do state interests reflect individual preferences. Traditional theory considers only a specific case; according to it, the dependence between public and individual preferences is always functional. Hence follow the comments by Polterovich and Stiglitz on Arrow's theorem.

We believe that this theorem should be interpreted absolutely differently. Unlike Stiglitz, we suggest that in a theoretical model the state must be personified and regarded as an autonomous market agent pursuing its own specific interests. In this regard, a negative result obtained by Arrow – like it has happened many times in other disciplines – helps understand the limitedness of the customary axioms. If under the set conditions it is impossible to make a correct 'social choice', we should give up the excessively restrictive basic assumptions, not the idea of the rational behaviour of the state. We mean the same assumption – the reducibility of

---

[175]We do not consider any degenerate cases here when the said unanimity is reached due to the dictatorship or individuals' 'mass consciousness'. We also leave aside the possibilities of hypothetical consensus, analyzed in the previous chapter, whose achievement is connected with the Rawls' 'veil of ignorance'.

[176]North D. Op. cit., p. 66.

public needs to individual preferences – which we consider excessively rigid and not adequate to the reality.

In this context, Arrow's theorem has a double meaning. First, we can interpret it as the evidence of the existence of social interests not reducible to any function of individual needs. Hence, on the assumption of the state's rational behaviour, in a general case one should proceed from the existence of its autonomous interests which are not directly connected with other market agents' preferences. Second, this assumption changes neither contents of Arrow's theorem, nor its proof. With the same three participants having two alternative preferences each, having identified the state as one of them, it is possible to achieve the same result and prove the impossibility of a correct agreement of interests of all market agents.

Thus, it is impossible to find a solution which would fully meet the interests of all individuals and the state. The second version of Arrow's theorem clearly indicates the fact that the conflict of interests of market agents (including the state) can be successfully resolved only as a result of some compromise, implying that all participants (including the state) can maximize their utility functions only within the limits set by the well-known Pareto scheme.

In this connection, the suggestion that rational behaviour is determined only by individual utility becomes quite vulnerable. We believe that another theoretical construction is needed, one that takes into consideration the simultaneous presence of all socialized agents on the market. Results of their activities should be considered from a more general point of view; attention should be paid to goods' ability to realize the interests of not only individuals but also social groups and society as such. In other words, we have the right to assume existence of such autonomous interests of society that are not revealed in individual needs. Any attempts to absolutize the reducibility hypothesis do not bring the neoclassical model closer to the reality.

Therefore, in cases when the society's needs can be reduced to individual preferences, and demand for goods and services completely 'dissolves' in these preferences, the market can indeed give answer to all questions[177]. Coming across irreducible public needs, the 'invisible hand' starts to fail. M. Blaug writes, 'We have come to the conclusion that the "public nature" of some goods restricts "the theorem of the invisible hand" in a way Adam Smith didn't have any suspect of'[178]. Generally speaking, Blaug merely establishes here what is already well-known: the 'invisible hand' can't reach many areas of the economy. This 'discovery', as we noted before, has led to a narrowing of the market sphere.

Meanwhile, the said restrictions can be overcome correctly, if the state (a bearer of irreducible public interests) is included in the number of market agents and 'the theorem of the invisible hand' is reformulated respectively. We proceed from the fact that in a generalized model of a competitive market, in which individual agents with their needs and the state with its irreducible needs operate simultaneously and whereby all of them try to maximize their own utility function,

---

[177]Samuelson P.A. Economics. – Moscow, 1992. V. 2., p. 395.
[178]Blaug M. Op. cit., p. 551.

the self-regulation mechanism can ensure efficient market equilibrium without any essential exceptions.

Treating the state as an agent of a competitive market, where, along with its other agents, it tries to maximize its own utility function, removes the hindrance for operation of the 'invisible hand'. In other words, turning the state into a market player can produce a mechanism providing that reducible public needs are reflected in individual preferences, the state is 'responsible' for the irreducible ones, and the emerging equilibrium is accompanied by the Pareto-efficient allocation of resources.

It is clear that this approach, based on the recognition of the category of irreducible, societal needs and the notion of the state as a market agent, is hardly possible without radical modernization of the neoclassical model. We associate this modernization with the concept of *economic sociodynamics*, developed by us, which is to be considered in the following chapter.

4 The Principles of Economic Sociodynamics

In 1898 Thorstein Veblen's monograph *Why is Economy a not evolution science?* and the second collection of works by Leon Walras *Etudes d'économie politique appliquée*[179] were published. These are two books whose authors are not usually mentioned together. One of them used physical analogues in his analysis and thought about economic development exclusively in terms of the general equilibrium equation; the other treated such views of the world ironically and believed in the institutional bases of a socium and viewed the evolution of the economic system and wildlife according to similar, if not the same, laws. With one hundred years having passed, we can state that these two standpoints developed into alternative theories.

Though Walras also insisted that all social phenomena – religion, politics, economy, and spiritual life – are closely interrelated, this *interrelation imperative* has not been realized in neoclassical theory. Despite all further achievements and constant declarations about relations of the economy and different aspects of social life, the dominating concepts are still individualistic. As before, such fundamental categories as 'need', 'utility', 'price' and 'equilibrium' are almost always treated by this theory in the context of methodological individualism, from the standpoint of a separate person regardless of the socium to which he or she belongs.

The end of the 20th century is marked with a crisis of the dominating economic theory[180] and obvious revival of interest in institutionalism[181]. Compared to the time of Walras and Veblen, the role of social factors in the economy has become much more important, which encouraged us to make another attempt to incorporate it into economics, and is an essential market theory.

We believe that the general theory of well-being developed by Vilfredo Pareto, Walras' successor at the chair in Lausanne University, may lay the groundwork for such synthesis. Here we are referring to the system of axioms and the principle of optimum, mentioned in the previous chapter. According to Pareto, every person is

---

[179]This publication continues the research begun in his first collection of works – *Etudes d'économie sociale - 1896*.

[180]Please, refer to the special report by Viktor Polterovich, which he presented at the seminar 'Unknown Economy' in January 1997: Polterovich V.M. Op. cit., 1998, pp. 46–66.

[181]In connection to this, please pay attention to the Evolution Economics Centre established in 1995 by the Russian Academy of Sciences and an international symposium arranged by this Centre in Pushchino. Refer to the 'Voprosy Ekonomiki', No. 3, 1997 and No. 8, 1998.

the best judge of his own well-being (1); the well-being of separate people cannot be compared with each other (2); and society's well-being is determined by the well-being of separate people (3). The allocation of resources is considered optimal if it is impossible to improve anybody's well-being without impairing the well-being of another individual[182].

The principle of optimum and the axioms suggested by Pareto have become a philosophical foundation for neoclassical theory. Moreover, from the standpoint of methodology, Pareto optimality has turned into a specific criterion of economic concepts' correctness. However, we see the core point in another aspect. In our view, the mere concept of Pareto-efficient allocation of resources has a much greater potential than neoclassical theory – with its individualistic outlook – has been able to use.

The requirement, contained in the formulation of the optimum, to take into account interrelations between market agents suggests the possibility of building the Pareto scheme for more general conditions, when the state becomes one of them. In this connection we suggest the category of *social utility* and the concept of *economic sociodynamics*[183] in general with its basic axioms: *the postulates of social utility, social motivation and social immunity.*

4.1 The Postulates of Economic Socio-Dynamics

Here we wish to emphasize again that the repudiation of the universality of the reducibility hypothesis and recognition of the existence of autonomous interests of society as such make the basic thesis for our concept of economic sociodynamics. Accordingly, any good can realize the interests of qualitatively different market players, including society as a whole. We call the assumption of ability of any good to meet irreducible social needs the *postulate of social utility*[184]. We are going to give a number of examples illustrating the said ability.

---

[182]Pareto V. Manual of Political Economy. – New York: Augustus M.Kelley, 1971 Also: Blaug M. Economic Theory in Retrospect. Fifth English edition. Cambridge: Cambridge University Press, 1997 (Russian Edition – Moscow, 1994, p. 545).

[183]We should note that the term 'sociodynamics' was introduced in the scientific terminology long ago (see, for instance, Moll A. Sociodynamics of Culture, – M. 1973). It is widely used to characterize changes in the public environment. The adjective 'economic' shows the synthetic nature of our concept, considering the economy in the social context. We also draw attention to another meaning that we attribute to the category of 'sociodynamics'. We want to emphasize its similarity to 'thermodynamics', characterizing the states of energy equilibrium in physical systems and the processes of transition from one state to another. We believe that there exists an analogue of the physical energy in social systems: interests of individuals, their various aggregates and interests of an aggregation of people as a whole. Proceeding from this, we regard economic sociodynamics as a concept describing economic patterns of dynamic processes in a socium.

[184]The category of social utility was first suggested for the theoretical substantiation of subsidizing the producers of cultural services (Rubinstein A. On the Theory of Prices, Sub-

Example 4.1. *The first artificial satellites of the Earth.* On October 4, 1957, the first sputnik was launched in the USSR. Later, a similar launch took place in the USA. We consider this extraordinary event the most vivid evidence of the existence of a society's irreducible need and, at the same time, an example of a good able to meet the said need and, consequently, possessing the social utility.

We would like to emphasize that the age-old 'dream about stars' cannot be in any way equated with the market players' needs influencing their rational behaviour. Even in the end of the 20th century, when spaceship launches became purely utilitarian actions with purely technical objectives, the 'dream about stars' was not included in individual utility functions. In the 1950s, such opportunity for practical use of space simply did not exist. Therefore, there could be no individual need for launching artificial satellites.

As for the public need for creation and launch of spacecraft, in the middle of the century the respective interest of societies as such was so great that the USSR and the USA devoted enormous budget funds to its realization. It is clear that due to the above circumstances the said interest could not be reflected in individual preferences. Thus, considering the first artificial satellites, we have the right to regard them as a textbook example of a good possessing the social utility, i.e. able to meet an irreducible public need.

The above is an example of production of the goods *originally possessing* the social utility. And now we are going to describe another mechanism for satisfying a society's irreducible need. Instead of producing goods that directly meet irreducible needs (like artificial satellites), the state, being a market agent, can realize its autonomous interest indirectly, using the market mechanism. It can always create the conditions encouraging individual market agents to produce and consume the goods that eventually ensure satisfaction of the respective society's need.

Example 4.2. *Production and consumption of automobile catalysts.* Recently, the number of automobiles in many countries has increased at such a rate that a serious environmental danger emerged. In particular it was discovered that the exhaust aggravates the so-called greenhouse effect, which – as was scientifically proven – caused a number of destructive floods and droughts. Thereby, a specific societal need appeared to protect the atmosphere from pollution. It was also determined that this need could be technically met, if special devices – catalysts – were installed in cars. However, it was hardly possible to expect car owners to start buying catalysts on a mass scale to prevent the atmospheric temperature from increasing. Perhaps one day installing catalysts will turn into a moral requirement (according to Sugden). As for now, like several years ago, such motivation (even under the 'veil of igno-

sidies and Rent // Economics of Culture: Intensification Issues. – Moscow 1986, pp. 39-41; Rubinstein A. 'Introduction into Economics of Performance Art. Moscow 1991, pp. 18-22, 188-190).

rance') seems an illusion. International practice shows that this abstract interest to protect against the greenhouse effect is not manifested in individual utility functions. The pure atmosphere is still only a societal irreducible need.

However, though individuals are not interested in liquidation of the greenhouse effect, the state can stimulate their demand for catalysts required for purification of the exhaust. Actually, this is what governments in many countries do, introducing fines for driving cars not equipped with catalyst, and in some cases subsidizing manufacturers of catalysts. In this situation, an individual's desire to purchase a catalyst is caused by his rather practical interest in reducing expenses for his car's operation, since the price of a catalyst is usually lower than the fine for its absence. Individual consumption of catalysts provides the possibility for meeting the society's irreducible need to reduce emission of carbon dioxide. In other words, we see the good able to realize the interests of qualitatively different market agents. Thus, it is possible to state that an automobile catalyst possesses social utility along with the individual one.

It is important to emphasize that there is no functional dependence of social utility on individual preferences because the base of social utility is formed by irreducible social needs that are only postulated for the aggregation of individuals as a whole. Indeed, the independence of social utility makes the government an equal participant in the market, where individual subjects act simultaneously according to their specific needs and the government – according to its irreducible interests, all of them trying to maximize their utility functions.

Such interpretation of the market model evidently requires the revision of its basic premises. In this context a question arises: is it possible to preserve the notion of equilibrium and the principle of Pareto optimality, having given up one of the key theses of Pareto's concept? We are referring to the reducibility hypothesis (implying the functional dependence of the public well-being on individual well-being), which, according to our notions of society's irreducible needs, should be replaced by the *postulate of social utility*. However, before answering this question, it is necessary to analyze Pareto's other basic assumptions, which also require modernization.

As for Pareto's first axiom, by which every individual is the best judge of his own well-being, it can be preserved, but the institutional paradigm of the socialization of economic subjects should be applied. According to this paradigm, every person, remaining a judge of his own well-being, belongs to a social group and adopts some value judgements and norms of economic behaviour characteristic of it. Therefore after institutionalists, we have to recognize that the behaviour of any market agent has a strong foundation of social experience, seriously impacting the subjective vision of personal well-being.

But the socialization paradigm also allows a new theoretical generalization. In particular, its use allows for a broadening of the composition of participants in market relationships. Therefore, in our interpretation, every bearer of a distinct interest, including separate individuals, their groups and society as a whole, appears as an independent actor in the market attempting to realize this interest. All market agents, including the state, are the best judge of their own well-being. We call the above thesis *the postulate of social motivation*. It is supposed to replace Pareto's first axiom in the suggested concept. Below you will find an example of market activities of a specific agent representing corporate interests of a certain professional group and having noticeable influence on the formation of the market environment, the Russian Union of Theatrical Workers.

Example 4.3. *The Russian Theatrical Workers' Union*. More than a hundred years ago, a great Russian actress Maria Ermolova organized the first mutual aid fund for the 'stage community'. Later it was transformed into the Russian Theatrical Society, and then into the Union of Theatrical Workers. Nowadays, this professional union is the bearer of a distinct group interest. It is enough to read the Charter of this creative association to find the specific interests of the theatre community, which are irreducible to its members' needs, such as preservation of the Russian theatrical school, development of the theatrical art, support for young actors' activities, etc. It is evident that these interests, however close they may be to those employed in this sphere, cannot be revealed in individual preferences of actors, directors, artists, etc[185]. Realizing the said group interests, the Union of Theatrical Workers therefore acts as an independent market agent.

In this case, the number of market agents indeed increases; in addition to theatres and theatrical organizations, a new powerful player appears. While analyzing the market situation, one cannot fail to consider this player's actions, aimed at accomplishing specific interests. In today's Russia, every theatre feels the influence of the Union of Theatrical Workers on the process of creative staff reproduction, volume and structure of audience's demand, and – the most important thing – on the formation of the rules of economic behaviour beneficial to theatres and people involved in this sphere. Pursuing group interests related to the preservation of the Russian theatrical school and development of the theatrical art, the Union of Theatrical Workers always lobbies these interests in governmental structures, tries to get necessary tax benefits and suggests respective amendments to the Russian legislation[186]. These activities impact the situation on the theatrical market considerably. In this respect, the neoclassical model – dealing only with individual market agents (like theatres) and ignoring those players representing group

---

[185]In pursuing the said goals, the Union of Theatrical Workers spends considerable funds to arrange creative laboratories and master classes, to organize theatre festivals and contests, etc.; the interest of their participants in the communication with outstanding theatre masters is conditioned not by the general ideas of the development of theatrical art and preservation of the Russian theatrical school but purely by personal motives (professional growth).

[186]Here it is sufficient to remember a number of special governmental decrees, aimed at supporting the theatre, and the draft of the Federal Law of the Russian Federation 'On Theatre and Theatrical Activity', which was initiated and prepared by the Union of Theatrical Workers and submitted to the State Duma in December 1999.

interests (like the Union of Theatrical Workers) – is not suitable for an adequate description of the reality.

Considering Pareto's second axiom on the impossibility of interpersonal comparison, we must keep in mind that this 'taboo' was overcome sixty years ago in the above-mentioned article by Bergson. In our interpretation, the admissibility of the comparison of separate individuals' well-being is directly connected to the existence of irreducible public needs. In fact, the existence of these needs as such entails the recognition of the possibility of interpersonal comparison. However as a German proverb says, 'the devil is hiding in the details'. The question is, when such a comparison is possible. We believe that the mentioned taboo is correctly overcome only in the preliminary phase – in the process of actualizing and postulating on autonomous public interests.

Another assumption of economic sociodynamics is of extreme importance in this regard, the postulate of social immunity. This postulate, reflecting the operation of a teleological mechanism, establishes that every society possesses immunity objectively. Put differently, inherent interests exist and forces arise within society that are directed toward its self-preservation and development, to guaranteeing its 'leaps onto new levels of complexity'[187].

The immune force of self-protection, in particular, compels us to compare individual well-being; based on the mechanisms of a positive reverse interdependence to form, at different points in history, such social directions and distinct interests of the state, including its specific interests of 'efficiency' and 'equity' that have often been impossible to predict[188]. We are going to give a specific example to ensure a better understanding of the postulate of social immunity.

Example 4.4. *Structural policy in the coal industry in the Federal Republic of Germany.* In the early 1960s the pursuit of the policy aimed at opening the internal markets in Western European countries resulted in growing international competition practically in all economic areas. The coal industry of the FRG found itself in an especially difficult situation (in Germany the costs of coal mining were always relatively high due to natural conditions). Since the imported coal was cheaper, serious difficulties arose in the selling of German coal. Individual consumer preferences and market mechanisms actually 'con-

---

[187]We wish to remind the reader of the philosophical interpretation of Ilya Prigogine's theorem that 'legalized' the combination of necessity and chance, negative and positive reverse interdependence in any complex system, including the socium.

[188]Following Toffler, now in the context of our concept, we draw attention to the fact that the purposes of society are often formed by chance. It is here that necessity combines with probability. Something similar can be seen in the physics, where, according to Toffler, 'before appearance of the quantum theory, many believed that chance played insignificant or null role in changes, the initial conditions of the process predetermining its development (*we wish to emphasize the similarity of this thesis to the fundamental theorems of well-being – R.G., A.R.*). Nowadays, in the nuclear physics, for instance, the belief that chance dominates in changes is widespread' (Toffler A. Op. cit., p. 496).

demned' the coal industry of the FRG to a 'lifelong' recession. The danger of an avalanche-like closing of coal mines, which used to play an important role in the German economy, was getting more and more real and threatened mass unemployment, especially in the Ruhr region.

The danger of the respective social tension triggered the mechanism of social immunity and activated self-protective forces of the society. As a counterweight for the market requirements, public interest aimed at preserving jobs emerged, which could not, however, be reflected in individual preferences of producers and consumers of German coal. Numerous strikes in Northern Rhine-Westphalia, pressure of the German Trade Union Association, and political debate in mass media were the manifestations of the positive reverse interdependence, which ensured detection and actualization of the respective irreducible public need. After becoming a subject of discussion among the general public and in *Landtags* and Bundestag, this need was recognized at the national level.

As a result, the government developed and approved a program which suggested carrying out a structural reconstruction of the coal industry. This program sought the realization of two primary goals. On the one hand, the gradual reduction of the number of coal mines was admitted as reasonable. On the other hand (and this being the main objective), it was decided to provide governmental subsidies to the coal industry. Thus, the functioning German mines got a chance to set competitive prices, which prevented their avalanche-like closing. Besides, the federal government ensured the conditions necessary for a socially-acceptable transfer of the released labour force to other economic sectors.

In irreducible public needs 'legitimated' by social immunity, the results of interpersonal comparison of utilities that actually determine the public interest of 'equity' are always reflected. Moreover, such a comparison is an integral part of institutional environment. As for the stage at which market agents' interests are realized, comparison is impossible: if every market player is the only judge of his well-being, the extent of the realization of his interests cannot be compared with that of other market agents.

Strictly speaking, here we face sociodynamic cycles, within which the 'permission' for utility comparison is replaced by its 'prohibition', and the prohibition, in its turn by a new permission. It applies to all market agents, including the state, which seek to maximize the social utility. This considered, Pareto's third axiom should be formulated in relation to our concept as follows: *the well-being of individual market agents are not comparable, and the social utility is incommensurable with the individual one.* The second part of this logical formula is especially important for us, and we shall return to it.

Considering the basic assumptions of our concept in general and comparing them with Pareto's famous axioms, we can make the following (preliminary) conclusion. Pareto's basic axioms are replaced by an essentially different system of postulates; we have called these economic sociodynamics. We would like to repeat its main propositions. The postulate of *social motivation* suggests the socialization of market agents and an aggregated treatment of the interests of these agents, bearers of distinct interests; the postulate of *social immunity* determines the mechanism for the formation of public needs and social and economic purposes of the state activities; the postulate of *social utility* establishes the existence of irreducible social needs and social utility of goods.

4.2 Equilibrium and Evolution in Economic Sociodynamics

Now we shall try to answer the question raised in the previous paragraph regarding the equilibrium and existence of Pareto optimality. Having transformed Pareto's axioms into the postulates of economic sociodynamics, we are going to mark out two important theses.

First, though the state is included in the number of common market agents, its 'uncommonness' should be emphasized. It is conditioned by the qualitative difference between social and individual utilities. While individual utilities that join the market flow are reduced to an average on the whole set of individuals, social utility that reflects the goods' ability to realize interests of their aggregation as a whole is not involved in such reduction. These are qualitatively different types of utility, each of them having its own metric. Therefore, any summing of these utilities, including that using weight functions, is inadmissible[189].

Second, in dealing with socialized economic agents that have replaced traditional 'homo economicus', it is impossible to rely on the permanency of the preferences of separate individuals, their groups and society as a whole. On the contrary, according to institutional doctrine, the cumulative causation effect should be kept in mind, i.e. an endogenous mechanism of 'consecutive changes regarded as self-sustaining, self-developing and lacking the final goal'[190]. Taking this into consideration, we should proceed from the fact that both social and individual utilities are continuously changing.

We wish to note that the energy of cumulative causation is supported by the mechanism of social immunity, involving continual comparisons of individual well-being[191], stimulating changes in the interest of 'equity'. Other public needs are similarly emerging and changing, including the interest of 'efficiency', connected

---

[189]We consider this to be the main mistake of Margolis. Assuming the possibility of the existence of an autonomous interest of society, he started to sum this interest with individual interests using the weight function. In other words, assuming the existence of an irreducible interest of the aggregation of individuals as a whole, he started to reduce this need to the interests of separate individuals.

[190]Veblen T. The Place of Science in Modern Civilisation and Other Essays. – New York: Huebsch, 1919, p. 37.

[191]Our friend, a famous philosopher, likes repeating, 'We live in the world of ratios, not levels, in the world of consequences, not causes' (principle of 'social envy' by Vladimir Pokrovski).

with the competitive environment, reproduction of production factors, structural shifts in the economy, etc. It is evident that dynamics of the institutional environment adjust individual preferences of market players as well. We stress again that all changes in a socium are subject to the general teleological pattern combining necessity and chance, energy of a negative reverse interdependence, serving the system's tendency to equilibrium, and positive reverse interdependence, responsible for the society's development vector and 'leaps onto new levels of complexity'.

Thus, the use of the socialization paradigm and introduction of the postulates of economic sociodynamics make it necessary to update both the initial premises and the notion of equilibrium itself, giving rise to doubts as to the possibility of achieving Pareto optimality. When in addition to households and firms, other market agents act (including the state), all of them maximizing their utility functions (including the social one), the social utility cannot be summed with the individual one and all utility functions are not permanent. It is obviously impossible to reach the state corresponding to Pareto optimality, since under these conditions there is always a possibility of Pareto-improvement.

This conclusion absolutely agrees with institutional doctrine regarding the equilibrium only as a nontypical state accompanied by the 'blocking effect'. In our interpretation, this specific case is conditioned by a situation in which certain stability of the institutional environment emerges, temporarily fixing the existing formal and informal norms, thus impeding or suspending the process of evolution of social and individual utilities. Only when the energy of a positive reverse interdependence depletes and determinism comes into its usual force, is it possible to speak about equilibrium in its traditional sense.

Assuming the reducibility of public needs and basing itself on the reduction of social utility, the neoclassical market model defines the condition of equilibrium as equality of marginal costs to the marginal individual utility. In this case the price of any good corresponds to the standard model of demand and supply. But since in this model there is no place for budget subsidies, tax benefits or any other forms of the state involvement, the practice deviates from its theoretical construction, the evidence of this deviation being provided by the mere fact of the state budget expenditures reflecting the 'format' of irreducible public needs[192].

According to the postulates of economic sociodynamics, all market agents, including the state, pursue their own interests in the process of exchange, and their aggregate demand is conditioned by individual and social utilities. Therefore, the conditions necessary for equilibrium are met only when *the marginal costs equal the marginal individual and marginal social utilities*. Attention must be given to the conjunction 'and', since we speak not about a simple sum or weight function,

---

[192]We wish to emphasize that the introduction of the category of public goods 'adopted' by the neoclassical model (Lindahl's equilibrium) does not resolve all contradictions but in some cases brings this model even further away from reality. It happens every time we face the aforesaid 'quasi-public goods', which habitually include many paid services of education, theatres and concert organizations, and whose producers, in addition to the revenues from selling them, enjoy tax benefits and/or budget subsidies. The merit goods demonstrate the limitedness of the neoclassical model even more vividly.

but about the conjunction, i.e. logical summation of qualitatively different and ir-reducible utilities[193]. This interpretation of equilibrium also changes the traditional notion of the state as bearer of the social interest. Its activity, including the forma-tion and spending of budgetary funds is not regarded as interference in the market sphere any more; it becomes an integral part and condition of equilibrium.

This considered and in accordance with the postulates of economic sociody-namics, the basic theorems of the theory of well-being should be reformulated. The first theorem, in our version, can be worded as follows: any competitive equi-librium of the market where the state acts as one of the agents is Pareto-efficient. Modification of the second theorem is reduced to the conclusion that for any com-petitive equilibrium (Pareto optimality) of the market where the state acts as one of the agents, there is an option for resource reallocation with a corresponding Pareto optimality.

We believe this creates a real basis for the resolution of an age-old conflict be-tween 'efficiency' and 'equity'. If the state, the bearer of the interest of 'equity', is a market player, then an emerging equilibrium brings into optimal correlation those resources at the disposal of the whole aggregation of market agents and the degree of equity as for the allocation of results of their use (the first theorem). Any at-tempt to increase this degree – i.e. obtain 'more equity', 'more satisfaction' of pub-lic needs – requires reallocation of resources (the second theorem).

Assuming that the theorems of the theory of well-being are still true in a case in which the postulates of economic sociodynamics are introduced, and keeping in mind that the state becomes a market player, it is possible to reword Arrow's statement that has been already quoted. If the degree of the realization of an irre-ducible public interest is evaluated as insufficient, the available resources should be reallocated by introducing additional taxes, and then the market should be al-lowed to function freely[194]. We agree with Arrow that after resource reallocation, and also without it (when it is not required), there is no need for any nonmarket 'price regulation or rationing'.

We would like to emphasize again that in general, the teleological combination of energies of negative and positive reverse interdependences always results in dynamic processes of utilities' changes. In short, this leads to the disappearance of old irreducible public needs and the actualization of new ones – which makes every equilibrium an infinitesimal moment of history –, and their sequence forms

---

[193]We shall further show that the difference in the metrics of two types of utility that do not allow their simple summing can be overcome by means of a special mechanism we call the *sociodynamic multiplier* (see paragraph 4.4 hereof).

[194]It should be reminded that in speaking about reallocation of resources aimed to increase equity, Arrow means 'a one-stroke free transfer of respective quotas'. Though the state is not explicitly present here, it is difficult to imagine that such reallocation can be carried out without the state's involvement. In our market model, the state is originally responsi-ble for realization of the public 'interest of equity'; therefore, resource reallocation may not be needed. And if this necessity arises, the problem is resolved with the help of the traditional mechanism of taxation providing the possibility for the differentiated contri-bution of separate individuals to the formation of state resources.

the trajectory of evolution. For this reason, Pareto optimality exists only in the form of 'absolute truth' or predetermined harmony within our theory, whereas the striving for this end represents the essence of evolution.

Attention should also be paid to regularly emerging opportunities for Pareto-improvements, ensuring the allocation of resources as a result of which an improvement in the well-being of some market players *(including the state)* does not worsen that of other players *(including the state)*. Here an additional commentary is required. Having declared the state[195] a normal market agent, we must clarify our standpoint regarding two fundamental questions: WHAT should be thought about state property and HOW should state expenditures be treated?

The answer to the first question is quite evident, and no misunderstanding should arise here. Although the state becomes a market agent, this cannot generate any additional motives for nationalization of the private property. Moreover, we share a well-known thesis about the presumption of state property inefficiency and believe that the state should have minimum property at its disposal.

Strictly speaking, the state as a market agent acts as a typical *non-profit organization,* which does not strive to gain profit, using all available funds to fulfil its tasks. In this context the issue of state property should be considered from another standpoint. The state needs only that movable and real property which is necessary for it to meet irreducible social needs. There is actually nothing new within this argument; this is a traditional interpretation of the famous subsidiarity principle originating from the medieval philosophy of Catholicism.

The core of the state's market activities is an exchange of its tax revenues for respective social utilities. Actually, it is in this act of market exchange that budget funds are spent. Whatever the purposes of the state, neoclassical theory regards the state expenditures as merely a *deduction* from the national wealth. Even those sensible people convinced by the necessity of state expenditures for science, education, culture, public health, etc. usually recognize that these expenditures make an additional burden on the budget. As for ideologists of radical reforms, they directly call for the reduction of the social sector[196].

---

[195]Using such terms as 'state' and 'society', we certainly keep in mind that they are not identical. At the same time, having included the state as a market agent, we are entitled to affirm that it operates on the market exclusively in the interests of society and in this regard tries to meet its irreducible needs. We also understand that in reality correspondence of the goals of the state with those of the society is constantly violated by the interests of 'special groups'. However, such violation can be regarded as an ordinary theoretical error, which will be considered further in the form of a special case.

[196]We cannot agree with this opinion. However, this is the scenario according to which the situation develops in Russia, where the social sphere is sacrificed to radical reforms. Even ten years after the beginning of reforms, despite the declarations about governmental measures to support culture, science, education and public health, the state of affairs does not change. It is enough to mention that when the federal budget was executed for 70% between 1996 and 1998, the actual level of funding for culture had, for instance, never exceeded 35% of the approved expenditures for this sphere. Such budget expenditures are among the state's most 'unneeded' needs. Those employed in the sphere of culture are in the end of the queue for public goods; their average wages make about 50% of

Rejecting this view, we are going to formulate our response to the second question about the rationality of state expenditures. We are confident that expenditures devoted to the satisfaction of irreducible public needs always result in the social and (let us specially emphasize) economic progress. We are going to prove that the satisfaction of the said needs generates a specific social effect that gives birth to the phenomenon of self-sustaining growth of the national wealth when interacting with the institutional environment. Let us consider this process in greater detail and first pay attention to the specifics of the realization of social interest as such.

4.3 Characteristics of the Realization of Autonomous Social Interest

When describing a market model in which individual subjects with their needs and the state with its irreducible interests operate, the following fundamental conclusion should be made. To implement the interests of separate individuals and society as a whole, the goods whose consumption generates *two qualitatively different effects* should be supplied for market exchange.

First, let us single out a thoroughly-examined effect emerging in the process of individual consumption and measured by 'pleasure and suffering', namely individual consumer effect. Economic theory has never suggested anything else, since it has always proceeded from the 'reducibility hypothesis', which implies that any beneficial result can be presented as a function of individual consumer effects. Admitting that the zone of applicability of this hypothesis is quite narrow, we must thus recognize that a consumer effect which cannot be reduced to the said function may exist[197].

In a general case the, aggregate consumer effect therefore consists of two parts, one of them embracing *individual consumer effects,* the other representing an additional effect of the interests of society as such being realized. Actually, the fact of meeting specific public needs is evidence of this additional effect. Hence it is possible to state that the aggregate consumer effect is a sort of combination of individual benefits and the *social consumer effect* derived by the state. To specify the described picture, answers should be given to three key questions: WHAT are consumer effects, WHEN do they emerge, and WHO appropriates them?

We proceed from the assumption that the basis of any useful result, whether it be individual or social consumer effect, is the consumption of goods by market

---

average wages in the economy in general. Moreover, this figure has been decreasing on an annual basis: 62% in 1993 and 1994, 61% in 1995, 55% in 1996, 52% in 1997 and 51% in 1998.

[197]We substantiated the limitedness of this hypothesis in the previous sections of the book. But if then, while analyzing public interests, we established the fact of the existence of *irreducible public needs,* now we analyze consumer effects including the *irreducible constituent of an aggregate consumer effect.*

agents. Moreover, the social effect, being supplementary, usually appears after individual effects[198]. It therefore makes sense to classify these qualitatively different effects on a chronological basis; as such, we shall call individual and social effects primary and secondary effects, respectively.

After dividing consumer effects into primary and secondary ones, we should break the process of forming consumer effect into two stages. This necessity is conditioned by the fact that there are qualitative differences between the agents appropriating consumer effects. Separate individuals and society as a whole participate in this appropriation. Without affecting the generality of analysis, we assume that at each stage consumer effects cannot be obtained by both types of consumers at the same time. They are appropriated by individuals *or* their aggregation. Actually, this is the reason for dividing the process under consideration into two stages. Let us give two examples demonstrating the simplest cases when the consumption brings about only one effect: either primary or secondary.

Example 4.5. *Fashionable clothes* – only the primary consumer effect (pleasure and comfort) and its appropriation only by separate individuals at the first stage. The secondary effect lacks here, since wearing such clothes has no consequences except for personal satisfaction.

Example 4.6. *National defence* – only the secondary consumer effect (state security) and its appropriation by society at the second stage. In this case there is no primary effect, since the good itself is originally designed for realizing the interests of society as a whole and cannot be consumed by separate individuals.

However, a more general case is possible, goods that simultaneously satisfy the interests of separate individuals and society as a whole. We have already mentioned that two different effects emerge here. There is a pronounced causal relation between them; a social (secondary) effect, except for degenerate cases, always emerges after and as a result of individual consumer effects. An example illustrating the existence of primary and secondary consumer effects follows.

Example 4.7. *Library services* – two stages of the formation of consumer effects. First, emergence of the primary effect (pleasure and information) and its appropriation by individuals – readers – at the first stage. Second, the distant secondary effect from reading and its appropriation by society as such. It is the social effect manifested in an increased educational and intellectual level of the population (growth of 'human capital'). This effect obviously emerges at the second stage only after and as a result of the realization of individual interests.

---

[198]We should mention an exception to this general rule. This is a situation in which the primary consumer effect does not exist, since the good itself is *not designed* for individual consumption (for instance, the national defense, Example 4.6).

Now it is possible to answer the question, who appropriates primary and secondary consumer effects appropriated when. In our opinion, the primary effect is appropriated only by individual market agents at the first stage, and the secondary (social) effect is appropriated by the state at the second stage, with this effect manifesting itself in some *improvement in public environment.* Therefore, the secondary consumer effect relates to all market agents. In this sense, the social effect has the classical characteristics of a public good: no one can be deprived of the benefits resulting from a public environment improvement, and every one may get equal use of them.

Being a consequence of the realization of a public need not reflected in individual preferences at the first stage, the social effect (improved public environment) becomes a 'property' of each and everyone at the second stage. Thus, the state activity aimed to bring about irreducible public interests creates opportunities for its members to get potential, or secondary, benefits. Let us illustrate it with the example of vaccination.

> Example 4.8. *Mass vaccination during an epidemic.* First, there emerges the primary effect (health preventive measures) appropriated at the first stage by individuals, consumers of a vaccine. The risk of illness does somewhat decreases among other market agents (a well-known phenomenon of externality). Nevertheless, until the number of consumers of a vaccine reaches the critical point, the said externality cannot prevent those not vaccinated from getting ill during an epidemic. Trying to meet the irreducible public need for the removal of this threat, the state provides subsidies to producers of a vaccine, thus ensuring the required scale of vaccination. The social effect, emerging at the second stage, therefore conditions a public environment improvement in the form of epidemic discontinuation and leads to a reduction in the level of illness with all positive outcomes and secondary benefits for each society member.

At the same time, a more precise answer to the question, who appropriates consumer effects when, requires an additional analysis. It mostly concerns the social effect, appropriated by the state on behalf of society. It is noted that upon this effect's emergence, the process of the appropriation of consumer effects does not discontinue. The social effect, manifesting itself in an improvement of the public environment, creates new opportunities for the appearance of individual benefits, those being additional potential advantages, which individuals may have as a result of consuming the goods whose supply is a direct consequence of the said improvement in public environment. Consider a quite traditional example.

> Example 4.9. *Educational services.* Besides some obvious individual benefits at the first stage (getting a high-paying job) and the social effect at the second stage (a public environment improvement due to an increased educational level of the population and growth of 'human capital'), we can see the third stage of the formation of consumer effects. A higher level of education and an increased intellectual and technological potential of the country ac-

celerate scientific and technological advancements, materializing in the form of goods and services whose production and consumption generate new benefits for individuals. For instance, invention of innumerable household appliances in the 20th century can be regarded as a direct consequence of higher general educational levels. It is also evident that these goods provide direct benefits for their producers and consumers. Thus a 'self-sustaining growth' of an aggregate consumer effect can be observed at the third stage, i.e. emergence of additional secondary benefits along with individual (the first stage) and social (the second stage) consumer effects.

It is important the keep in mind that the potential for social effect – advantages of an improved public environment – cannot be exhausted, since its consumption by one of the market agents does not reduce the possibility of its consumption by others (which is characteristic of public goods). Evidently, the results of meeting irreducible public needs such as a high level of employment, stable situation in the monetary system, fundamental research, education, cultural heritage, etc. do not diminish in the event of their individual use. This reminds us of the well-known words of Rene Char, 'Art is a *realized* desire which still *remains* a desire'. Taking this specificity of the social effect into account, we can state that every time certain conditions emerge, a new stage of self-sustaining growth of an aggregate consumer effect is reached, and at this stage the use of the social effect produces additional secondary individual benefits.

Attention should be paid to the phenomenon of individualization of a social effect, to its transfer from one metric to another. In this respect, the appropriate question is: how, given the irreducibility of public needs to individual ones, can secondary individual benefits appear? How is a social effect 'transformed' into individual ones? It seems this phenomenon contradicts our statement about the irreducibility of public needs, whose satisfaction actually generates the social effect. In reality, there is no contradiction.

The point is that the social effect itself, being part of an aggregate consumer effect, remains within the original metric of irreducible public needs. In speaking about its individualization, we are referring to its ability to generate secondary individual benefits that, due to their nature, are always considered in the same metric as usual consumer effects. Only in this sense is it possible to discuss the mechanism for overcoming the initial differences in the metrics of individual and social effects. Though it is impossible to sum individual effects with a social one, the secondary benefits generated by the latter should be undoubtedly summed with individual consumer effects.

We wish to emphasize that the desire to take advantage of an improved public environment – let us call this desire a *'creative inclination'* – is inherent to every market agent. This inclination directly proceeds from the fundamental postulate of the rational behaviour of a person, maximizing his individual utility. It is this creative inclination together with the preservation of the social effect potential that determines the above process of cyclic self-sustaining growth of an aggregate consumer effect that does not differ from the multiplier mechanism. Taking into consideration that this is based on the principles of economic sociodynamics, let us call this process the *sociodynamic multiplier of economic growth (Figure 4.1)*. The exceptional theoretical significance of this multiplier requires special discussion.

4.4 The Sociodynamic Multiplier of Economic Growth

Depending on social and economic characteristics and specifics of goods' production and consumption, it is possible to single out several types of the sociodynamic multiplier of economic growth. Setting aside the problem of their typology for the time being, we shall give a number of examples characterizing various aspects of the public life.

> Example 4.10. *Sociodynamic multiplier of research and development.* It is already a commonplace that fundamental research and technological progress connected with it are the most essential factors of renovation and diversification of the world of goods and services. It is also well-known that fundamental research eventually determines economic growth and people's well-being. With the help of this example we shall only show the *mechanism* of growth of material wealth due to research and development.
>
> Apparently, there is no need to prove that along with individual needs for specific results of research and development, there is a public need for growth of scientific knowledge as such, this irreducible need not being reflected in individual preferences and hence inevitably requiring state support for its satisfaction[199]. This support brings about a social effect, i.e. an improvement in the public environment in the form of growing scientific knowledge. It is also evident that the use of this knowledge by individuals provides them with additional benefits without diminishing the social effect potential; these are scientific and technological advances, improvement in engineering and technology, development of new goods and services, providing their producers and consumers with additional benefits (*Figure 4.1*).
>
> For instance, government financing of research and development in chemistry resulted in the development of new polymeric materials, whose use (in nylon shirts, hoses and raincoats, plastic bags and housewares, etc.) became 'El Dorado' for their producers and consumers already during its initial stages. In the course of time, scientific achievements in the chemistry of polymers generated new opportunities for their use (units and parts for machinery and equipment, plastic pipes, window-frames and roofing materials in construction, furniture items, etc.). Here again additional individual benefits appeared. This multi-stage process of self-sustaining growth of an aggregate consumer effect does not seem to have any limits.

---

[199]The lack of state support for science usually results in its underfinancing. Mark Blaug, in particular, convincingly demonstrated this pattern using education as an example (Blaug M. Op. cit., p. 550).

Similar processes can be observed in other fields of fundamental and applied research, in which the spiral of sociodynamic multiplier of economic growth also keeps untwisting. Due to this multiplier of research and development, taxpayers' resources, invested in research and education, are repaid to them hundredfold in the form of additional economic benefits.

Besides the state's concern about growth of scientific and technical potential and its materialization in the production of new goods and services, there is an equally important need for preservation of conditions for the free functioning of the economy as a whole. One may oppose this statement, referring to F. Von Hayek, who argues that the best means of creating such conditions is the state's non-involvement in economic life, and that any forms of its involvement always result in resources being wasted. We have doubts as to the universality of this view; in our opinion, the situation is more complex.

Is it still impossible to assume that state interference connected, for instance, with protecting the environment, preventing negative consequences of economic globalization, ensuring employment of the population and maintaining stability of the monetary system, stimulates growth of national wealth? The textbook example of this kind is governmental regulation of effective demand. We describe this case using the respective sociodynamic multiplier.

Example 4.11. *A special case of sociodynamic multiplier – Keynes' multiplier.* Reminded that according to Keynes, the main instrument of state anti-recession interference in the market mechanism is budgetary financing of job creation aimed at increasing the aggregate effective demand. The multiplier's action in this case is characterized by the cyclic self-sustaining growth of the aggregate consumer demand: the state finances job-creation – personal incomes grow – an additional effective demand appears – production of goods and services grows – new jobs are created – personal incomes grow further – an effective demand increases, etc. We are going to show that the self-sustaining growth of personal incomes, determining the aggregate effective demand, is a particular case of the sociodynamic multiplier of economic growth.

In our paradigm, budgetary financing of job creation is nothing but the realization of the respective irreducible interest of society. This irreducibility directly arises from the fact that during a prolonged recession, 'blind' market forces make the majority of firms reduce their production. Under these conditions, they certainly have no interest in taking on more people. In this case, the social effect is directly expressed through an increase in employment, i.e. through the improvement in public environment that creates real conditions for the manifestation of individual creative inclination.

This inclination in combination with an increased number of jobs causes production and personal incomes to grow, thus ensuring the cyclic self-sustaining growth of the aggregate consumer demand. In other words, realization of the irreducible public need for new jobs 'triggers' the respective sociodynamic multiplier (*Figure 4.1*). It is also easy to notice that the application of this multiplier to the aggregate effective demand makes it identical with Keynes' multiplier. In this context, the latter can be treated as a particular case of the sociodynamic multiplier of economic growth.

Returning to Keynes, we would like to repeat that the 'true' market adherents still regard state regulation as the 'absolute evil'. By the way, Russian reformers of the 1990s liked to theorize on the harmful consequences of state interference. However, even the staunchest defenders of the market – when faced with reality – have to put up with the inevitable presence of the state in some spheres of economic life. In particular, it is now a commonplace to recognize the legitimacy of its interference in the production of public goods, though this 'difficult' decision is also accompanied by regrets regarding inefficient public expenditures, and the ideological thesis of the state's total harmfulness for the economy does not allow the recognition of many positive results of its activities. We shall show it using the sociodynamic multiplier of public goods.

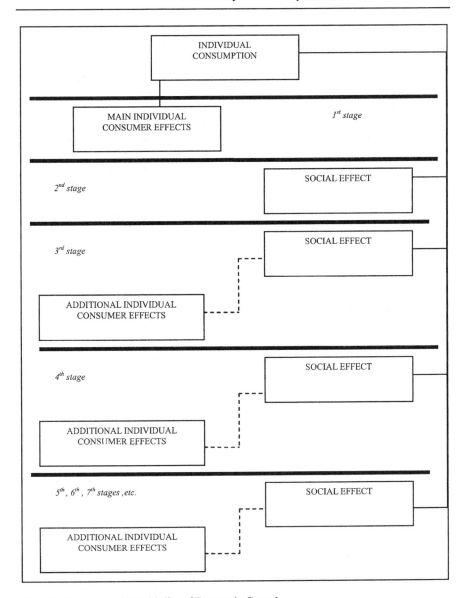

Fig. 4.1. Sociodynamic Multiplier of Economic Growth

Example 4.12. *Sociodynamic multiplier of public goods.* Consider a classical public good, a lighthouse. Imagine the situation when a traditional sea route between two commercial ports took several days. At the same time, there was a shorter but less safe route involving the risk of running aground or striking a reef. A number of shipwrecks forced sailors to give it up, but some time later men of enterprise started choosing this route again, and wrecks became as frequent as before. Impelled by a concern for people's lives, the state faced the option of either prohibiting navigation along the short route or ensuring its safety. If we proceed from the choice made in favour of a shorter and more beneficial route, the following conclusion can be made. Not resorting to bans, the state thus recognized that construction of a lighthouse met the irreducible public need for safe navigation.

The social effect in the form of safe navigation along the shorter route, which was produced by satisfaction of this need, provided the public environment improvement that created additional opportunities for revealing the 'creative inclination'. An opportunity to reduce costs by reducing the duration of the sea journey together with the safeness of this route triggered the mechanism of self-sustaining growth of the aggregate consumer effect *(Figure 4.1)*. The use of the lighthouse (a classic public good) by some sailors does not diminish the social effect (not decreasing the safety of other transportation using the short route). The preservation of the initial potential of this social effect accompanied by the regular generation of additional individual benefits actually characterizes the sociodynamic multiplier of economic growth.

Having demonstrated the unwinding spiral of the sociodynamic multiplier using concrete examples, we must now pay attention to a factor that, to a great extent, conditions the process of self-sustaining growth of the aggregate consumer effect. Economic history has always demonstrated fundamentally different outcomes of the *same* state actions in *different* countries over different periods of time. This fully applies to the sociodynamic multiplier of economic growth. The international practice of state interventionism in particular shows that the most necessary state initiatives and the most reliable state instruments often do not produce the desirable self-sustaining growth of aggregate consumer effect.

State actions fail every time when they are not adequate for society's institutions. This phenomenon is especially evident during economic reforms, when many governmental actions are not backed by the respective institutional reorganization. We wish to quote Valery Makarov, who wrote, 'Institutions and economic freedom are two sides of one medal. One side is useless or absolutely inefficient without the other. What happens when one of them – economic freedom – exists, and the other one – market institutions – doesn't exist, can be seen in our country'[200]. Makarov is absolutely correct. The inefficiency of Russian reforms is caused first of all by the undeveloped institutional structure of society. It is not only the correctness of the reforms that matters. An adequate institutional environment itself is a fundamental factor of economic growth.

One should always remember that a social effect and individuals' creative inclinations are not sufficient to take advantage of an improved public environment and to turn potential individual benefits into actual ones. To make it possible, special *channels* are required that 'connect' individuals having creative inclinations with the respective advantages of public environment. Such channels obviously include value orientations, customs and traditions, legislation, behavioural norms

---

[200]Makarov V.L. Why is the Russian Economy Inefficient // Vlast, 1998, No. 6, p. 17.

and various organizations. It is clear that the process of social effect channeling is rigidly tied with the institutional structure of a society. The more developed this structure, the higher its degree of adequacy to the current requirements of economic growth, and the larger the additional individual benefits generated by a social effect.

Culture plays a specific role here. Everybody knows that we should treat its invaluable heritage with care. But in practice this incontrovertible imperative is often ignored. Moreover in Russia, for instance, there is the wide-spread opinion (throughout the society, even among those employed in the sphere of culture) that any expenditures for the maintenance and recovery of cultural heritage are only a subtraction from the state budget, waste of scarce public resources. It has even ceased to be a disgrace to word this indecent thesis from high rostrums[201]. Actually, various demagogic statements – such as 'first, people should be fed, and then we can think about museums and palaces' – are not only doubtful both ethically and aesthetically, but they are also economically inefficient. To prove the fallacy of such views, we shall show that the mechanism of self-sustaining growth of aggregate consumer effect ensures benefits considerably greater than the expenditures for the preservation of cultural heritage.

> Example 4.13. *Sociodynamic multiplier of cultural heritage.* Along with the needs felt by individuals to preserve cultural values in their possession, there is an interest of society as such in the preservation of architectural monuments, works of art, libraries and museum funds, etc. This irreducible public interest cannot be reflected in individual preferences; hence its realization inevitably requires an appropriate state support. Realization of this public interest generates the respective social effect, manifesting itself in the preservation of achievements of human artistic genius that creates new (sometimes unexpected) possibilities of their involvement in active cultural life. Use of these possibilities by the individuals with 'creative inclinations' provides them with additional benefits, the potential of social effect being preserved. With respect to this, we are referring to the commercial use of architectural monuments, national parks, masterpieces of art, and related goods and services that provide their producers and consumers with additional individual consumer effects.
>
> An illustration of the efficient functioning of the sociodynamic multiplier of cultural heritage is Arena di Verona, which was built in the 1st century A.D. and 2,000 years later was given its second birth by famous opera festivals. The society's efforts to preserve this cultural monument produced con-

---

[201]If we consider another group of politicians, who, to the contrary, widely use the 'cultural rhetoric', we see the same situation. Despite regular 'ritual' declarations about the originality of the Russian culture, about its significance for the country's life, the cultural heritage is still in a miserable situation, and this condition is getting progressively worse. About 2,000 valuable monuments of Russian history and culture perish every year, and the resources allocated for the maintenance of cultural heritage are not sufficient and have been reduced on an annual basis.

siderable individual benefits in the 20th century. The revenues from tickets during one festival exceed USD 15 billion. If we add revenues from the whole infrastructure providing services for the festival (tourism, hotels, restaurants, TV, transport, souvenirs, etc.) and the benefits from additional jobs, it is obvious that the social effect of the preservation of this ancient architectural monument triggered the mechanism for self-sustaining growth of aggregate consumer effect.

We can see the same effect at Sotheby's auctions in London, where annual volumes of deals compare with some countries' budgets. As a matter of fact, the mechanism of sociodynamic multiplier of economic growth is a drive for the development of the whole industry of mass tourism. By the end of the 20th century, total world turnover within this ever-expanding industry, which has been functioning in the sphere of cultural and natural heritage for a long time, exceeded the revenues of the world aggregate export of machinery and equipment.

Societal expenditures for the maintenance of cultural heritage have always generated new opportunities for its involvement in active cultural life (adjustment of ancient buildings for restaurants and hotels, opening of new museums, printing, mass media channels, Internet, etc.). At each stage of self-sustaining growth of aggregate consumer effect, the social effect in the form of preserved and reconstructed cultural monuments ensures additional individual benefits. And we have no reasons to doubt the endlessness of this multi-stage process.

However important the practical use of architectural monuments created in previous ages may be, we see the main significance of the cultural heritage in its unique institutional contents. Being able to pass information 'preserved' in the cultural monuments – about old times, its spirit and intellectual achievements, value orientations and customs[202]– from one generation to another, cultural heritage ensures favourable institutional environment for *all creative actions*. Improving conditions for the operation of other sociodynamic multipliers, the sociodynamic multiplier of cultural heritage acts as a catalyst for them and as an accelerator of economic growth.

Here we emphasize again that the additional specific of the sociodynamic multiplier of cultural heritage is its close relation to the processes involved in the formation of society's institutions. It would be a gross error to assume that these are unchanging. We should bear in mind the explicit evolutionary nature of the institutional environment, continual changes of formal and informal rules and restrictions and shifts in social postulates and individual preferences. These institutional dynamics involves two essential consequences.

---

[202]We would like to emphasize that we share views of institutionalists. See, for instance, Boyd R., Richardson P.J. Culture and the Evolutionary Process. – Chicago: University of Chicago Press, 1985; Johansson S. The Computer Paradigm and the Role of Cultural Information in Social Systems //Historical Methods, No 21, 1988.

First, institutions' continuous evolution causes the transformation of market agents' notions of rational behaviour and permanent adjustment of individuals' creative motivation. Second, institutional changes generate new opportunities for the channeling of social effect. Strictly speaking, it is the evolution of institutions that determines the stages in the process of self-sustaining growth of aggregate consumer effect, this process being described in our concept by the sociodynamic multiplier of economic growth.

Let us summarize. One of the key notions of economic sociodynamics, the sociodynamic multiplier of economic growth, characterizes the phenomenon of self-sustaining growth of aggregate consumer effect. The multiplier itself is the result of the interaction of three constituent elements: social effect, individual creative inclination and institutions of society. Under the concept of economic sociodynamics, the social effect results from actions of the state intended to satisfy irreducible public needs and to manifest itself as a public environment improvement. There are always some individuals with the explicit creative inclination, whose self-interest energy stimulates them to avail themselves to the advantages of an improved public environment.

We face more difficulties when dealing with institutional conditions. Institutions are able to channel the social effect, creating and maintaining the conjoining of individual creative inclinations and advantages of an improved public environment. Yet if the institutions are not adequate for an emerging social effect, they can impede its transformation into secondary individual benefits. There are many examples of social effects that bring about economic growth in some countries whilst producing no positive results in others. In other words, in 'unsuccessful' cases an improved public environment finds no interested user. If the institutions ensure the indispensable interaction between individual creative energies and the advantages of an improved public environment, however, the sociodynamic multiplier mechanism automatically sparks economic growth. From this moment, the implementation of social interests begins to produce individual benefits.

When all three elements are 'combined successfully' in the single mechanism of this multiplier, economic evaluation of the consequences of the realization of social interest fundamentally changes. Giving up traditional negative attitude toward any state interventions and their association with the waste of pubic resources, one should legitimate the rational behaviour of the state acting as an autonomous market agent, ensuring Pareto-improvement.

In this regard, it is necessary to prove that the realization of social interest that requires respective expenditures – including tax expenses of individuals – generates such economic consequences – including secondary individual benefits – that the wealth of every market agent is not diminished. Economic sociodynamics, possessing such means of analysis as the sociodynamic multiplier of economic growth, makes this proof possible. Here the core is still the analysis of the economic consequences of the realization of social interest. We are going to discuss it in the next chapter.

5 The Realization of Social Interest

Starting to consider the economic consequences of the realization of social interest, we should again point out one more methodological difficulty that we mentioned in the previous sections of the book. In particular, we have stated that the social effect and individual benefits cannot be summed. Like two types of utility, they exist in different metrics. That is why we seek to pay attention to another essential specific of the sociodynamic multiplier of economic growth, as it allows us to overcome this obstacle.

It was shown in the previous chapter that the sociodynamic multiplier's ability to conjoin individual creative inclinations and advantages of an improved public environment on the institutional basis conditions the social effect's transfer from one metric to the other, i.e. its conversion into individual secondary benefits. The latter can be summed with individual consumer effects without reserve. All this allows us to regard the sociodynamic multiplier of economic growth (Ψ) as a kind of *transformer* of the social metric or a process of the social effect individualization.

Taking into account the above and bearing in mind the economic contents of the Sociodynamic multiplier, let us record two interdependent equations:

$$I = I_I + \Psi I^S \tag{1}$$

and

$$\Psi I^S = \Psi [I^S, \eta^I, \Omega] = \Sigma I_k \tag{2}$$

where: I – aggregate consumer effect
I_I – individual consumer effect
I^S – social effect
I_K – secondary individual benefits at k stage
η^I – individual creative inclination
Ω – institutional structure of the society
Ψ – sociodynamic multiplier

It should be noted that the letter Ψ identifies a *process*, not a functional reducing of the social effect to individual ones. If we now go back to Margolis' model and recall his attempts to sum social and individual interests, we can express them in the form of another simple equation:

$$I = I_I + \lambda I^S \tag{3}$$

where: I – aggregate utility function
I_I – individual interest (consumer effect)
I^S – social interest
λ – social interest weight

It is easy to see that the difference between our approach and Margolis' model, based on the reducibility hypothesis, is conditioned by the difference between the sociodynamic multiplier Ψ and weight factor λ. Therefore, Margolis' model can be regarded as a particular case of economic sociodynamics, corresponding to the situation when the public interest can be reduced to individual interests. Under such circumstances, all needs originally exist in one metric, and the sociodynamic multiplier *degenerates* into a constant characterizing of the weight of social interest. In this particular case, equations (1) and (2) are reduced to the equation (3). It is also clear that Margolis' model is valid only in the zone where the reducibility hypothesis is true.

Another preliminary note: In the traditional market model, there is no problem with summing, since when all needs are reducible, all consumer effects are measured according to one system. The flip side of the coin is the inability of the neoclassical model to 'see' *all consequences of social effects* and evaluate them correctly. If the reducibility hypothesis is absolutized, any social interest always dissolves in individual benefits completely. This means that the neoclassical model cannot 'notice' the part of an aggregate consumer effect that is not revealed in primary individual benefits. This gives rise to the theoretical underestimate of state actions aimed at the realization of its specific interests, i.e. the state falls victim to the classical paradigm.

As for the concept of economic sociodynamics in general and one of its instruments (sociodynamic multiplier of economic growth) in particular, they allow for the exculpation of social interest. Using this multiplier when evaluating state interference makes it possible to take into account not only tax expenses of market agents but also secondary individual benefits from the realization of social effect. Let us consider this extremely important issue in greater detail, using graphic analysis.

5.1 The Traditional Model of State Intervention

Let us first dwell on the traditional graphic model, using such instruments of analysis as indifference curves, budget lines, equilibrium points, demand and supply curves.

Consider *Figure 5.1*. In its first part (a) we measure quantities of the good x_i from the set X on the horizontal axis. Quantities of the other good x_j from the same set X are measured on the vertical axis. The good x_j, without affecting the generality of analysis, can be replaced by a set of goods and services – 'other consumption'. It should be assumed that x_i and x_j are substitutes.

Indifference curves labelled I_1, I_2, I_3 show equal utilities for an individual consumer (individual utilities) of different combinations of goods x_i and x_j. Z_1, Z_2, Z_3 are budget lines, showing the maximum combinations of goods x_i and x_j that an individual can purchase given the available budget. It can be considered, without affecting the generality of analysis, that if the price of the good x_i decreases, the budget line Z_1 changes its slope and transforms into the line Z_3, and if this price increases into Z_2.

In full accordance with the canon, it is possible to expect that the individual's rational behaviour should result in the maximization of his individual utility, this maximum being attained at the point where the indifference curve intersects the budget line. In *Figure 5.1(a)*, such maximum points in cases of different budget constraints are **A**, **B** and **C**.

Consider the point **A** in *Figure 5.1(a)* and the corresponding market equilibrium point **R** in *Figure 5.1(b)*. At the point **R** the demand curve **D** and the supply curve **P** intersect, and the individual shows demand for the good under consideration x_i^R at a price p_i^R. It is clear that the individual's expenses are determined by the area of the rectangle $Ox_i^R Rp_i^R$. As a result of consumption, the individual gains consumer income corresponding to the area of the triangle $p_i^R RJ$.

Now let us analyze the situation when the state, realizing the interest of society as such, induces the individual to a higher level of consumption of certain goods and services. Suppose the state measures were efficient and the individual started to consume the good in question in volume x_i^m. According to the demand curve **D**, he is ready to purchase this volume of the good x_i^m only at a price p_i^m. Therefore, 'voluntary' individual expenses for the purchase of the good in volume x_i^m equal the area of the rectangle $Ox_i^m Rp_i^m$. Taking this into consideration and according to the supply curve P, this quantity of the good is sold on the market only at a price p_i^P. Thus the state measures inducing the individual to increase his consumption from x_i^R to x_i^m must include subsidies equal to the area of the rectangle $p_i^m FRp_i^P$.

If we assume that these subsidies are provided to the producer to ensure market supply of the good in volume x_i^m at a price p_i^m, the subsequent reduction of prices (by the difference $p_i^P - p_i^m$) changes the budget constraint of the individual. The budget line Z_1 changes its slope and transforms into Z_3. In this situation, maximum individual utility of the consumer of the good x_i^m is attained at a higher indifference curve (I_3) at the point where it touches the budget line Z_3 (the point **C** in *Figure 5.1 (a)*).

Under such circumstances, each consumer's income obviously increases. A comparison of *Figures 5.1 (a)* and *(b)* allows this to be seen. If the consumption grows from x_i^R to x_i^m, the individual's consumer income increases, equaling the area of the triangle $p_i^m FJ$ at the expense of subsidies (the area of the rectangle $p_i^m FR_m p_i^P$).

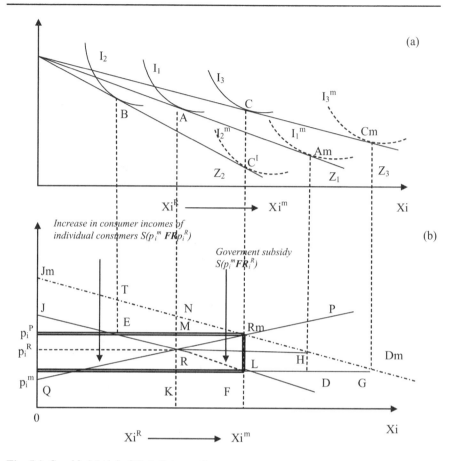

Fig. 5.1. Graphic Model of State Intervention

The time has come to explain what lies behind the state's desire to increase good's consumption from x_i^R to x_i^m. As we do not want to overstep the traditional model for the time being, a meritoric motivation usual for such cases should be assumed here. Following Tietzel and Müller, we proceed from the assumption that consumers show fictitious preferences for some goods and services, and the state, even without having a clear idea about the true preferences of individuals, can stimulate an increase in these goods' consumption, at least up to the level of 'political decisions'[203]. Without affecting the generality of analysis, it is possible to consider that this is the case of specific state actions through which individuals are stimulated to such consumer behaviour, as though their true preferences for goods x_i and x_j corresponded to indifference curves I_1^m, I_2^m and I_3^m.

---

[203]Here we purposefully repeat the graphical construction by Tietzel and Müller from their famous article on meritorics (Tietzel M., Müller C. Op. cit., p. 89-91). One of the purposes of our analysis is to demonstrate the limitedness of both this construction and subsequent conclusions.

In the case of these individual preferences, another demand curve labelled **D** should be considered. According to it, the individual would be ready to show the demand x_i^m at a price $p_i^{Dm} = p_i^p$. Under such conditions, the maximum individual utility is attained at the point $\mathbf{C^I}$, where the indifference curve I_2^m touches the budget line Z_2. In this case and as a result of the consumption of the good x_i^m at a price p_i^m, the individual obtains consumer income equal to the area of the triangle $p_i^p R_m J_m$.

It is not difficult to show that in the case of such state behaviour and the respective subsidizing of the good's production aimed at increasing its consumption from x_i^R to x_i^m, each consumer would obtain such income as though his true preferences corresponded to the 'political' ones $(S(p_i^p R_m J_m) = S(p_i^m FJ))$. However, in the case of voluntary consumption of the good x_i^m at a price p_i^m, individuals would have to cover all expenses equal to the area of the rectangle $O x_i^m R_m p_i^p$.

That is why every individual consumer eagerly agrees to state actions if they require from him only a part of expenses equal to the area of the rectangle $O x_i^m F p_i^p$; the other part equaling the area of the rectangle $p_i^m F R_m p_i^p$ is covered at the expense of other taxpayers[204]. In this case, according to Tietzel and Müller, 'a consumer is catapulted onto a higher utility curve I_3'[205]. Due to the subsidy, the price he has to pay for the good decreases from p_i^p to p_i^m and his budget line therefore shifts from Z_2 to Z_3. Having summed each individual's increase in incomes – caused by an increase in the good's consumption from x_i^R to x_i^m – with his tax expenses, one can find out that aggregate consumer income growth, being a result of the implementation of the interest of society as such, is less than the governmental subsidy required for this implementation[206]; the difference corresponds to the area of the irregular pentagon $p_i^R RFR_m p_i^p$.

The analysis usually ends here, and the conclusion sounds like a condemnation of state support for the consumption of any goods or services. From the viewpoint of the whole economy, governmental subsidies aimed at increasing the consumption of certain goods result in an obvious Pareto deterioration; the taxpayers' resources can be spent more efficiently, bringing them higher consumer incomes.

We doubt this verdict and suggest continuing the graphical analysis, having brought the state out of the 'parallel world' and into the real arena of market relations. We wish to repeat that the state's needs differ from individual needs. The former are based not on a good's consumption by separate individuals but on the opportunity for a group of people or the whole society to consume this good in a certain quantity.

---

[204]We proceed from the usual assumption that all taxpayers participate in financing governmental subsidies through taxation.

[205]Tietzel M., Müller C. Op. cit., p. 91.

[206]There is nothing unexpected in this. This conclusion completely corresponds to that directly arising from the fundamental theorems of the theory of well-being. Here, we come across one more graphical version of the traditional assumption about the inefficiency the state interference.

5.2 A Neo-Pareto Analysis of the Realization of Social Interest

In the second part of our analysis of economic consequences of the realization of social interest, we go beyond a limit set by the traditional model with its compulsory reducibility of any public need to individual preferences. With this in mind, we are going to revise both the composition of the participants in market relationships and the basic assumptions regarding the motivation for state actions in the market.

Speaking about a neo-Pareto analysis, we are referring to a number of aspects. First, we examine the postulates of economic sociodynamics considered in the previous chapter, which have replaced Pareto's axioms. Second, the social generalization of the principle of Pareto optimality and its application to the case when the state, seeking to realize specific interests of society as such, participates in the market exchange along with households and firms. Third, the sociodynamic multiplier mechanism, ensuring the transfer of social effect from one metric to the other and its conversion into secondary individual effects. And finally, evaluation of the changed positions of individual market agents, taking into consideration their tax expenses devoted to the realization of the public interest, and the sum of primary and secondary benefits they enjoy as a result of this realization.

Let us hereby assume that along with the pleasure individuals get from consumption of a good, there is the satisfaction of their aggregation as a whole with the good's availability for each of them. In other words, from our viewpoint, the state's purpose is not to ensure a transfer from the false individual preferences to the true ones but to realize its own interests, that of meeting its specific needs regarding the level of consumption.

From this position, consider *Figure 5.2,* including four diagrams. Having labelled the above-considered diagrams (b) and (c), we add two more diagrams: (a) and (d). As before, we are going to use indifference curves in the analysis, but this time these will be curves I_0^S and I^S in *Figure 5.2 (a)*, showing the same utility of different combinations of goods x_i and x_j for *a state* (social utility). Let Z_0^S and Z^S represent budget constraints, i.e. variants of state funds available for meeting its irreducible needs for the goods x_i and x_j. In the case of budget constraint represented by Z^S, maximum social utility is attained at the point C_S, corresponding to the consumption of the good x_i^m. On these assumptions, let us analyze the consequences of the realization of society's interest as to the consumption of the good x_i.

Not to encumber the analysis through too much reasoning, we proceed from the assumption that the good's consumption less than or equal to x_i^R is beyond the zone of the state's interest. In other words, let consumption x_i^R in *Figure 5.2 (a)* correspond to the frontier of the society's immune activity; to the left of it, indifference curves I_0^S and I^S exist only in the latent form (dotted line), and to the right explicitly. If we label an increase in this good's consumption Δx_i and shift the beginning of the vertical axis $\mathbf{O^i}$ to the point where this increase is zero $(x_i = x_i^R)$, the new vertical axis will coincide with the immune activity frontier and divide the plane of values of the good's consumption x^i into two parts, the zones of latent and real preferences of the state. In *Figure 5.2 (b)* and *(c)* the extension of this vertical axis marks the frontier of the public interest regarding the good x_i.

Now, by analogy with the analysis of individual behaviour, it is possible to draw the state's demand curve for the good x_i. *Figure 5.2 (d)* shows this curve as the piecewise continuous line $Ox^iR_sD_s$ with the only point of discontinuity in case $x_i=x_i^R$. According to this curve, the state shows positive demand for the good's individual consumption $x_i>x_i^R$ and is ready to 'buy' this consumption level at a price d_i^m. In other words, if a producer ensures market supply $x_i^i>x_i^R$ at a reduced supply price $p_i^{Pm}=p_i^R$, the state is ready to pay him the difference between the market and reduced price ($d_i^m=p_i^P-p_i^{Pm}=p_i^P-p_i^R$) for each sold unit of the good.

Therefore, it is clear that in the zone of latent preferences (to the left of the frontier of the society's immune activity), i.e. within the interval from 0 to x_i^R inclusive, state demand is zero, and if $x_i>x_i^R$, this demand is plotted by the sloping line $\mathbf{D}_s$.

It is also clear that if $x_i>x_i^m$, the demand curve $\mathbf{D}_s$ and the supply curve P intersect at the point $\mathbf{R}_m$, where the state shows demand for the 'level of good's consumption' x_i^m at a price $d_i^{Rm}=p_i^P-p_i^m$. Therefore, its expenditures devoted to the realization of social interest (an increase in the good's consumption from x_i^R to x_i^m) are represented by the area of the rectangle $p_i^m FR_m d_i^{Rm}$. Having provided the satisfaction of this public need, the state obtains an income equal to the area of the rectangle $d_i^{Rm}R_m R_s d_i^{Rs}$. Let us substantiate this conclusion.

Consider the zone of the state's latent preferences, i.e. the parts of *Figure 5.2 (a)* and *(d)* showing production and consumption of the good in the volume less than or equal to x_i^R. Since within the interval from 0 to x_i^R in the case of the state's zero actual demand indifference curves I_0^S and I^S still exist (though in the latent form)[207], we assume the existence of an analogous form of the state demand. *Figure 5.2 (d)* shows it as $J_S R_S$.

We repeat that it is only a latent form of demand, which is not accompanied by any real state expenditure. However, some individuals, according to their personal preferences, realize their demand for the good also within the said interval, thus conditioning the achievement of a certain level of this good's consumption. In other words, we may conclude that in the zone of latent preferences the state actually behaves as a usual *'free rider'*, obtaining consumer income (though latent) absolutely free. *Figure 5.2 (d)* shows the state's latent income (given the good's consumption $x_i<x_i^R$) as the area of the triangle $d_i^{Rs}J_S R_S$.

To the right of the frontier of society's immune activity, i.e. within the zone of real preferences, upon reaching the consumption level $x_i=x_i^m$ the state's actual consumer income equals the area of the triangle $d_i^{Rs}R_m J_S$. In other words, it is possible

---

[207]We proceed from the assumption that many goods, such as educational services, science and culture, possess social utility. However, it takes time for a society to realize it. Not very long ago in Russia the state support for education was therefore an exception rather than a rule. Only in course of time and often upon reaching a certain level of consumption – as a result of action of the mechanism of social immunity revealing the respective irreducible need – can this good's social utility, which has previously been 'dozing', starts to form the state's real preferences.

to state that the subsidy required for the realization of social interest, being equal to the area of the quadrangle $p_i^m FR_m d_i^{Rm}$, ensures not only an increase in individual consumer incomes (the area of the quadrangle $p_i^m FRp_i^R$ in *Figure 5.2 (c)*) but also an additional state income, corresponding to the difference between the areas of the triangles $d_i^{Rs} R_m J_S$ and $d_i^{Rs} J_S R_S$, equaling the area of the quadrangle $d_i^{Rm} R_m R_S d_i^{Rs}$ (*Figure 5.2 (d)*).

Now, let us return to the state's motivation. After repudiating the traditional understanding of state interventionism as activities aimed at revealing the true individual preferences and attributing to the state's behaviour other, exclusively egoistic, interests connected with meeting the society's needs, we must find out what makes the state give up its 'free rider' status and try to increase the level of a certain good's consumption.

To that end, let us turn again to *Figure 5.2 (a)* and analyze the case of the good's consumption x_i^R. If we assume that at the moment of making a decision on the expediency of stimulating the good's consumption, social immunity has already actualized the respective irreducible interest of society; the latent curves of equal social utility get transformed into the real indifference curves, defined on the whole set of x_i. Hence it becomes possible to define the curves I_0^S and I_1^S at the points A_S^0 and A_S, where $x_i = x_i^R$.

Let us first consider the degenerate case in which maximum social utility is attained already at the initial level of consumption $x_i = x_i^R$. According to our assumptions, this consumption level is ensured without any special actions of the state; therefore, the said maximum is attained at the point A_S^0, where the curve I_0^S and the budget line Z_0^S cross the horizontal axis $O^{II} x_i$. In such a situation, Z_0^S conditions the achievement of the maximum only at a zero level of social utility.

It means that even though the irreducible need is actualized by social immunity, the state has no resources to stimulate the good's consumption. Continuing to act as a 'free rider', the state obtains the income which was not identified before. In this case, it has no reason to change the situation and hence no motive for meritoric actions, since any increase in the good's consumption would require additional state budgetary resources, which it does not possess.

The situation is absolutely different if Z^S lies above Z_0^S. This is possible, for instance, when the state budget grows due to taxes. In this case, the budget line Z^S enables the state to 'catapult' onto a higher utility curve I^S (remember Tietzel and Müller), and the initial consumption level $x_i = x_i^m$ will correspond to the point A_S on this curve. Given the budget Z^S, it is obvious that a rationally-behaving state will strive to shift from A_S to C_S, where social utility reaches its maximum at consumption level x_i^m. This is actually a direct motive for state activities in such situations.

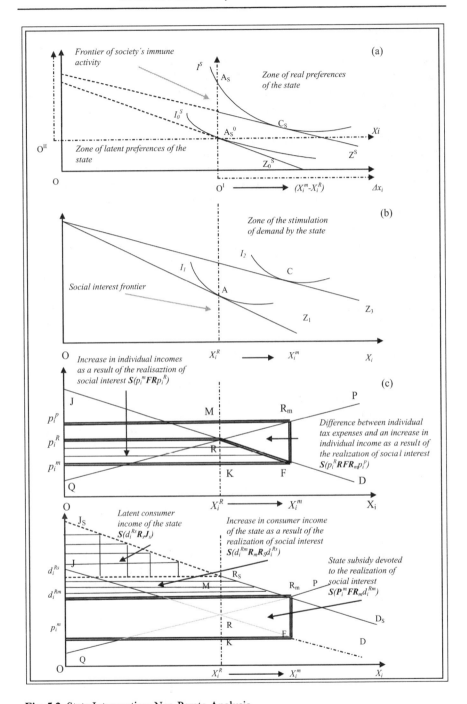

Fig. 5.2. State Intervention: Neo-Pareto Analysis

It is stimulation of the good's consumption by providing subsidies $S(p_i^m FR_m d_i^{Rm})$ *(Figure 5.2 (d))* that ensures – as we have already shown – an increase in individual consumer incomes $S(p_i^m FRp_i^R)$ *(Figure 5.2 (c))*. Assuming that through the taxation mechanism all individuals are involved in the financial provision of said subsidies, and subtracting the value of an increase in individual consumer incomes from their total tax expenses, we can evaluate each individual's loss (this is what is usually done in such analysis). In *Figure 5.2 (c)*, this corresponds to the pentagon area $p_i^R RFR_m p_i^P$. But if we continue the analysis, we can extend the traditional computations and compare these losses with the additional income $S(d_i^{Rm} R_m R_S d_i^{Rs})$ *(Figure 5.2 (d))* obtained by the state maximizing its function of social utility. Such comparisons make it possible to answer the basic question: does the governmental support for goods' consumption always mean Pareto deterioration?

With this in mind, consider *Figure 5.3*. Its left part *(a)* shows the state's expenditures for and incomes resulting from the realization of social interest and corresponds to *Figure 5.2 (d)*; its right part *(b)* shows individual expenses and incomes and corresponds to *Figure 5.2 (c)*. Trying to fulfil the above formulated task to compare the negative and positive results of the realization of social interest in an increase in the good's consumption, we will try to combine both parts of *Figure 5.3*. We must note that the possibility of a direct comparison of all positive results of the realization of social interest with its costs is limited.

It is connected to the fact that individual and social utility functions exist in different metrics. However, while the social effect remains in the initial metric of society's irreducible interests, the secondary benefits generated by it are treated in the same terms as individual consumer effects.

We would like to repeat the conclusion made in the previous paragraph. Despite the fact that the social effect cannot be summed with individual ones, the secondary benefits corresponding to it can be summed with individual consumer effects.

Now we are going to resort again to the sociodynamic multiplier of economic growth, which helps overcome the difference in the metrics of individual and social effects. We labelled this process ψ. Using this symbol, for any k stage of the formation of final consumer effects it is possible to record the following important equation: $Y_k[S(d_i^{Rm} R_m R_S d_i^{Rs})] = S(p_k R_S^k Fp_i^m)$[208]. We wish to repeat that we use 'ψ' to indicate the *process*, not the functional reducing the social effect to individual ones. We will return to it later, and now we would like to turn to *Figure 5.3(b)* and try to show secondary individual benefits resulting from the functioning of the sociodynamic multiplier ψ.

---

[208]Without affecting the generality of analysis, we assume that $k=n+1$; by substantiating the sociodynamic multiplier in the previous paragraph, we associated the first stage of the formation of consumer effect only with primary consumer effects obtained by separate individuals.

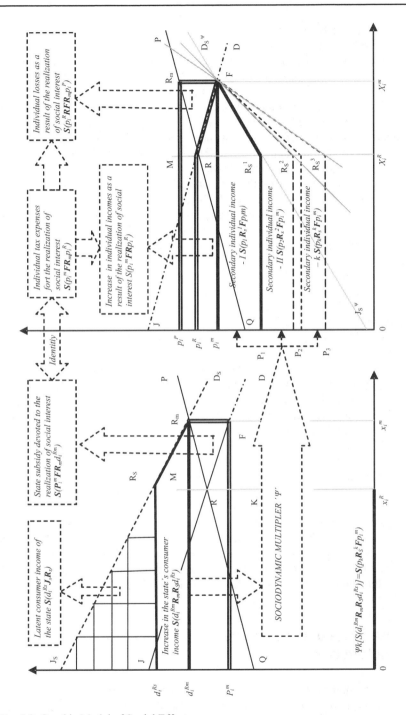

Fig. 5.3. Graphic Model of Social Effect

To show the state's income in *Figure 5.3 (b)*, where individual expenses and incomes are presented, we build quadrangles $p_k R_S{}^k F p_i{}^m$, corresponding to the secondary incomes obtained by individuals at k stage of formation of consumer effects. Purely geometrically, these quadrangles can be obtained by the reflection of the quadrangle $d_i{}^{Rm} R_m R_S d_i{}^{Rs}$ with respect to the axis $d_i{}^{Rm} R_m$ and its translation to the line $p_i{}^m F$. Taking into account that the potential of social effect cannot be exhausted, we can sum up the secondary benefits emerging at different stages of the formation of consumer effects and, without affecting the generality of analysis, consider that each of the built quadrangles characterizes the secondary individual income with progressive total $S(p_k R_S{}^k F p_i{}^m)$.

Now we are able to compare the costs and effects of the realization of social interest, including the benefits connected with an improved public environment. For this purpose, it is enough to compare the pentagon area $p_i{}^R R F R_m p_i{}^P$, showing individual costs of the realization of social interest, with the area of the quadrangle $p_k R_S{}^k F p_i{}^m$, corresponding to the secondary individual incomes (with progressive total), obtained as a result of this realization.

The condition under which the realization of society's specific interests is not an unavoidable evil, but a matter of rational behaviour of the state – trying to maximize its utility function and ensure Pareto-improvement – can be presented as the following inequation: $S(p_k R_S{}^k F p_i{}^m) > S(p_i{}^R R F R_m p_i{}^P)$. It is clear that its left part refers to the illustrative aspect of the analysis, since the geometrical plotting of the individual secondary effects only conditionally reflects the real sociodynamic multiplier mechanism. Though the polygon area $p_k R_S{}^k F p_i{}^m$ does not show the true value of secondary effects, it is possible to assert that circumstances exist when this inequation is true. We would like to emphasize again that these effects are fully determined by constituents of the sociodynamic multiplier of economic growth and conditions under which it functions.

Rehabilitation of the state in economic sociodynamics indirectly justifies meritorics considered above. At the same time a neo-Pareto analysis of the state activity allows us to free this concept merely from the accusations directly connected with the underestimation of the results of meritoric actions. The above-mentioned critique of the motivation for meritoric interference is still in force. Taking this into consideration, we should return to the concept of merit goods and determine its 'legitimate' place in the context of economic sociodynamics. It is especially important as the solution of this issue requires a more thorough examination of the key problem of economic sociodynamics, the nature of the formation of social interest in the context of the modern state's functioning.

5.3 The State and its Interests in Economic Sociodynamics

Returning to meritorics, we emphasize the main point which we cannot agree with, namely individuals' 'double-think' accepted under this concept. What fundamentally distinguishes our concept is not the denial of ambivalence in the evaluation of goods and services – to the contrary, this is the key issue of economic sociodynamics – but another understanding of the nature of this ambivalence. In our approach, such attitude to goods is caused by the existence of *two different* sources of their evaluation, not by the double-think of one and the same individual[209].

In economic sociodynamics, the state is the second source of evaluations – independent of individuals – that acts as an autonomous market player expressing the interests of society as a whole. Besides, we proceed from the model where some goods have social utility in addition to their ability to meet individual needs. Such goods and services' aggregate consumer effect combines individual benefits and a social effect, the latter, as it has already been shown, manifesting itself as an improved public environment, potentially affecting all market agents, all members of society.

However, the existence of social effect is not sufficient for the transformation of potential consumer income into actual individual benefits. For this to take place, an adequate institutional structure that encourages market agents to avail themselves of an improved public environment is necessary and it should make the connection between the social effect and personal benefits 'visible'. When there are such institutions (for instance, the postulate of the benefits of education, dominating in the post-industrial society), the prerequisites arise for the personalization of social effect, and market agents start to evaluate goods 'correctly'[210]. In a general case, however, the institutional environment is not 'visible'. Actually, the irreducibility of needs arises because the secondary benefits of social effect are 'invisible' for the majority of individuals. These benefits are visible only for those called philosophers by Plato[211], 'informed people' by Musgrave[212] and 'politicians' by Schmidt[213]. For us it is important that those are the people who form the state's interests, and we are going to consider them in greater detail.

---

[209]We have already paid attention to this in considering the Bergson-Samuelson model and Margolis' two utility functions, which oblige an individual to have two evaluation systems. A broader approach to this problem allows us to see the philosophical background of the double-think. We should be reminded that in his *State,* Plato pointed out the double nature of a person, being a person and a citizen at the same time (Plato. Der Staat. Zürich: Artemis-Verl., 1950 (Russian Edition – Moscow, 1971, V. 3(2), pp. 91-454)). Obviously, an alternating personality suggested by Plato best corresponds to the double-think accepted in meritorics, considering individual evaluations through the prism of a 'person and a citizen'.

[210]When 'all the benefits of education' are seen by uneducated people its social utility disappears, completely dissolving in individual preferences. Then the conditions for termination of state support of education arise, except for the cases concerning support for the indigent, who correctly 'see' and evaluate the benefits of education but cannot pay for it. These individuals can be provided with necessary benefits and grants.

[211]Plato. State (473 d) // Vol. 3 (1), p. 275.

[212]Musgrave R.A. Op. cit., 1969, p. 16.

[213]Schmidt K. Op. cit., 1988, p. 384.

Skipping over the issue of the 'correctness' of politicians' outlook[214], we note it is here that the main dividing line between meritorics and economic sociodynamics is drawn. In meritorics, the state's interests are interpreted as 'true' preferences of individuals or 'common values', which all individuals are ready to recognize as their own interests. This interpretation entails the 'double-think' of market agents, generating an absolutely artificial problem of their 'self-command'[215].

It is impossible to get out of this dead end, where an 'individual has an opinion but does not agree with it', without conceptual losses. This is why Margolis has to add the weight function, thus reducing two individual evaluation systems to one; Taylor has to look for the way to coordinate the public interest with individual ones by applying the 'community behaviour' to the whole society; and the representatives of constitutional theory, striving for a hypothetical consensus, are ready to put all individuals in prison cells or cover them with the 'veil of ignorance', whose size even Rawls could not imagine.

We proceed from the assumption that the state has its own autonomous interest rooted in the fact that *the real institutional environment does not make it possible for all individuals to 'see' all benefits of all goods.* This generates the society's irreducible needs for at least some goods and services,[216] which provides no ground for dividing individual preferences into 'false' and 'true'. The substitution – traditional for meritorics – of interests of society as such for allegedly existing 'true' individual preferences is nothing but an attempt to *reduce the irreducible public needs.* Groundlessness and hopelessness of such attempts are evident. To defend

---

[214]We shall return to this issue later, and now we wish to note that the teleological nature of the postulate of social immunity conditions such democratic mechanism that, on the one hand, reveals and actualizes irreducible public needs and, on the other hand, forms a safety system ensuring the 'correction' of wrongfully-chosen purposes. According to this postulate, in the long run any 'wrong priorities' inevitably come into collision with the laws of socium's development.

[215]Besides the above work by Koboldt (1995), we wish to reference the survey by Schelling, whom Tietzel and Müller consider the author of the notion of 'self-command' (Schelling T.C. Ethics, Law and the Exercise of Self-Command // Choice and Consequence. — Cambridge-London, 1984, pp. 83–112).

[216]We would like to draw attention to the closeness of this conclusion to the interpretation of the state meritoric interference suggested by B. Priddat in the early 1990s: 'When individual agents declare that their '*rational competence*' as for actions is not sufficient to maintain the level of incomes and employment, and that they lack any means to increase this competence, when they are not able to improve their situations on their own, then – it is an ethical requirement – the state faces the task to provide them, by means of merit goods, with a 'credit', which should be regarded as an investment in their future *production competence* – herein lies an economic solution' (Priddat B.P. Op. cit., p. 255-256). We assume that individuals' inability to see all benefits of some good's production and consumption (according to Priddat, lack of their rational competence) should not necessarily be ascertained by individuals. To decide on meritoric actions, the 'public desire' to compensate the objectively 'invisible' consequences of individual behaviour is sufficient. This applies to a wider range of motives than just the maintenance of income and employment levels.

the universality of the reducibility hypothesis actually means to recognize Plato's ideal state or to believe in the existence of a communist society, in which all individuals develop harmoniously, and the adequate institutions ensure the absolute 'visibility' of all goods' consumer effects.

There is another aspect of this issue to which neither Musgrave nor his supporters and critics have paid adequate attention, but which is extremely important from the standpoint of economic sociodynamics. We mean the factor of time; that is, the dynamics of preferences of individuals and society as a whole. During the forty-year discussion of meritorics, none of its participants was interested in this topic, but implicitly all of them considered a *moment* when all goods and services are divided into merit and usual goods. Meanwhile, it is an evident simplification of the problem. Even without considering the motivation behind state activity, it is possible to assert that the merit nature of goods and services is not their inherent quality. Any good can become a merit good any time and then return to the category of usual goods.

In economic sociodynamics this issue is rather important, since the mechanism of social immunity continuously transforms the society's preferences, reduces or liquidates some of its interests and actualizes new irreducible needs. This process is to a great extent conditioned by the dynamics of institutional environment. Institutions (current value orientations, behavioural norms, formal and informal rules) determine the degree of 'visibility' of consumer effects for individuals. The institutions condition a component of an aggregate consumer effect that is 'invisible' for most of market agents, this component manifesting itself in irreducible public needs. Therefore, the joined impact of an ever-changing institutional environment and mechanism of social immunity can move some goods and services into and out of the zone of state interest, 'non-transparent' for the majority of market participants.

This fundamental proposition is connected with a broader understanding of meritorics itself as the existence of goods and services *temporarily endowed with social utility. To make a good merit means to meet an actualized irreducible public need.* The main characteristic of this interpretation is the transient nature of meritoric actions concerning any good. They remain rational only until the irreducibility of the need for this good fails to persist due to either a rejection of the former goals by the society or changes in the institutional environment, which transform the society's interests into individual preferences. We are going to give some examples to make it more obvious.

> Example 5.1. *Meritoric actions concerning a vaccine.* Expanding on Example 4.8 – which demonstrates the endowment a vaccine with social utility and the emerging ability of this good to meet the society's irreducible need for putting an end to epidemic –, we wish to point out the 'meritoric nature' of this situation. We suppose that Musgrave would also regard subsidies to producers of a vaccine as a typical case of meritoric actions of the state encouraging individuals to increase this good's consumption. However, Musgrave passes over something rather important. It is evident that when the threat of epidemic disappears, the respective irreducible need is gone, and the society

gives up its specific goals formulated under the former conditions, the consequence being the vaccine's transformation into a usual good and simultaneous ceasing of state subsidizing for its producers.

Example 5.2. *Meritoric actions concerning the coal industry in the Northern Rhine-Westphalia.* We are going to continue considering Example 4.4, relating to structural policy. In this example the situation looks more complicated. Unlike the usual case of meritorics in which the state correcting the 'consumers' excludability', we can see here society's 'struggle' with 'producers' excludability' – an attempt of the FRG government to preserve the volume of Ruhr coal extraction. This irreducible need became current in the 1960s, when, after the European domestic markets were opened, a threat of widespread mine closures and subsequent mass unemployment due to an abrupt fall in demand for the German coal appeared. The measures taken by the FRG government (subsidies to coal producers) aimed to preserve jobs and improve the competitiveness of German mines should be also regarded as the state meritoric actions.

This example demonstrates the functioning of the teleological mechanism of social immunity that conditions detection, actualization and – in no way less important – the 'dying off' of irreducible needs. Having detected the vital public need in a timely fashion, it signaled the need for a necessary structural reorganization of one of the basic industries. In proportion as the identified irreducible need for the social protection of miners was being satisfied through meritoric actions concerning the German coal and the implementation of the structural reorganization program, the volume of subsidies for the coal industry was continuously decreasing. Today one can observe a significant fall in the number of unprofitable mines along with the contraction of state meritoric interference in this sphere. In the near future, we can expect German society to give up the goals formulated in the middle 1960s and German coal to move back to the 'transparent' zone of usual goods and services.

Example 5.3. *Meritoric actions concerning education.* Education is traditionally referred to as a typical merit good by Musgrave himself and by all participants in the discussion of meritorics. Moreover, education is often regarded as the main sign of a 'double standard' in individual preferences. Musgrave's famous formula stating that 'uneducated people cannot appreciate all benefits of education' has become key in legitimating state actions in the 'pathological case' considered above. We therefore continue the analysis of educational services that began in Example 4.9. In particular, we stated that the social effect of education recognized by all economists is the improvement of public environment in the form of an increased educational level of the population and growth of 'human capital'. In our interpretation, this effect is the evidence of the social utility of education and its ability to meet irreducible public needs (here we repeat that 'uneducated people cannot appreciate all benefits of education').

Consider another important circumstance. Whatever the motive for state action in the sphere of education (an irreducible public need or correction of individual preferences in the 'pathological case'), history knows numerous examples of both governmental support for education and individual responses to this support. In the end of the 20th century one could observe certain shifts in the institutional environment connected with changes in value orientations and social postulates regarding education. In addition to 'visible' individual benefits (a highly paid job), individual time and money investment in education became a behavioural norm for the majority of individuals in most developed countries. In other words, if an individual still 'does not see' all benefits of education, the institutions start to 'work' for him after transforming an 'invisible' link between education and well-being into an evident fact recognized by the majority of the population.

However, it is when 'visible' channels link the social effect of education with secondary individual benefits created (so that even uneducated people start 'seeing' them) that the social utility of educational services begins to disappear. Eventually, it gets completely dissolved in individual preferences. Then the conditions emerge for ceasing governmental support for educational institutions and education's moving out of the 'invisible zone' of merit goods. In this situation, support for consumers of educational services can be continued. However, this would involve support for the indigent, who can be provided with certain benefits and grants. This is, however, another case of meritoric actions.

Example 5.4. *Meritoric and demeritoric actions concerning money.* A broader understanding of meritorics allows us to regard state monetary policy as such actions. In this sense, any reduction of the interest rate can be interpreted as setting reduced prices for loan money to stimulate investment. And vice versa, an increase in this rate should be interpreted as pursuing a policy restricting the use of credit funds aimed at 'cooling' the investment climate. Legitimation of these irreducible public needs lies in the area of macro-regulation theory and practice, without which no country can manage.

One may succeed in constructing another artificial model with a new 'veil of ignorance' to legitimate the interference in question from the standpoint of normative individualism. What really matters, however, is that money can be regarded as a merit good. It is probably an example of the most short-term meritorics or, to be more precise, an endless succession of meritoric and demeritoric impulses of the state. Actually, it is in this succession of increasing and decreasing the interest rate that state monetary policy is implemented. Here we come across the process of endowing money with social utility and respective dynamics of this utility, reflecting changes in the institutional environment and targets of society.

Strictly speaking, a broad understanding of meritorics erases its boundaries. In principle, any goods and services can become merit one day. We repeat that it depends on society's institutional structure and purposes dominating at every moment. Marginal cases are well-known. These are the centralized economy (the state regards all goods as merit; market forces are almost completely neutralized) and its antipode – the so-called wild market (everything is left to the 'invisible hand'; the state does not implement its own interests and there is no place for merit goods).

Each of these actually degenerate economies has its own institutional environment, ensuring its functioning for the time being. Both cases involve the negative aspects so well-known that their analysis makes no sense here. We would merely like to emphasize that in the course of time, the teleological forces of social immunity and changing institutional environment generate obstacles such economies are unable to overcome.

When analyzing meritorics in the context of economic sociodynamics, we should bear in mind the problem of the *scale* of state involvement in market relations. While in Marxism this scale is maximal (the state almost completely substituting for the market), and in traditional Anglo-Saxon economics it reaches the absolute minimum (the society just having to put up with the unavoidable evil of state presence), the German economic thought proceeds from the principle of subsidiarity and the idea of 'state orderliness'. In our paradigm, the question of whether 'there should be much or little state' makes no sense. The state is a market player like all others, and the scale of its meritoric actions at any given moment is conditioned by the current political system and the mechanism of social immunity.

Our last remark refers to the 'relationship' between meritorics and economic sociodynamics. Treating Musgrave's concept with all due respect, we still think it occupies an intermediate position in economic theory and has disadvantages usual for such 'middle-of-the-road' theoretical constructions. On the one hand the concept of merit goods reflects actual economic life better than the neoclassical model and treats the state more adequately. On the other hand this concept is still connected through the umbilical cord of normative individualism with the neoclassical model, limiting the state's functions to the correction of market failures. The natural outcome of this fundamental contradiction is the assumption of market agents' 'double-think' concerning evaluation of goods and a wrong understanding of the motivation for state meritoric actions.

But if we update the traditional contents of meritorics and use the key postulates of economic sociodynamics (the existence of irreducible public needs and social utility of goods) when determining the actual motives for the state activities, then 'adjusted meritorics' will not differ much from economic sociodynamics. Moreover, in this case economic sociodynamics absorbs meritorics, the latter becoming its part. And then, paraphrasing Tietzel and Müller[217], we can say *all that is valid in meritorics is already contained in economic sociodynamics.*

However, it is possible to evaluate the relationship between meritorics and economic sociodynamics from another standpoint. The concept suggested by us can

---

[217]Here we refer to the following conclusion of Tietzel and Müller, 'All that is valid in meritorics is already contained in other theories; all that is new in it is not valid from the individualistic viewpoint' (Tietzel M., Müller C. Op.cit., p. 124).

be regarded as an extension of the German tradition[218] and the further development of Musgrave's approach. One should clearly understand that economic sociodynamics has absorbed all basic ideas of meritorics and, foremost, that idea that points out that the demand for some goods by private market agents lags behind that 'desired by society'. Actually, our 'social utility' is derived from the category of 'merit goods'. According to economic sociodynamics, all four types of societal desires – in the cases of 'pathology', 'weak will of Odysseus', 'material assistance', and 'common values' – have the same nature, connected with the existence of irreducible public needs and some goods' ability to meet these specific needs.

In conclusion, we emphasize that in our concept, considerable opportunities for economic development arise from the self-sustaining growth of the aggregate consumer effect, i.e. they are connected with the functioning of the sociodynamic multiplier of economic growth, this process being completely determined by the interaction of three constituents. We would like to reiterate that these are the social effect, individual creative inclinations, and the institutional structure of society, which, in fact, channels the social effect, creating and maintaining communications between creative inclinations and advantages of an improved public environment.

The special place in this specific triad is occupied by the state. Meeting the irreducible public needs, it ensures the said improvements in public environment and actually 'triggers' the sociodynamic multiplier of economic growth. Thus, it is the state that ensures positive economic consequences for the realization of social interests. Hence it is ensuring the state's rational behaviour that should prove to be a considerable resource for sustained economic growth.

Long ago Adam Smith understood himself and made others understand that lack of individual freedoms characteristic of feudalism is the main hindrance for economic development; today something similar occurs in relation to the state. The restricting concept of the state, dominating in the mainstream, is also a hindrance, making it impossible to use societal resources efficiently. Economic sociodynamics is aimed at eliminating this hindrance. It is clear that such theoretical construction requires the modernization of notions of state structure and functioning. The final chapters of our book are devoted to this important issue.

---

[218]This yields reference to the German financial science (Finanzwissenschaft) and its most famous representatives: Lorenz von Stein, Albert Schaffle and Adolf Wagner.

6 The Individual, the State and Society

In the preface to the English translation of *Studies on Theory of Finances* by Knut Wicksell, James Buchanan called on economists 'first to construct a model of state or political structure, and only after that start analyzing the results of the state activity'[219]. Following this methodological postulate, he developed his own model of the state and institutional theory of constitutional economics. As we also claim to create a general theory and plan to analyze state activity in this chapter, we shall follow Buchanan's advice and first discuss our vision of the contemporary society and democratic state, our views of people's coexistence in a socium.

'We live together because the social organization provides us with the effective means to reach our personal goals, not because the society provides the means to attain some abstract general happiness'[220]. These words open *The Limit of Liberty* by Buchanan. It is difficult to find a person who disagrees with this assumption. Indeed, most of people, unable to imagine themselves out of society, do no't expect any abstract happiness from it. However, there are few people who think about efficiency of the means it provides to reach their personal goals. We live together because this is the only way of life possible for us.

But there have always been people who have tried to understand why it is *necessary* to live together and how personal and collective aspects correlate in this forced communal life. In other words, they tried to find out how to make individual choices without infringing upon others' freedom of choice, and how to maintain social unity, preventing its collapse and chaos. We do not simply live together; we live in the state, which arranges our life one way or another. By setting the general rules, it forces us to give up some of our personal interests, and we certainly would like to think that our sacrifice is justified. We even have a hope (or an illusion?) that state interference can always be presented as our own *individual choice*. This is the secret of popularity of 'methodological individualism', postulating state policy as a 'process of coordinating our preferences'[221]. Obviously, rea-

---

[219]Buchanan considered this call so important, that he repeated it in his Nobel lecture (Buchanan J.M. The Constitution of Economic Policy, American Economic Review, 1987, Vol. 77 (3) (Russian Edition – Nobel Prize Winners in Economics. James Buchanan. – Moscow, 1997, p. 18)).

[220]Buchanan J. The Limits of Liberty: Between Anarchy and Leviathan. Chicago: The University of Chicago Press, 1975 (Russian Edition: Nobel Prize Winners in Economics. James Buchanan. – Moscow, 1997, p. 212).

[221]Buchanan J. The Limits of Liberty, p. 212. Buchanan wrote, 'The term "methodological individualism" should not be confused with "individualism" as a norm of society's or-

sons also exist for the tremendous popularity of Buchanan with his contract paradigm and *institutional Utopia of unanimity*.

Criticizing the formerly popular 'organic concept' with its obviously outdated understanding of public interest, he conceived of another utopian idea about a society as an aggregation of individuals *inevitably* capable of unanimity. Dashing aside from any 'social interest' like the devil from the incense, and fearing to 'let some organic concept in through the back door'[222], Buchanan reduced everything to personal preferences, to an agreement between individuals and a consensus achieved when people voluntarily give up some of their personal interests. Of course, we dare not 'suspect' Buchanan of the teleological justification of this unanimity – especially as he has always been against teleology –, unfortunately repudiating the possibility for the formation of any objective goals of society different from subjective interests of individuals[223]. That is why he has nothing to do but to speak about the inevitability of consensus and repeat like an incantation, 'It is an agreement between people, inherent to any type of exchange'[224].

The German scholar, J. Habermas, actually speaks about the same 'great present', albeit in different words. He suggests a model of compromise between individual preferences based on the so-called 'discourse' and people's readiness for self-modification[225]. In his theory, consensus is an inevitable result of people's co-existence, and he is absolutely confident that compromise between personal interests is possible. Setting aside the paradox of non-teleological belief in consensus for the time being, let us return to Buchanan's 'ideological phobias', paying greatest attention not to the organic concept but to the topic of our concern, the problem of public interests and the legitimacy of state actions aimed at their realization.

Rejecting the category of public interest, Buchanan, like other economists, sees only its specifics reflected in Marx' social and philosophical doctrine, regarding 'society as a single organism irreducible to a sum of individuals, developing according to objective laws regardless of people's will and consciousness'[226]. In other words, he treats the notion of social interest only as an integral part of the 'organic concept'[227]. Meanwhile, we would like to once again stress that this approach no-

---

ganization. The analysis from the standpoint of "methodological individualism" is an attempt to reduce all problems of political organization to the issue of individual choices between different options'. (Buchanan J., Tullock G. The Calculus of Consent: Logical Foundations of Constitutional Democracy. Ann Arbor Paperbacks, 1962 (Russian Edition: Nobel Prize Winners in Economics. James Buchanan. – Moscow, 1997, p. 35)).

[222]Buchanan J., Tullock G., The Calculus of Consent, p. 50.

[223]Buchanan J. Constitution of Economic policy, pp. 19-20.

[224]Ibid., p. 25.

[225]Habermas J. Zur Logik der theoretischen und praktischen Diskurses // Riedel M. (Hrsg.) Rehabilitierung der praktischen Philosophie. Bd. 2. - Freiburg, 1974, pp. 381-402. Also see: Habermas J. Legitimationsprobleme im Spätkapitalismus. — Frankfurt a. M., 1973.

[226]See notes to the Russian translation of *The Calculus of Consent* (Buchanan J., Tullock G., The Calculus of Consent, pp. 48, 491).

[227]This postulate is shared by Kurt Schmidt, one of the most 'experienced' examiners of public interests (Schmidt K. Op. cit., 1964, pp. 335-362), and by some other economists analyzing meritorics. Richard Musgrave belongs to the opponents of this view. The cate-

ticeably limits the possibilities of analyzing the modern society and does not allow the recognition of other aspects of collective interest. Without repeating what was already said about irreducible public interests in the previous chapters hereof, we note the following circumstances overlooked by Buchanan and his followers.

First, let us consider the notion of society. Rejecting the 'organic concept' without reserve and reckoning ourselves among Buchanan's followers as for an understanding the society, we also believe that it is 'populated' by people with their own goals, acting both individually and within a group[228]. Thus, we deal with a multitude of interacting individuals, each of them having personal interests. But understanding society as such an aggregation not structured in a single organism does not require the recognition of the universality of the reducibility hypothesis. This is why we cannot agree with Buchanan, recognizing only the interest corresponding to a consensus of individual preferences as a public one. It is evident that according to the holistic outlook any aggregation of individuals, including that not forming a single organism, manifests its qualities differently from those of its components. Hence it is possible to speak about the interest of society as such, staying outside the 'organic concept' and not necessarily treating society as a single organism, developing according to its own laws.

Second, the irreducibility of social needs does not mean that society's targets do not depend on the 'people's will and consciousness'; this simplified interpretation is also connected with the 'organic concept'. But if we base the repudiation of the universality of the irreducibility hypothesis not on an artificial model of a society – in which consensus among individuals rules – but on the real market relations, clearly understanding that in the process of individuals' interaction not every need can be revealed, we have only two options: either to assume that there are no irreducible interests of society[229], thus limiting the possibilities of analysis; or to recognize, assuming the existence of these interests, that for the time being they are 'detected' by statistically small groups of people. The will and consciousness of these specific 'mediums' of a society (passionaries) not noticed by the market are a source of drive and energy for the formation of irreducible social interests. Thus, the second argument of those rejecting the existence of social interests proves to be unsubstantiated.

Third, consider the process of the formation of public interests. We have already noted in the previous chapters that we associate this phenomenon with the teleological principle, the mechanism of social immunity. Here we evidently disagree with Buchanan, who, not recognizing teleology, substitutes it for a contract paradigm and the confidence in the attainability of a consensus.

We wish to stress the radical difference between our concept and Marxism, also using the teleological principle. Marxism deals with a single public organism, gaining energy for its development not in individual 'will and consciousness' of

---

gory of 'common needs', suggested by him, demonstrates other opportunities for defining the public interest. (Musgrave R.A. Op. cit., 1987, pp. 452-453).

[228]Buchanan J., Tullock G., The Calculus of Consent, p. 50.

[229]This is an assumption of the majority of neoclassical concepts, theories of well-being and institutionalism.

separate market players but in the class struggle, reflecting antagonisms between productive forces and production relations. Not evaluating this idea here, we want to emphasize that in our case an individual is a bearer of public interest.

Later we shall describe the processes for identification and actualization of social interests, as well as the mechanisms for their spread in the socium from the few passionaries and statistically-insignificant groups of individuals to general public. Now, let us consider different models of society and state along with the evolution of theoretical notions of the individual, simultaneously acting as a private person having personal interests and a member of a social organization having collective goals. A brief historic overview of some concepts of social philosophers will help us to understand this matter more clearly.

6.1 Between an Ideal State and the 'Hand of Providence'

Since the 18th century, when the differentiation was made between the state and society as autonomous systems, organizing people's communal life, and between the ideas of a human being as a *'citoyen'* (a member of a socium) and a *'bourgeois'* (a separate economic agent), an ideal integral civil community was often associated with the Athenian city-state in the time of Solon. But Plato believed that the unity of civil community was not attained in the city-state. In particular, this is clear from an abstract from his *Protagoras*, a dialogue between Socrates and Protagoras containing a mythological interpretation of people's ability to unite.

> Example 6.1. *Myth about the universality of civic virtues.* Socrates and Hippocrates, having learned about the arrival of the famous sophist Protagoras, come to his place and get engaged in a controversy with the philosopher to gain knowledge from him. Their dialogue starts with the issue of the 'Origin of Virtue in Society and Individuals'[230]. Since Socrates doubts the possibility of learning virtue, Protagoras suggests proving it using the 'myth told by the old people to the young'[231].
>
> After Prometheus gave people the fire and the skills of Hephaestus and Athena, they 'invented dwelling, garments, footwear, beds and obtained food tilling the land. Having settled down like that, people first lived scattered (there were no cities), getting killed by animals, since they were weaker, and the skills of processing, though they helped them well to obtain food, were not enough to fight animals: people had no skills of living in a society, a part of which is soldiery. So, they started to try to live together and build cities for their safety. But hardly had they got together, they started to offend each other, since they had no skills of living together; and again they had to go live away and die.

---

[230]Plato. Protagoras, Philebus, and Gorgia. Amherst, N.Y.: Prometheus Books, 1996 (Russian Edition – Moscow, 1968, Vol. 1, pp. 199-211).
[231]Plato. Protagoras (320 c), p. 202.

Then Zeus, being afraid that all people would die, sent Hermes to introduce shame and virtue among people, so that they adorn cities and friendly relations. Hermes asked Zeus how to endow people with shame and virtue. "Should they be distributed like skills are distributed? And the skills are distributed like that: a person who gained full skill in healing is many times as endowed as a person ignorant of it; and the same applies to other skilled people. So, shall I allocate virtue and shame among people like that or shall I endow all of them equally?"

Zeus said, "Let all the people have them; there will be no states if only some people have them as they have skills. And establish the law on my behalf, saying that everybody without shame and virtue will be killed as ulcer of society' "[232].

But Socrates does not want to recognize that Protagoras is right. Defending his point of view, he persists in saying that 'it is impossible to learn virtue'[233] and interprets the myth otherwise. Finishing the dialogue, Socrates and Protagoras partially recognize each other's arguments, and Plato words the following fundamental conclusion about people's ability to reach unanimity: though it is possible to learn virtue, *it is not equally attainable for everybody*. In his *The State* and *The Laws*, Plato gives the same interpretation of individuals' ability to evaluate public utility.

Noting that people are different (everybody cannot have equal civic virtue) and being sure that all individuals, being egoists, contribute to the destruction of their community, Plato sets the tasks of a state. 'Can there be a greater evil for a state than the one resulting in the loss of its integrity?.. Can there be a greater good than the one that unites the state and contributes to its integrity?'[234] Therefore, given the division of labour and the evolution of autonomous personal interests, the maintenance of the state's integrity requires a policy ensuring the settlement of the conflict between the private and the public.

Plato realizes this harmony according to the ancient Greek tradition, excluding any possibility of a person's individualization and not understanding all significance of personal freedom. This is the reason why the first model of a state – an ideal state of Plato – has become a repulsive Utopia, in which it is impossible for a person to choose his trade and estate, to have family and children, and where there is no place for private property, the 'principle of singleness is suppressed'[235] and 'all people are recognized only as general people'[236].

---

[232]Plato. Protagoras (322 b-d), p. 204.

[233]Plato. Protagoras (361), p. 252.

[234]Plato. Der Staat. Zürich: Artemis-Verl., 1950 (Russian Edition – Moscow, 1971, V. 3 (2), p. 260).

[235]Hegel G.W.F. Vorlesungen über die Philosophie der Geschichte, in Hegel G.W.F. Werke, Bd.12. Frankfurt/Main: 1969-1971 (Russian Edition: Collected Works. – Moscow, 1932, V.X, p. 222).

[236]Ibid., p. 217.

Now we know that Plato is wrong. But how can society's heterogeneity be neutralized? How can one compensate people's basic incapability of an equally correct evaluation of the surrounding world and the consequences of their actions? How can one coordinate the behaviour of many individuals and avoid chaos, given that all individuals are different (in particular, their 'personal judgements regarding the good and evil differ'[237]), and that knowledge, will and resources are distributed unequally among them?

Answering these fundamental questions, Thomas Hobbes suggested his formula that supreme power equalizes everybody. According to his theoretical constructions, social differentiation and 'bellum omnium contra omnes' can be overcome only by the state, behaving like a sovereign possessing supreme power. 'The supreme power is the source of all honours. Virtues of a lord, duke and prince are created by it. Like a servant before his master, subjects in the presence of their sovereign are all equal and have no honour'[238]. According to Hobbes, the state is therefore omnipotent and looks like an ominous Leviathan. Here, it makes sense to digress and discuss the allegory suggested by Hobbes, which has been used by social philosophers and economists for more than three hundred years.

Example 6.2. *Myth about Leviathan and its conceptual transformations.*

Prologue. According to a Ugaritic pagan myth, Leviathan was a sea monster, representing the Chaos against which the Most High fought. According to the modern sources, 'the fight of Leviathan and other monsters with the God is a plot of many myths, widely spread in the Middle East, about the initial animosity between the God and the powers of the sea representing the Chaos, which the God must defeat to create the well-ordered universe'[239]. Thus according to pre-biblical cosmogonic myths, the first page in Leviathan's biography was marked by his absolute animosity to the God and direct relationship with the Chaos.

Biblical period. The second period in Leviathan's history started when he got mentioned in the Bible, whose monotheistic grounds required a certain modification of the myth. Leviathan lost his godlike status and turned into a sea monster or 'whale' (Gen.1:21). Establishing the idea of the Almighty God, the Genesis emphasizes that the sea monsters were not rival gods, rather they were created by the God. As a result of such evolution, Leviathan appears in the Bible only as an allegory. The Book of Psalms, for instance, calls the Egyptian Pharaoh – a cruel oppressor of Jewry who was punished by the God – Leviathan, 'Thou didst crush the heads of Leviathan, thou didst give him as food for the creatures of the wilderness' (Ps. 74:14), and in the

---

[237]Like Plato, Hobbes regarded the belief that everyone can correctly evaluate public utility as one of the most 'poisonous' illnesses of the state, resulting in its disintegration (Hobbes T. Leviathan. Hamburg: Meiner, 1996 (Russian Edition – Moscow, 1991, V. 2, pp. 251-252)).

[238]Hobbes T. Leviathan // V. 2., p. 142.

[239] Society on Research of Jewish Communities. Brief Jewish Encyclopaedia. Jerusalem, 1988, V. 4, p. 722.

book of the prophet Isaiah, it is a symbol of the hostility of the Babylonian empire to Jewry: 'In that day the Lord with his hard and great and strong sword will punish Leviathan the fleeing serpent, Leviathan the twisting serpent; and he will slay the dragon that is in the sea' (Is. 27:1). During the biblical period of Leviathan's biography, his image was localized and transformed into a symbol of a hostile power or hostile state. We would like to stress that this is not any state, but only a hostile one.

Life in the world, or the history of one delusion. A new page of Leviathan's conceptual evolution is opened up in the famous book by Hobbes. Explaining his comparison of a state with the monster, he indicates that he took this comparison 'from two last verses of *Job 41* where the God, depicting Leviathan's great strength, calls him the king of pride'[240]. Strictly speaking, Hobbes' association relates only to those features of Leviathan which characterize its tremendous power, the hostility of the state, characteristic of the previous comparisons ('he is king over all the sons of pride' (Job 41:34)), vanishing and ceasing to condition the use of this allegory. It is here that the second conceptual transformation takes place. In the new history, Leviathan becomes a prototype of all sources of power and every state; according to Hobbes, in other words, any state viewed as a social institution appears as a monster, representing absolute evil.

It should be mentioned that this symbol of a state has been widely used by economists, who, in spite of their inclination to mathematical precision, seem to get great satisfaction 'under the veil' of figurative thinking, applying such emotional concepts as 'the invisible hand' or 'hand of providence', 'free rider', 'prisoner's dilemma', 'night watchman', etc. Leviathan as an allegory of the state belongs to such concepts. We are not experts in Hobbesian works, and we cannot say whether the said comparison was made by mistake, or whether it was the author's intention. In any case, let us pay attention to a peculiar change in the biography of Leviathan.

We'd like to remind our readers that, according to the legend, Leviathan was a monster representing the Chaos, which the God had to defeat to establish order. Taking into consideration that the Supreme Power (according to Hobbes) also fights with the Chaos, the association of the state with Leviathan does not seem quite adequate. Here we face an obvious substitution of concepts; instead of struggle with the Chaos, the state starts to be an accessory to it. However, we wish like to repeat that Hobbes might have taken a perspective which we are unaware of, thereby explaining such substitution (for example, Leviathan's victor becomes Leviathan himself).

Having considered the dramatic history of the state's symbol suggested by the English philosopher more that three hundred years ago, we are going to consider his model of the state. Based on the principle of Supreme Power of the sovereign, equalizing all subjects, it can nevertheless be regarded from the opposite stand-

---

[240]Hobbes T. Leviathan, V. 2, p. 249.

point, as an ideological foundation for a legal state[241] in which Law always rules. Everybody is equal before the Law, ensuring the necessary integrity of the society 'through compulsion and fear of power'[242]. Actually, Hobbes, like Plato, enhanced his model of the state with the idea of 'the second best'[243], according to which an ideal state (or supreme power) is restricted by the laws it itself establishes.

If Hobbes' construction is absolutely rigid and based on the principle of compulsion of individuals to the adherence to rules of community established by the power, John Locke[244], unlike Plato, implicitly assumes that everybody possesses equal civic virtue; due to his reasonableness, a person is social by his nature and therefore is able, 'proceeding from the correctly understood interests of his own and using his intellect, to realize the necessity of the state association'[245]. Strictly speaking, we can see the same motif of the expediency of obedience to the power in Hobbes' works: the losses caused by civil status that limit individual freedoms are less than those emerging from the unrestricted 'bellum omnium contra omnes'.

The main assumption made by Hobbes and Locke is that only *compulsion* can neutralize the forces of the self-interest, thereby destroying the society. And though Bernard Mandeville also basis his analysis on the power of compulsion[246], his notion of the state reveals his understanding of the importance of egoistic interests and their teleological relation with the social utility. Mandeville's famous formula, *'private vices – public benefits'[247]*, later complemented with the category

---

[241]We wish like to mention Macpherson's work, which studies the relationship between individualism and power (Macpherson C.B. Die politischen Theorie des Besitzindividualismus. Von Hobbes zu Locke. — Frankfurt a.M., 1973).

[242]Koslowski P. Op. cit., p. 157.

[243]In the fifth book of *The Laws*, the Athenian says: 'However, when one thinks and observes, he will agree that we are building the state which is only the second compared to the best one' (Plato. Laws. Amherst, N.Y.: Prometheus Books, 2000 (Russian Edition – Moscow, 1971, V. 3(1), p. 213)).

[244]Locke J. Two Treatises on Government, 3 Vols. – Moscow: Mysl, 1988, V. 3.

[245]Koslowski P. Op. cit., p. 159. Interpreting Locke, Peter Koslowski draws a connecting line between the views of this philosopher of the 17th century and contemporary economic ideas. It is interesting that *these* views have outlived Locke. Actually, the assumption that individuals recognize public interests as their own interests is one of the most popular in theories of the public well-being (Samuelson and Bergson), institutionalism (Sugden and Taylor), and constitutional economics (Buchanan) nowadays.

[246]Actually sharing Hobbes' views, he writes about it even more forthright, 'The state is the society where a person, either subdued by the superior force or brought out if his wild state by persuasion, has become an obedient creature' (Mandeville B. The Fable of the Bees. Harmondsworth: Penguin, 1970 (Russian Edition – Moscow, 1974, p. 310)).

[247]Due to this maxim, a number of authors, Hayek in particular, include Mandeville among the theorists of liberalism and pioneers of the principle of *laissez-faire* (Hayek F.A. Freiburger Studien. – Tübingen, 1969, p. 112). We cannot agree with this, since, according to Mandeville, spontaneous order is impossible. Without the fear of compulsion, 'a hundred people will never be able to stay together awake, even for two hours, without quarrelling' (Mandeville B. Op. cit., p. 310). His model of the state requires power and compulsion in the form of 'skillful politician'.

of 'skillful politician'[248], actually means that individuals' egoistic striving to achieve their *personal* goals can ensure the *public* well-being as well, provided that political power acts skillfully.

In ascertaining the essentiality of personal motivation while rejecting any possibility of spontaneous order, Mandeville stays within the previous concepts of the state and society, and suggesting a scheme of mediating individual interests by state interventions, he shows himself to be a direct successor of Hobbes, who, like the majority of his predecessors, failed to 'see' the teleological potential of the social ordering in individual interests.

Smith managed to do this however. He was the first to see the creative role of individual freedom and find the substitute for power able to overcome the chaos. The main point in Smith's surmise is the teleological mechanism of self-regulation, taking the energy of equilibrium from the 'natural inclination to trade and exchange'[249]. The ideas purporting that self-interest does not result in anarchy but, to the contrary, contributes to spontaneous order, and that egoistic actions of each separate person and of all people together are coordinated by the 'invisible hand', became a key postulate of the liberal doctrine, ruling on theoretical Olympus for more than two hundred years.

Among Smith's arguments, there are objections to Mandeville. Rejecting the postulated capability of a 'skillful politician' to transform private vices into public benefits, Smith explained his critical attitude to state interventions by the fact that the state lacks the information required for such intervention. 'The sovereign is completely relieved from the duty, whose proper performance is inaccessible for any human wisdom and knowledge, to manage private persons' labour and direct it to the activities satisfying the society's needs better'[250]. According to Smith, only the heuristic abilities of the 'invisible hand' generate the *a posteriori* knowledge for 'what is good and bad'. This information always appears after an equilibrium emerges, and therefore an economic order, conditioned by the force of self-interest, cannot be predicted even by the most 'skillful politician'.

Thus according to Plato, the power required to ensure society's integrity, absolutized in the form of the sovereign state by Hobbes, and transformed into a 'skillful politician' by Mandeville, was completely delegated to the 'invisible hand' by Smith. The teleological potential of ordering, discovered by Smith in individual freedom, moved the state to the periphery of the social structure. However, he complemented the priority of private interests by morale, ensuring the mediation of individual subjectivity by an 'unprejudiced observer everyone has in his heart'[251]. Therefore, those having such observers in their hearts and being guided by the 'invisible hand' need the state only as a guard for their property and laws.[252]

---

[248]Mandeville B. Op. cit., p. 318.

[249]Smith A. An Inquiry into the Nature and Causes of the Wealth of Nations. London: Dent, 1981 (Russian Edition – Moscow, 1962, p. 27).

[250]Smith A. Op. cit., p. 497.

[251]Smith A. The Theory of Moral Sentiments. Cambridge: Cambridge University Press, 2002 (Russian Edition – Moscow, 1997, p. 150). Please pay attention to Koslowski's remark that Smith differentiates private interest from moral universality (Koslowski P., Op.

Some economists still regard this minimum set of functions as optimal for the state, where freedom and private initiative, due to the Most High will of the 'invisible hand', must lead society to consensus and harmony. This notion of the state has impacted the 'destiny' of Leviathan, who has undergone a new transformation.

> Example 6.3. *Myth about Leviathan. Under the pressure of the 'invisible hand'.* In the contemporary history (after Smith) Leviathan underwent new, not less surprising, transformations. Gradually losing his power, based on the Supreme Power of sovereign, the state finally yielded to the teleological force of the 'invisible hand'. Along with the state, Leviathan was defeated. While at first he was defeated in the form of the Chaos, this time he lost personifying the Order. But even at a new stage of history, he was defeated by the same force, having evolved from the God, Creator, to the teleological principle of pre-established harmony. Actually, this is the manner through which Leviathan was eventually transformed into a 'night watchman' – a modest security guard, who, when out of duty works as a 'janitor' on the competitive market, cleaning it up from continual failures of the 'invisible hand'.

But good hopes did not come true. There is no consensus, no harmony even in the most developed countries and democratic societies. And the two-century way has not brought about the formation of moral imperatives able to play the role of an 'unprejudiced observer'. Unequal 'distribution' of civic virtue among members of a society still thwarts the hopes of filling individual interest with altruism. In other words, infringement of the postulate of the universal morale (the ethical component of Smith's liberal doctrine) results in the disturbance of anticipated harmony.

---

cit., pp. 181, 330). Strictly speaking, Smith substitutes Mandeville's 'skillful politician' not only for the 'invisible hand' but also for morale, which 'ennobles' personal interests. Strange though it may seem, that Smith assumes all individuals have equal civic virtue – an 'unprejudiced observer'– to ensure the universality of the morale, is the evidence of this.

[252]Here we mean the state's duties that are well-known and widely quoted by economists: 'first, to protect the society from the violence and intrusion of other autonomous societies; second, to protect, whenever it is possible, every member of society from injustice and oppression by other members, or to establish strict and unprejudiced administration of justice; third, to establish and maintain certain public institutions' (Smith A. An Inquiry into the Nature and Causes of the Wealth of Nations, p. 497).

6.2 From an Institutional Utopia to a Realistic Model of the State

This is especially evident if we consider the goods whose production and/or consumption is accompanied by externalities. The egoistic inclination of individuals to behave like 'free riders' disarms the 'invisible hand' and conditions market failures, i.e. such market zones where the teleological mechanism of pre-established harmony obviously fails, the state having to respond with interventions to all market failures. Here, the requirement for the 'skillful politician' arises.

In the case of the universal moral norm excluding the 'free rider' behaviour, as well as in all other cases in which there are no externalities and market transaction is a matter of agreement between two agents, the market mechanism of self-regulation is able to ensure equilibrium without any governmental interventions. But as soon as we return to the real world, where the universality of morale and isolated market transactions with internalization of all their externalities are only to be desired, state interference becomes inevitable, and its legitimacy evident.

The second half of the 20th century provides a good example of continuously expanding state interference despite strong ideological pressure of liberal doctrine in most countries with developed market economies and mature democracy. All we can hear in response to this phenomenon are irritated voices of those dissatisfied with the real world[253].

An attempt to resolve this evident controversy was made by Buchanan, who suggested a different view of market relations, his own understanding of a society and a special model of the state. Buchanan calls the *contract*, based on the above 'agreement between people, inherent to any type of exchange', a possible and theoretically desirable substitute for governmental interventions, at least with respect to the achievement of market equilibrium. Here is an example demonstrating the nature of this contract and its contents, based on the well-known model by Buchanan[254].

> Example 6.4. *Model of the contract between two individuals.* Buchanan considers individuals *A* and *B* and assumes that there is a rare good *T*, in which both of them are interested, that is somehow allocated among them according to 'anarchic equilibrium', i.e. the 'natural state' of humanity (Cell I, Table 6.1)

---

[253]Here we can refer to Buchanan, who wrote, 'The state machine directly disposes of one third of the national product' (Buchanan J., Tullock G. The Calculus of Consent. p. 57), and other adherents to individualism ('There are the reasons to assume that the continuously increasing share of the state is a result of meritoric actions concerning the technically private goods. Meanwhile, this trend basically contradicts the individualistic principle of minimum compulsion' (Tietzel M., Müller C. Op. cit., p. 112)).

[254]We intentionally repeat the scheme by Peter Koslowski (Koslowski P. Op. cit., p. 164), revealing the essence of Buchanan's model, and use the tables and their interpretation suggested by Buchanan (Fig. 2.1 and 4.3 in *The Limit of Liberty*) (Buchanan J. The Limits of Liberty, pp. 244, 292-293).

In the case of a natural allocation of the good *T*, when neither of the parties recognizes anyone's right to this good, the utility level for individual *A* is 9, for individual *B*, 2. Under such circumstances, individual *A* tries to occupy the position corresponding to Cell II *(A=22, B=1)*, and individual *B* the one corresponding to Cell III *(A=3, B=11)*. Here they face the 'prisoner's dilemma'. The optimal resolution of this conflict of interests is corporate behaviour; both individuals, having partially given up their intentions, prefer the allocation of the good *T* according to the conditions of Cell IV *(A=19, B=7)*. If this equilibrium (Cell IV) is instable or is not reached (Cell I), and 'bellum omnium contra omnes' takes place, they are forced to spend certain resources to protect their share of the good *T* or seize another person's share. Buchanan believes that at some stage of this conflict, the rationally-acting individuals will inevitably realize the usefulness of observing each others' rights, recorded in the respective agreement. In other words, the parties will reach consensus, having understood that the expenses for the seizure and protection of the good *T* may exceed the utility levels corresponding with the current allocation of this good. This situation makes Buchanan conclude that a stable agreement is inevitable.

Table 6.1. Model of the Contract Between two Individuals

		Individual B	
		Does not observe rights	*Observes rights*
Individual A	*Does not observe rights*	Cell I **A=9, B**=2	Cell II **A=22, B**=1
	Observes rights	Cell III **A=3, B**=11	Cell IV **A=19, B**=7

In this model, 'each individual realizes that his behaviour directly affects further behaviour of the other'[255]. However, in case the number of parties to the agreement grows, this interdependence becomes weaker, being absolutely insignificant when the whole aggregation of individuals gets involved. Taking this into consideration, Buchanan makes the fundamental conclusion that implementation of the agreement on a society-wide scale requires the involvement of an external institution[256]. He actually means the state, though in a narrow model, which establishes ensuring the observance of laws as the state's only function[257].

---

[255]Buchanan J. The Limits of Liberty, p. 294.

[256]Ibid., p. 297.

[257]Here Buchanan went further than Smith, in particular, releasing the state from its third duty; that is, 'to establish and maintain certain public institutions'.

Buchanan's radical individualism[258] and reluctance to see the state as an institution striving to realize public interest reduces it to an ordinary 'referee, its only task being to ensure the observance of the agreement'[259]. But even here, Buchanan remains faithful to his marginal philosophical doctrine, declaring individual freedom the only highest value. For this reason he regards any institution of power and any restriction on personal freedom as a monster. Though he means only a contemporary understanding of Leviathan[260] (quite an 'old' monster, whom he associates with the bureaucracy), the state, in the opinion of this theorist, remains hostile to the individual. In this connection, let us continue our story about Leviathan's evolution.

> Example 6.5. *Leviathan as a scarecrow.* One has to admit that economists cannot forget Leviathan, who left the deep long ago, transformed and far from being frightful. When it appeared on the cover of one of the most significant books of the end of the 20th century, it became clear that the original idea of the pre-biblical myth was completely forgotten. This is how James Buchanan motivates his reference to this symbol of first the Chaos, then a *hostile* state and later *any* state, establishing order using the power of compulsion: 'Dictionaries define Leviathan as a "sea monster, personifying the evil". In 1651, Thomas Hobbes applied this name to the sovereign state. Three and a quarter centuries later we use it only to speak pejoratively of the state and political processes and to draw attention to the threat connected with the growing state sector'[261]. Leviathan is therefore far from personifying the Chaos, it is actually the opposite to it; Buchanan searches for the limits of liberty somewhere between the Chaos and Leviathan, this monster being not a state any longer but only a *pejorative* allegory of the state and political processes. Actually, now he is just a scarecrow in a perfect suit and white collar of a faceless and heartless bureaucrat.
>
> *Epilogue.* From a godlike creature in a Ugaritic pagan myth to a simple bureaucrat in the institutional Utopia of Buchanan, this is the conceptual evolution of Leviathan during several millenniums, the result of his being defeated in the battles for regulating the world, in which he was the symbol of each antagonistic party at different moments of history.

Now we wish like to point out the most important thing. We have been living together for a long time. 'We' are a lot of people possessing different knowledge, will and resources, having personal interests and specific ideas of the good and evil; 'we' are a multitude of interacting individuals. We really want our communal life to provide all of us with 'effective means to reach our personal goals'. But our

---

[258]We would like to draw attention to the critique of Buchanan's exaggerated individualism by one of the founders of the theory of public choice, K. Arrow, and refer the reader to the review by N.Milchakova (Milchakova N. Development of Neoclassical Theory in Studies of Kenneth Arrow // Voprosy Ekonomiki, 1995, No. 5, pp. 108-113).

[259]Buchanan J. The Limits of Liberty, pp. 296-297.

[260]Ibid., p. 398.

[261]Buchanan J. The Limits of Liberty, p. 396.

personal desires disagree with each other very often, and the Chaos, looking like Leviathan in his pre-biblical years, is always on the lookout for 'the limits of liberty' of our relatively well-ordered social life. Therefore, the real dilemma any society faces is not Buchanan's institutional choice 'between anarchy and Leviathan' the state, but rather the choice between Leviathan the Chaos and dictatorship, ensuring the order by the supreme power of a sovereign. It is here that the real limits of liberty lie. Rejecting both the 'power of arbitrariness' and 'arbitrariness of power', we are sure that harmony is necessary.

Searching for harmony, thinkers of the past discovered different means of fighting with the chaos. First, only the sovereign power of compulsion seemed to be a possible option, then it was almost completely replaced by the teleological mechanism of the 'invisible hand', and after that, their various combinations were tried. And every time thinkers came across the power setting limits to freedom, they sought to minimize its influence and regroup the available 'forces of order', including teleological mechanisms, so that as many decisions as possible were made on the basis of individual choice. This is how political philosophy developed, which produced various theoretical models of the society and state. Let us consider this process from other standpoints.

If we admit that political philosophy, legalizing the economy as a society's constituent, begins with Hobbes, this period can be used as a starting point of the search for efficient distribution of 'forces of order' between the power and teleological mechanisms of socium. First, Hobbes developed the mode of the state where only the Supreme Power possessed the 'energy of order'. Then there appeared the model of the state suggested by the author of *The Fable about Bees*, where the power of compulsion still dominated but acted taking into consideration the *'laissez-faire'* principle. Actually, Mandeville's formula *'private vices – public benefits'* confirmed the redistribution of the energy of order from the power to the teleological mechanism. And finally, the 'forces of order' were regrouped in Smith's liberal doctrine – almost everything was left to the 'invisible hand', the power preserving only a few functions reducible to those of a 'night watchman'.

Considering further evolution of the notion of state, we could speak about a triumph of liberal theory, if it were not for a number of annoying circumstances we come across in our daily life, being the evidence of a still continuing 'struggle with the chaos'. Market failures and interests of society not detected by the market are evidence of system failures in the mechanism of the 'invisible hand', making us consider further redistribution of the 'energy of order'. But this redistribution does not imply moving backwards from the market self-regulation to a wider zone of state decisions. To the contrary, we consider it necessary to create the conditions for purely authoritative powers to be reduced, and the power itself along with its targeted behaviour to be transferred to the market exchange zone, in which the state becomes one of market agents whose actions are coordinated by the teleological mechanism of self-regulation. In this case the 'invisible hand' has to share the 'energy of order', concentrated in it not with the power of compulsion but with another teleological mechanism. We are going to explain our conclusion.

Since Smith, the 'natural inclination to trade and exchange' was considered the basis for a spontaneous order, identifying the goals and resources for their achievement, ensuring well-being of the whole society. Meanwhile, as our analysis has shown, the mechanism of the 'invisible hand' servicing this process fulfils this task only in the zone where public needs are reduced to individual interests. Any infringement of the universality of the reducibility hypothesis takes revenge through an expansion of state powers and growing interventionism, i.e. results in the actual redistribution of the 'energy of order' for the benefit of the power.

That in one teleological mechanism, in a general case, society's goals and resources for their achievement are not separated, does not allow it to ensure the desirable harmony. In this connection, we are reminded that the mechanism of the 'invisible hand', reflecting negative reverse interdependences, allows the adequate representation of only the sociodynamic processes that correspond its movement to society's movement towards equilibrium, and the second component of the society's life, connected with 'leaps onto new levels of complexity' and reflecting the phenomenon of transformation of the energy of positive reverse interdependences into respective social interests, cannot be embraced by this teleological mechanism[262].

We see the solution of this problem in supplementing the 'invisible hand' with another teleological mechanism that is able to detect and actualize irreducible public needs. It is the mechanism of social immunity, involving the sociodynamic processes characterized by a decrease in the entropy and formation of societal interests as such. In a certain way, this teleological mechanism possesses the largest potential of ordering, since it allows for the structuring of fluctuation energy, 'spread' in the socium, in distinct interests of society. Unlike the 'invisible hand', the teleological mechanism of social immunity is not aimed at equilibrium. Acting in the opposite direction, it is responsible for the vector of the society's development.

We shall discuss this important issue in the next section of the book in the context of contemporary state functioning. To conclude this paragraph, we wish to formulate the general view of the state. In our model a state and its directed actions exist in three dimensions: the social immunity reveals irreducible public interests and forms the goals of a state, the power of compulsion provides it with necessary income and ensures the fulfillment of generally- established rules, and the mechanism of the 'invisible hand' realizes the optimum allocation of resources, including the allocation of government funds.

In our opinion, this approach allows the considerable advancement in a protracted dispute about the extent of the state involvement in the economic life. However paradoxical it may be, Friedrich Von Hayek's remark, saying that 'what really matters is not the scale of state activity but its form', is especially topical in the context of this (anti-Hayek) concept, if we consider different forms of the state activities in the context of social immunity: first, in the sphere of realization of powers; and second, in the area of market exchange.

---

[262] We spoke about this in greater detail in Chapter 3 whilst considering Prigogine's theorem of thermodynamics of non-equilibrium processes and its analogue for social systems.

6.3 The State and Social Immunity

Strictly speaking, the teleological mechanism of social immunity is all-sufficient. In any society, social immunity belongs to the sociodynamic processes that, absorbing the energy of external disturbances and positive reverse interdependences, eventually ensure the detection of the true interests of society as such regardless of the state's current position. In this sense, the state's role is always secondary. At the same time, the efficiency of this mechanism depends to a great extent on the social and political environment in general and on a degree of the society's democratization, in particular. From this viewpoint, it is difficult to overestimate the state's significance. These circumstances actually determine the possibilities of analyzing the behaviour of a state in the context of social immunity, reflecting the processes of formation and actualization of irreducible public interests.

Discussing the process of identification of societal goals, let us return to the myth about the 'universality of civic virtues' and reconsider Plato's conclusion. Taking the side of Protagoras in his dialogue with Socrates, let us show the ambiguity of the main thesis of Socrates. As we know, he came to a conclusion that 'it is impossible to learn virtue'[263]. We are going to refute this conclusion.

To that end, we refer to Hegel, who pointed out the capability of people, 'with all their interests and passions, to make something sensible of themselves'[264]. Actually, we would like to consider the most general assumption which was formulated by Locke as an individual's ability to 'realize the necessity of the state association'; by Habermas, as an inevitable result of a discourse (compromise)[265]; and by Buchanan, as a 'rule of universal consensus'[266].

As we see, in different versions the same thing is actually meant; social 'adjustment' of people, realization of the teleological potential underlying their individual desires, the possibility of reaching pre-established harmony in a socium. With regard to this, Plato is wrong: it is possible to learn virtue. We proceed from the assumption that in the process of people's 'social education' and self-adjustment of their preferences, their individual judgements are spontaneously coordinated. This is how the teleological principle manifests itself, ensuring an agreement between all or most people; this is how the 'civic virtue' can become universal or nearly so.

However, this approach is not identical to 'Plato's belief in the existence of truth in the politics, which should be just revealed and then can be explained to sensible

---

[263]Plato. Protagoras (361 a), p. 252.

[264]Hegel G.W.F. Vorlesungen über die Philosophie der Geschichte, in Hegel G.W.F. Werke, Bd.12. Frankfurt/Main: 1969-1971 (Russian Edition: Collected Works. – Moscow, 1932, V.X, p. 222).

[265]Habermas J. Legitimationsprobleme im Spätkapitalismus. – Frankfurt a. M., 1973, p. 155.

[266]Buchanan J., Tullock G. The Calculus of Consent: Logical Foundations of Constitutional Democracy. Ann Arbor Paperbacks, 1962 (Russian Edition: Nobel Prize Winners in Economics. James Buchanan. – Moscow, 1997, p. 129).

people'[267], denounced by Buchanan. We certainly do not share this simplified view. Moreover, we agree with Buchanan that 'the search for any "social interest" independent of specific interests of individual subjects of public choice... is like the search for Holy Grail'[268]. We are absolutely sure that there can be no *a priori* interests of society or 'pseudo-objective norms'[269]. Irreducible public needs, like market equilibrium prices, always exist only *a posteriori*, being formed in the process of a teleological response of socium, which reveals interests of society as such in people's behaviour and actualizes these interests, thereby ensuring their recognition by the majority of individuals[270].

Not everyone is able to perceive a public need and 'see' any other utility but a 'here-and-now' personal benefit. Therefore, if it makes sense to consider the phenomenon of political truth, it should be done only in terms of a public agreement, representing the result of coordination of individual preferences in the process of 'social education'. First, very few people and their groups 'catch' a 'hormone' of a distinct interest produced by the immune system of society. Having adopted the social goals, they persuade other citizens of their importance; in this discourse, as a result of modernization and the accumulation of social experience, individuals come to an agreement, giving up their own preferences in their striving for it[271]. This agreement determines the situation whereby certain collective needs start dominating in the minds of those making decisions on behalf of the whole society. The more perfect its institutions, the shorter this way and the more adequate the social goals.

Now let us consider 'civic virtue', which can be only *nearly* universal. Actually, this 'nearly' accounts for the main distinction of our notions of state from the views of Habermas[272] and Buchanan's model of the state. Repeating Buchanan's elegant formula – 'anarchy is ideal for ideal people; those endowed with passions

---

[267]Buchanan J. The Limits of Liberty: Between Anarchy and Leviathan. Chicago: The University of Chicago Press, 1975 (Russian Edition: Nobel Prize Winners in Economics. James Buchanan. – Moscow, 1997, p. 212).

[268]Buchanan J., Tullock G. The Calculus of Consent, p. 48.

[269]Again, we agree with Buchanan, who writes, 'Even for a person who considers himself an expert, any attempt to establish norms is, at best, useless... and at worst – detrimental, even pernicious' (Buchanan J. The Limits of Liberty, p. 212).

[270]To illustrate this conclusion, we quote Koslowski, who, comparing the views of Buchanan and Habermas, writes, 'Both of them reject the possibility of the existence of truth beyond contacts, beyond the discourse. Before completion of the process on the market, before reckoning up the results of communication, no need, no judgement can be regarded as *a priori* possessing the status of truth' (Koslowski P. Op. cit., p. 255). Obviously, the mechanism for the formation of social interest that we study conforms to this rule.

[271]Habermas defines the discourse as an 'ideal conversation', resulting in an agreement (Habermas J. Zur Logik der theoretischen und praktischen Diskurses // Riedel M. (Hrsg.) Rehabilitierung der praktischen Philosophie. Bd. 2. – Freiburg, 1974, p. 381–402).

[272]Here, we once again quote Koslowski who wrote, 'In Habermas' discourse theory, the problem of power moves to the background' (Koslowski P. Op. cit., p. 258).

must be sensible'[273]–, we emphasize that unanimity is possible only in an ideal society; therefore, the rule of universal consensus is only an 'ideal rule'[274].

All other rules are interpreted by Buchanan as its versions. Justifying their existence, he states, 'They can be rationally chosen not because the collective decisions made according to them will be 'better'... but because high costs of decision making according to the rule of consensus force to deviate from this ideal rule'[275]. Here, Buchanan supplements his 'universal consensus' with Plato's idea of the 'second best', which means that in reality a universal consensus gives place to majority voting. Therefore, the civic virtue is only *nearly* universal.

The same 'nearly' leads to the alteration of the notions of actual 'limits of liberty' and real distribution of the 'energy of order'. Taking into consideration that a consensus exists only as an ideal norm, and specific public interests are recognized only by the majority, stress must be placed on the fact that the realization of these interests is always based on the power of compulsion, that is compulsion of the minority of people, showing their inability to modify themselves (according to Habermas) and failing to see their egoistic interests in the current goals of society. To the extent that civic virtue is actually not universal, the power of compulsion must supplement the teleological mechanism of social immunity, which has determined and actualized public goals, ensuring their achievement in the form of the 'second best'.

We want to emphasize that any compulsion is fraught with two outcomes, and each of them should be considered separately. First, 'compulsion to happiness' of those who failed to see any link between personal benefits and the realization of collective interest continues the process of their forced 'teaching' by the state, making the said link more visible. The above sociodynamic multiplier mechanism can transform societal institutions so that the changed value orientations and behavioural norms bring public interest out of its 'non-transparent zone'[276]. Visible personal benefits would make the 'compelled minority' fewer in number and lead to universal consensus (in the limit). It is in this particular case that the public interest becomes reducible and completely dissolves in individual preferences, the 'second best' becomes the 'best' and there is no longer a need for power of compulsion. Habermas and Buchanan must have considered this situation when speaking about the inevitability of consensus.

Second, authoritative actions can generate quite the opposite situation when state involvement in realizing the interest of majority does not result in this inter-

---

[273]Buchanan J. The Limits of Liberty, p. 209.

[274]Buchanan J., Tullock G. The Calculus of Consent, p. 129.

[275]Ibid.

[276]We spoke about this in detail in the third chapter of this book, when discussing one of the key notions of our concept, the sociodynamic multiplier of economic growth. We showed, in particular, that institutions determine the extent of 'visibility' for individuals of the consequences of the realization of irreducible public interests. Modernization of the institutional environment due to the sociodynamic multiplier can alter behavioural norms in such a manner that collective needs will be perceived by separate individuals as their own interests and in this sense will become visible.

est's 'adoption' and individualization by the compelled minority. Correcting the state's mistakes, caused by the wrong understanding of society's interests or their distortion due to interests of 'special groups'[277], the socium's immune system detects a new interest of representatives of the compelled minority, alternative to the majority's preferences.

So, the society's teleological response to the suppression of its minority's interests may bring about the opposite results. In this rather common case it is easy to see the mechanism of positive reverse interdependence trigger the process of forming new social interests, of their gradual spreading and further recognition by the majority of people. Here it is also possible to eventually give up the society's current goals, thus achieving universal consensus on the basis of their denial on a higher level of complexity and adoption of new social interests.

We want to again emphasize that the socium's immune system is all-sufficient and eventually ensures the revelation of society's true interests. However the time this process takes depends on state actions. Therefore, its rational behaviour – contributing to the determination and actualization of public interests at early stages – requires an attentive and careful attitude towards the minority. This part of society is 'inhabited' by passionaries, able to 'see things covered by the veil of time' for most of people. Therefore, *support for the passionary minority (creation of the most favourable conditions for it)* is the most essential principle of the state's rational behaviour.

We will deal with this issue in the final chapter, in which we present the general principles of rational state behaviour in three spheres of its activities, connected with the issues of market exchange.

---

[277]Speaking about the state's mistakes, we are not going to compare them with market failures. We can refer to Buchanan, who sees intellectual bankruptcy in this shopworn comparison. 'In social and political regard, the 1970s could be called the years of intellectual bankruptcy. Economists adherent to the theory of well-being continue to discover sophisticated examples of market failures; those supporting the theory of public choice, who were accused of amateur involvement in "politics of well-being", supplement the work of advocates of "economics of well-being", giving their examples of state failures... In the 1970s an individual faces a dilemma. He understands that two great alternatives, *laissez-faire* and socialism, are dying, and we can hardly expect their revival'. (Buchanan J. The Limits of Liberty, pp. 429–430). In this case, the existence of the state's failures is important for us so far as it is essential for the description of the functioning of the teleological mechanism of social immunity.

7 The Rational Behavior of the State

Let us again refer to our concept of the state and its actions in three spheres: in the sphere of social immunity, where societal interests and the goals of the state itself are formed; in the sphere of the realization of state powers, which provide it with necessary income and ensure the fulfillment of generally established rules; and in the sphere of market exchange, within which the mechanism of the 'invisible hand' realizes the optimum allocation of resources, including the allocation of government funds. In brackets, we note that all types of state activities are somehow connected with its economic functions (that is, its behavior as an independent market player).

We certainly understand that the fundamental characteristics of a state – proceeding from the unique character of demand (irreducibility), the specific composition of income (collection of taxes) and concluding with the motivation for the expenditure of budget funds (in exchange for social utility) – demand the elaboration of an adequate mechanism for its market behavior. It should be kept in mind that the contemporary state is neither outside the boundaries of the market economy, nor above the market economy, but is built-in organically within its structures.

Here we wish point out the ambivalent characteristic of modern theory regarding state involvement in economic life. On the one hand, mainstream theory does not allow for state interventions; on the other hand theory following practice must consider the issues of stimulating an aggregate effective demand, employment, monetary and industrial policy, and other aspects of the economy's functioning. In these cases economists deliberately or unconsciously deviate from the canons of the mainstream and try to find sensible solutions based on the analysis of the economic practice or simply on common sense.[278]

---

[278]See Nekipelov A. Studies on Post-Communism Economics – M. 1996. Considering the seventh study on issues of state regulation in the post-communist economy and formulating the heretical question about the state in the market sphere – 'Night Watchman' or an active subject of economic life?' – the author summarizes his analysis, 'The state's objectives in the process of post-communist transformation must not be limited to the liberalization of economic activity' (p. 238). Moreover, contrary to the radical views of the adherents to market theory, A. Nekipelov insists on the necessity and expediency of state interference in the form of the regulation of aggregate demand (pp. 204–210, 240), control over privatization (pp. 213–216), and implementation of respective industrial policy (pp. 217–231, 239). We once again stress that most of the author's arguments are based on concrete analysis and common sense.

Meanwhile, the situation changes fundamentally if instead of a 'middle-of-the-road' wording ('active subject of economic life'[279]) we choose more definite positions of economic sociodynamics, proceeding from the assumption that the state is a market agent like all others. In this case there is a real opportunity to add the required theoretical generalizations to useful common sense. Then it would be possible to resolve the protracted dispute of whether there should be more or less state in contemporary economic life and what types of activities should be legitimated.

Let us make another preliminary remark. Analyzing the behaviour of the bearer of irreducible public needs, we try to answer two questions. What interests us is how the government funds are formed, and what the state should do for their optimum use. Like any other market player, the state has scarce resources that it spends on maximizing its utility. But, unlike ordinary market players, the state – though using the resources obtained from them – aims at maximizing the social utility, not individual ones. It is within this context that the main principles of contemporary state behaviour should be considered.

This approach allows not only the adequate evaluation of the role of a state in different spheres of its functioning but also, applying the Pareto scheme, the formulation an important definition relating to the criterion of its activities. *The behaviour of a state is considered rational if it implements Pareto-improvement while maximizing the social utility.* We are going to consider the state's functioning in the context of social immunity based on this criterion.

7.1 The Principle of Minority Support

We start with the point with which we finished in the previous chapter, having formulated one of the fundamental principles of state functioning connected with the creation of the most favourable conditions for the passionary minority. Taking into consideration the fundamental nature of this principle (for creating the channels for the revelation of irreducible public interests rather than for building a democratic society), allowing society to develop by ensuring its 'leaps onto new levels of complexity', we should consider specific mechanisms for the realization of this principle of rational state behaviour.

Before we discuss this essential topic in the context of the state's functioning as a market agent, however, we wish to examine the realization of this principle in specific examples, confirming our conclusion and demonstrating that when the state tries to support the minority and 'open' the channels between its passionaries and the whole society, it evidently wins.

> Example 7.1. *Glasnost in the USSR and its historical consequences.* Recalling the phenomenon of glasnost in the context of economic sociodynamics, the raising of the information blockade of Soviet citizens during the late 1980s should be regarded as the actualization of respective social interest.

---

[279]Ibid., p. 238.

'Charged' with the immune energy of the socium, its passionaries managed to breach a carefully guarded building of 'the only true' communist ideology. Andrey Sakharov, Peter Grigorenko, Andrey Sinyavsky, Yury Daniel, Vassily Grossman, Alexander Zinoviev, Roy Medvedev, Vladimir Bukovsky, Natan Shcharansky, Alexander Solzhenitsyn, Ernst Neizvestny, Victor Nekrasov, Yury Lyubimov with his Theatre, and a number of other outstanding representatives of the passionary minority, 'having opened many people's eyes', drew society's attention back to democratic ideas and liberal values. Under their influence, political discussions 'in the kitchen' and 'sam-izdat' (clandestine publication of banned literature) became so widespread that even the main bearer of totalitarian traditions – the state authorities – adopted the public need for removal of information bans, which was revealed through the mechanism of social immunity.

Glasnost, declared by Michail Gorbachev, opened informational gateways and over a short period of time changed public consciousness. Elimination of censorship, discontinued jamming of foreign radio stations, demonstration of formerly banned films, publication of formerly banned books, political activity in creative unions and an abrupt increase in international contacts ruined the monopoly on truth and radically changed the ideology of the Soviet society during the final period of its history. The country, which had for a long time been isolated from the rest of the world by an iron curtain, assimilated the ideals common to all mankind and humanistic values with an immense speed. It can be stated without reserve that glasnost, declared in the 1980s, became a decisive factor for the formation of the qualitatively new institutional environment in the changing Russia of the 1990s.

We do not approve of the policy chosen in Russia in 1992. Moreover, we are convinced that mistakes made in the economic reform process in the 1990s blocked its natural development for many years and conditioned Russia's lagging behind the majority of European countries possessing far smaller economic potential. In the 1990s, the country made an immense leap from the centrally planned economy to the market. Now that some time passed, it is evident that this mainstream of Russian society's development was prepared in the era of glasnost. It was the time when everybody got an opportunity to hear the voice of few, supporting the pluralistic democracy and market economy, and it was glasnost that conditioned the modernization of the institutional environment which made the system transformation possible.

Example 7.2. *Dissidents and reforms in post-socialist countries.* This example shows a connection between the suppressed dissent and decreased efficiency of market transformations in the countries of Central and Eastern Europe. In some socialist countries during the mid-1960s, the dissident movement started to develop, its participants vowing to protect human rights, the supremacy of the law and other liberal and democratic values. Since then up to the beginning of Gorbachev's era, these passionaries were continuously pursued and subject to repression by the state. For different reasons, the extent of power structure pressure on dissidents was not equal in all countries. In some of them – for example, Romania and Czechoslovakia (after August 1968) – the pursuit of dissent was the most consistent and tough; in others, like Hungary and Poland, the state allowed a wider space for individual freedoms and showed some tolerance towards passionaries' activities.

In the late 1980s – early 1990s, the wave of democratic revolutions, accompanied by the system transformation of the state structure and market reforms, radically changed the countries under consideration, and it turned out that the positive economic dynamics were characteristic of those countries having better institutional preparedness for market reforms, and to the contrary, in the countries where market reforms were not accompanied by the creation of an adequate institutional environment, GDP decline recurred. In Poland and Hungary, where market institutions therefore became firmly established, sustainable economic growth is reported. At the same time in Romania and even in the Czech Republic an adequate institutional infrastructure was not formed, which to a great extent predetermined negative social and economic dynamics in these countries during the last years of the 20th century.

In general, it can be stated that institutional progress in 'successful' countries was preceded by a relatively tolerant attitude to the dissent. Actually, a rather high level of tolerance by authorities in some socialist countries and opportunities for the spread of 'banned' liberal values formed the prerequisites for the adoption of the market and the respective behavioral norms of those brought up according to anti-market traditions. The dissidents-passionaries, breaching the ideological monolith of totalitarian regimes, gained a kind of institutional bridgehead for further market reforms. It is evident that market reforms had more chances to succeed in the countries where the pursuit of those dissenting was weaker.

Of course, we should not forget about the bloody suppression during the Hungarian revolution in 1956 and the introduction of martial law into Poland in 1981. However, unlike Czechoslovakia – where after suppression of the 'Prague spring', authorities started and for almost twenty years waged a total war against the dissident movement –, Hungary and Poland preserved at least a minimum degree of dissent in the public form. This 'gulp of freedom' sustained the 'dozing' public interest and to a great extent promoted the success of further reforms.

The 'delicate' treatment of the minority has always been characteristic of real democracy. The views of the 71st wise man in the great Sanhedrim of ancient Israel and the political structure of this supreme legislative and juridical body (with the main debater – *av-bet-din* – protecting the minority's positions), parliamentary opposition in modern political systems and, finally, the 'right to veto' in a number of international organizations – all prove that the issue of protection of minority's interest has always been the focus of attention in democratic societies. This fundamental component of the state structure is a matter of special concern for both social philosophers and economists.

Friedrich Von Hayek, writes about it maybe better (at least more passionately) than all others, 'No group of people is allowed to hold sway over others' thoughts and views. If the dissent is not suppressed in a society, there are always some people who doubt the ideas popular among their contemporaries and start to popularize new ideas, presenting them for others' judgement'[280]. An attentive reader must have already noticed that we actually spoke of the same when describing the mechanism of social immunity in the previous chapters. A teleological response of the society to ignoring the interests of its minority can lead to the formation of a new social interest and its gradual spreading among the citizens. Not to lose this opportunity vital for a socium, a rationally-acting state must support the passionary minority. We fully concur with these views of Hayek.

The conviction in the necessity of minority support along with the distrust of any democratic voting procedures makes this representative of the Austrian economic school go further and conditions his requirement to record the rights of the minority in the constitution. 'The choice is, either free parliament or free people. To preserve personal freedom, the power – even that of a democratic parliament – should be limited by the long-term principles approved by people'.[281] We will not deny that these views are especially close to ours, and that we are inclined to agree with almost all recipes of this kind.

Hayek's general principle is also manifested in his constitutional theory, where the traditional parliament is substituted for three representative bodies, 'the first meant for dealing exclusively with the constitution (it would meet at long intervals, only when amendments to the constitution are required); the second, for continuous improvement in the code of justice; the third for current rule, i.e. for managing the public resources'[282]. This system's specificity lies in its evident orientation towards the constitutional limitation of the 'arbitrariness of power', even democratic, and establishment of clear limits to its use by the state of its monopoly on compulsion.

Buchanan and Tullock are known for even more radical views. They wrote, 'Any concept of government activities dividing the society into ruling and oppressed classes and regarding the political process as a simple means of ensuring class domination should be rejected... in any case, regardless of whether the ruling class consists of owners of production factors, according to Marx, party aristocrats or representatives of the *unanimous majority*'[283]. We have italicized the last words in this quotation to stress Buchanan's maximalism regarding protection of the minority's interests. For the creator of constitutional economics, the only acceptable form of state policy is the one aimed at consensus or unanimity among all members of society.

---

[280]Hayek F.A. The Road to Serfdom. Chicago: The University of Chicago Press, 1994 ((Russian Edition – Moscow, 1992, p. 124).

[281]Hayek F.A. The political order of a free people, Chicago, Ill.: Univ. of Chicago Press, 1979 (Russian Edition – Society of Free People. Overseas Publ. Interchange, London, 1990, p. 155).

[282]Ibid., p. 69.

[283]Buchanan J, Tullock G. The Calculus of Consent, p. 48.

Not repeating what has already been said about the feasibility of this consensus, and moreover, regarding the unanimity as a plausible final result, let us pay attention to interim states of society. Here, the problem which Hayek is so worried about and Buchanan does not examine at all actually arises; it is then that the ruling majority, 'armed' with collective interests, compels the dissident citizens to 'happiness' quite democratically. In this common situation, the state should act as a guarantor of the interests of the compelled minority. We repeat that in our model, the principle of the most favourable treatment of passionaries is the basis for the rational behaviour of the state.

The realization of this principle requires the creation of institutions ensuring the protection of minority interests, constitutional norms and a system of formal and informal regulations covering all levels of government. Not going deep into problems of the constitution, transcending the topic of this book, and setting aside the formation of respective ideology, we shall only consider the regulations having juridical status.

Rather rich experience relating to this issue is accumulated both on the state level and on the level of territories and communities. It is enough to mention such protective norms as 'human rights' (now dominating all over the democratic world), 'qualified majority' in the management of joint stock companies in Russia and Europe, and the 'rule of twenty percent protest'[284] applied in the USA to see a wide spectrum of the state activities in the sphere of social immunity, in a sort of 'social broth' where the teleological mechanism forms collective interests.

Analyzing the rational behaviour of the state, we cannot ignore another essential issue: ensuring the freedom of speech and press, recognized throughout the democratic world. These are the institutions that to a great extent carry out a society's interest in support for its passionary minority. Developing and adopting laws on mass media, parliaments of many courtiers aimed to ensure independence of publishing, television and radio companies[285]. However, the historical experience of some countries, especially Russia, shows the vivid insufficiency of such measures. Political and economic interests of competing parties, as well as temptation for the state itself, turned out to be so strong that the 'independent' mass media have preserved their independence only in legal documents. Ignoring the fundamental norms of a democratic society that entails the information blockade of its passionary minority always results in impediments for society's development and the conservation of institutions harmful for the society. There is another example from Russia's recent past.

---

[284]We mean the rule according to which the use of any land property can be changed, the majority making the decision should overcome the 20% barrier. In other words, if one-fifth of neighbours consider that the decision imposed on them by the majority is not right, the state ensures protection of interests for the minority of land owners.

[285]In the Russian Federation, several special laws have this purpose: the Laws of the Russian Federation 'On Mass Media' (December 1991) and 'On Copyright and Related Rights' (July 1993), the Federal Law of the Russian Federation 'On State Support for Mass Media and Publishing Industry' (December 1995).

Example 7.3. *The mass media and the 1999 parliamentary elections in Russia.* In the summer of 1999, full control over the mass media was established by two concerned political clans. As a result of the establishment of a media holding by V. Gussinsky and acquisition of TV6 by B. Berezovsky, the electronic mass media completely lost their independence. Since then, ORT, RTR, TV6 and Culture channel actually became a mouthpiece of the governmental block, while NTV and TV-Centre started to service the interests of Moscow Mayor. Thus, by the beginning of election to the State Duma (1999) the 'political expediency' and 'friend-or-foe' treatment occupied the screen, and dissidents found themselves in the information blockade. Negative results of irrational actions of the state manifested themselves very soon.

Broadcasting was dominated by journalists fulfilling political assignments. Their programs, intentionally distorting the multi-coloured real world, propagated its black-and-white image, showing the binary logic of two rivalry clans' behavior, 'who is not with us is against us'. In a confrontation of election technologies without any moral limits, in a tough war of discreditable materials, the Russian society lost. It did not matter which of the political blocks won the elections or which one was more progressive. The whole society lost, and this defeat immediately revealed itself in a dramatic reduction of passionaries' influence, in the lessening of their energy vital for the socium.

When dissent is lacking, people are less able to independently evaluate the surrounding world and 'notice' a true public interest in time. This is the explanation for a radical change in the Russian society's attitude towards the first and second Chechen wars. And again what really matters is not who is to blame for these wars and whether they are aimed at national liberation or against terrorists. We have to state that a direct result of the information blockade of passionaries during the hostilities of 1999–2000 was the moral erosion of the society itself and total oblivion of humanistic norms, according to which death of innocent people can never be justified. There is no doubt about the state's responsibility for these negative shifts in the public consciousness.

Digressing from the election of 1999, such irrational behavior of the state that ignored the interests of the passionary minority and contributed to the journalists' voluntary repudiation of their professional duty in favor of 'political expediency' had brought about another negative result, the 'voluntary' adoption of the almost monarchic constitution by the young Russian democracy in 1993. Returning to an analysis of the situation of 1999–2000, we wish like to draw attention to the fact that after parliamentary elections and the resignation of Boris Yeltsin (December 31, 1999), the information blockade of the dissent continued. The voice of passionaries who called for the amendments to the constitution aimed at limiting the president's powers was once again not heard. In the first quarter of 2000, Russia missed its second chance for democratization, when instead of considering possibilities of redistribution of the president's powers in favor of the government and Duma, the country's political elite strove to improve its positions within the existing power institutions.

These facts from Russia's recent past show a common pattern of the weakening of the socium's immune system as a result of ignoring the voice of the passionary minority. Under such conditions, a society starts to lose its ability to resist antisocial forces. In other words, the immune system of a socium weakens so that there appears a threat of the conservation of institutions harmful for it. The historical experience shows that even in mature democracies it may result in the legalization or voluntary acceptance by the society of political dictatorship. This trend should always be resisted. Among the means of preventing such negative trends in societal development, a special place should be occupied by the determined actions of the state aimed at supporting the passionary minority.

It is no doubt that many other, not less striking, examples can be found. But this 'long story' about contemporary state activities transcends our study. In conclusion to this paragraph devoted to the rational behaviour of the state in the context of social immunity, we are going to show only one of the ways to apply the principle of the most favoured treatment of the passionary minority in practice.

The creation of the economic mechanism – in addition to existing legislation – could ensure the real independence of the mass media, maintaining a free tribune for the dissent so important for society. Though the sphere of market exchange should be a subject of special discussion, we shall demonstrate here the nature and contents of the said mechanism.

Here we wish to direct attention to state support for some mass media acting in the market environment. First, what are these media? Evidently, any autonomous market players whose activities are aimed at deriving profit should not be included in this category. Therefore, the object of state support is only printed and electronic mass media representing the so-called third sector, non-profit organizations[286]. But we should also exclude all publishing, tele- and radio broadcast companies supported in the form of direct subsidies, donations and price benefits provided by any legal entities and individuals. In other words, only those mass media financially independent of any political forces should rely on state support.

Of course, we do not insist on the correctness of our proposition. Moreover, it seems that in practice it is very difficult to formalize qualitative notions such as 'independence'. We merely seek to emphasize that the realization of the society's specific interest in preservation of independent mass media must not go beyond really independent printed and electronic media. With this in mind, state support for any private television broadcast company – for example, NTV[287] in Germany –

---

[286]Activities of these organizations are regulated in Russia by the Law of the Russian Federation 'On Non-Profit Organizations' (December 1993) and Articles 50, 116-123 of the first part of the Civil Code of the Russian Federation (October 1994).

[287]This refers to the benefits provided to this private television broadcast company in 1995, before the presidential election of 1996.

seems to be either unfair use of public resources or their absolutely impermissible squandering.

Second, consider the issue of the legitimacy of state support in a market economy. To see the rationality of such actions, one should understand that this is a market deal: a state exchanges a part of budget funds for the social utility of independent mass media. It is easy to show that in this case the state can ensure Pareto-improvement.

> Example 7.4. *State support for the independent mass media.* Suppose the marginal social utility complementing the marginal individual utility does not cover the marginal costs of services produced by a television broadcast company. This situation threatens a partial loss of independence by the television broadcast company in the case of 'acceptance of support' provided by some concerned political forces, the direct consequence being societal losses in the form of reduction of social utility of information services provided by the company in question. Therefore, an increase in budget subsidies or an expansion of other forms of state support for this company can be recognized as justifiable actions ensuring Pareto-improvement. Such behavior can be regarded as rational, since an improvement in the state's well-being does not result in worsening other market agents' positions, and their additional tax burden is offset by the secondary benefits from having an independent tribune for the dissent and ensuring the democratic foundations for the state.

Third, consider the forms of state support. We think that in this case the state has a rather wide range of instruments, from direct budget subsidies, price and tax benefits, to state orders for the implementation of special information projects. The general principle – spending budget funds for realizing the social interest – is still the main one.

In this section, we have considered only one specific situation concerning state expenditures for servicing the economic mechanism ensuring the most favoured treatment of the passionary minority, this mechanism being applied only to support for the mass media. However, the analysis of only one specific situation shows that any state activity requires respective funds. Let us therefore consider another sphere of state functioning, that sphere in which these funds are formed.

7.2 Realization of State Powers and the Principle of Correspondence

Any state behaviour depends on its goals not achieved in the process of satisfaction of individual needs, and on the available resources, including the ratio of private and public ownership for material and financial resources (production factors, real estate, revenues, etc.). We consider behaviour of a state rational only if it realizes Pareto-improvement along with maximizing the social utility.

In other words, any actions of the state connected with changing the ratio of private and public ownership must be in full compliance with the imperative of correspondence of the goals to the resources required for their achievement. It directly proceeds from the fact that if there is no such correspondence, it is always possible to reallocate resources between individuals and the state so that a new ratio of private and public ownership compared to the old one will be Pareto-improvement. Actually, this proposition reflects the second principle for the rational behaviour of a state, applying mainly to the sphere of realization of state powers.

Keeping in mind this imperative of correspondence between the goals and funds of the state, we'd like to note that its functioning reflects a process of the two-way movement of material and financial resources. In one case these are transferred from a separate individual to a group of people, their community and society as a whole, i.e. resources are socialized. In the other case, privatization in a broad sense takes place; material and financial resources flow from the society as a whole to communities, groups and individuals. For instance, the right to collect taxes is transferred to communities of a lower level and the total tax burden is lessened.

A decisive motive for the *socialization of resources* is the actualization of respective public interests and the impossibility of realizing them at a lower level of a community. The main directions of the socialization of resources are the nationalization of private property and introduction of additional taxes, duties and charges. It should be emphasized that not every act of resource socialization can be recognized as a state's rational action. The principle of correspondence requires that any actions of this kind ensure Pareto-improvement.

It is often impossible, however, to prove that positions of separate market players do not worsen when, using the power of compulsion and proceeding from its specific interests, the state takes away the resources owned by its subjects. Difficulties connected with the evaluation of the rationality of state behaviour as for its actions aimed at the socialization of resources are conditioned by the circumstances we considered in detail in previous chapters. Here we are referring to the 'non-transparency' of institutional environment, not allowing one to see many secondary benefits from the realization of the interest of society as such.

Actually, this is the reason why Pareto-improvement cannot immediately be seen in socializing a part of individuals' resources and their spending for fundamental research, education, culture, etc. It is possible to prove the fact of Pareto-improvement only using the sociodynamic multiplier mechanism. However, there are less complicated situations in which this relationship is more vivid. The following example demonstrates the rationality of state behaviour in the case of an additional tax introduction.

> Example 7.5. *Introduction of a 'tax on blank cassettes'.* We are going to quote a historical document elaborated on during the All-Russian Theatre Forum 'Theatre: Period of Change', which took place in Moscow on March 1–2, 1999. By that time, most repertoire theatres in Russia were close to the

poverty line. Therefore, the issue of additional budgetary support became vital for those employed in this sphere.

After discussing the state of affairs, the Forum participants approved an address to the President of the Russian Federation, the Federal Assembly and the Government of the RF, wherein they formulated a number of the most essential suggestions, whose purpose was to 'prevent the ruin of the Russian state repertoire theatre, at the same time providing living conditions for new theatrical entities, creating a competitive environment, which would provide an equal access to spectators and public resources for all those participating in the theatrical life regardless of their status. Only in this case the Russian stage can come up with new artistic ideas and achievements of actors and directors, for the sake of which the scenic art exists'. The society's actualized interest in the preservation of repertoire theatres required additional resources.

This famous address suggested concrete measures aimed at searching for new sources of budgetary financing, including recommendations to introduce special deductions (sales proceeds tax) paid by producers or importers of equipment (audio and video recorders etc.) and carriers (audio and video cassettes, CDs, etc.) designed for personal use. Considering the expediency of this tax introduction, one can show that this measure complies not only with the above principle of correspondence but also with the conditions for rational state behavior, i.e. the financial performance of the state and hence of the producers of cultural goods is improved, while the taxpayers' situation does not worsen.

This conclusion is based on the fact that, in the case of introduction of the 'tax on blank cassettes', the obvious internalization of externalities takes place, which in a certain sense fully corresponds with the conditions of the well-known Coase theorem. Here, we can actually speak about the specification of property rights (in this case the intellectual property rights). Inadequate regulation and ineffective protection of the rights of creators of art works and simplicity of 'free' appropriation of these rights through the recording or re-recording of art works on blank cassettes result in unreasonably high revenues for manufacturers and/or importers of audio and video equipment and carriers. Therefore, withdrawal of this 'unearned' income by means of the 'tax on blank cassettes' and its further reallocation through the state budget for the benefit of creators of art works is an evident Pareto-improvement[288].

---

[288] A kind of the 'tax on blank cassettes' was introduced in most European countries in the late 1970s – early 1980s. In a limited form this norm is recorded in Article 26 of the Law of the Russian Federation 'On Copyright and Related Rights': as 'deductions from revenues of manufacturers and/or importers of equipment and carriers based on contracts with organizations managing the property rights of authors, producers of records and performers'.

Along with a recovery of correspondence between the goals and resources required for their achievement, the rationality of *privatization* is tied with a presumption of the inefficient use of resources owned by the state, including municipal and other levels of realization of its powers. Privatization can be initiated by arising possibility of a transfer of public goals to a lower level of the community or to completely give up these goals in connection with increased abilities of individuals to satisfy their needs – formerly a matter of the state concern – on their own. Here is an example of denationalization meeting the criterion of the rationality of state behaviour.

> Example 7.6. *Privatization of the state property in Western European countries.* The waves of denationalization that swept across Great Britain and France in the 1980s can be regarded as an obvious success for the privatization of state enterprises. About one-third of all state enterprises were sold in Great Britain, providing a moderate increase in budget revenues but a considerable growth in production efficiency within those enterprises that became private. Actually, everyone benefited: the state, employers and employees. The shares of privatized companies were bought mainly by institutional investors (banks and insurance companies). Individual investors accounted for only about 20% of the shares. At the first stage of privatization the employees' wages remained unchanged, and they had some privatization benefits. For example, when British Gas stock was sold, all employees of that corporation were provided with 52 free shares each. In addition, two shares were given free with each one bought. It is important to remember that in Great Britain mostly non-competitive and unprofitable enterprises in the coal, electric and gas industries, as well as aviation and railway transport were privatized. As a result, most experienced increased production efficiency, wages grew and the gradual modernization of production facilities began.
>
> In France the mass wave of privatization, which also started in the second half of the 1990s, mostly covered highly profitable branches. Most international experts agree that the French Government managed to 'get rid' of its property at maximum prices. In any case, they were usually much higher than compensatory payments made during the nationalization, which had been carried out before. Over the said period, the treasury obtained about USD15 billion, which considerably reduced the burden of public debt. In this case we can also speak about the rationality of state behavior. Its position being improved, the well-being of employers and employees was maintained or even improved. Newly privatized enterprises remained actually as profitable as before, which could not but satisfy their new owners. As for the employees, they maintained their incomes and in addition obtained 10% of these enterprises' capital at a reduced price.

Realization of the principle of correspondence means, among other things, the establishment of a hierarchy of social goals: *on a higher level only those that are not achievable on a lower level can be recognized.* Recognition of the social goals on a higher level entails a transfer of the resources required for their achievement to this level. This relates to the whole system of federal, regional and local taxes. On every level of the hierarchy, members of the community are provided with 'service packages' meeting the social interests of that level.

Summarizing the motives for the socialization or privatization of material and financial resources, we would like to give another formulation of the principle of correspondence. An association of a higher level only possesses those material and financial resources that conform to the goals (interests) of this association as such and that cannot be realized on a lower level of association of people. As a matter of fact, this formulation is a projection of Pareto-efficient allocation of resources on state behaviour. If the principle in question is observed, and if the state, acting rationally, maintains the correspondence between goals and resources necessary to reach them, a firm basis for an equilibrium and further evolution appears[289].

When the correspondence between the goals and resources required for their achievement is upset, society starts to suffer from negative effects. Therefore, any excessive material and financial resource possessed by the state mean their direct squandering, since to infringe upon the principle of correspondence means to lose an opportunity for Pareto-improvement, i.e. an improvement in well-beings of ordinary market agents by means of returning to them a part of socialized resources without any detriment to the state's ability to meet irreducible public needs. In this case, rational state behaviour must be directed toward the liquidation of resource excess through privatization of the respective share of state property.

A specific situation is observed when the infringement of the principle of correspondence is caused by privatization. The incorrectly-performed privatization involving the transfer of state property to private persons at reduced prices (e.g. without taking into consideration the social utility of the privatized good) results in infringement of the principle of correspondence and generates a kind of *social rent*. Since we consider this fact theoretically and practically important, we are going to prove the 'theorem on social rent'.

Suppose that the good G, possessing the marginal individual utility MU_G and marginal social utility MSU_G, is owned by a state and, other things being equal, the principle of correspondence is observed. This means that, in addition to direct incomes from the individual use of the good, its being in the state ownership allows the realization of the respective goals of society, i.e. ensures appropriation of indirect incomes equal to the marginal social utility $P^2 = MSU_G$.

Now consider the situation when, as a result of privatization, a private market agent acquires the proprietary right to the good G at a price P^1, equal to the capi-

---

[289]The point of equilibrium that corresponds to the generalized Pareto scheme corresponds to the equation of marginal costs to logical sum of individual and social utilities. And only in a particular case when the state has no actualized need for a good and therefore no resources to meet it, the above condition turns into the classical equation of marginal costs to marginal individual utility. In general when setting a *price for any good, including that owned by the state,* the good's social utility must be taken into account.

talized revenue from this good[290]. Let the sale price of the good be lower than its full price P^1, since it corresponds only to its marginal individual utility: $P^1 = MU_G$. This privatization deal does not take into account the social component of the good G equal to its marginal social utility MSU_G. In other words, the following equations are true: $P^1 = MU_G$ (1) and $P = MU_G$ & MSU_G (2).

Evidently, the principle of correspondence is not infringed upon in only two cases. First, if in estimating the capitalized income both individual and social utilities of the good are taken into account. Second, if the sale of state property at a reduced price (without taking into consideration its social utility) is accompanied by the delegation to a new owner of tasks whose fulfilment allows the realization of the respective goals of society.

In the case under consideration, the principle of correspondence is infringed upon. State property is transferred to a private owner at a reduced price P^1 without imposing respective obligations on him. As a result of this deal, the privatized good G loses its social utility, and the state, having received one constituent of the revenue equal to P^1, is deprived of its other constituent equal to the marginal social utility of the good $P^2 = MSU_G$.

It is also evident that in this case the lost social utility of the privatized good MSU_G turns into excessive revenue of its new owner I_R. In other words, equations (1) and (2) allow us to conclude that the excessive revenue of the new owner is equal to the good's social utility lost by the state: $I_R = MSU_G$ (3). The revealed excessive revenue is rental in nature, and since it is equal to the lost social utility of the good, this revenue can be called social rent.

The provided proof allows the consideration of a rather wide range of application of this fundamental theorem. In fact, any privatization of state property aimed at economic growth – keeping in mind the presumption of inefficient use of resources owned by the state – can always have a reverse side, an infringement of the principle of correspondence and obtaining of excessive revenue (social rent) by a small group of people. Let us consider a number of examples illustrating the phenomenon of social rent arising in different sectors of the Russian economy.

> Example 7.7. *Privatization of an oil refinery.* Assume that 60% of shares of the *Petroller* concern (its annual output being 1 million tons of petrol) is owned by the state, which, according to the respective goals of society, pursues the policy of petrol price restrictions, reining in on the inflation growth of costs in the country's economy. Due to the reduced price level, income of *Petroller* is less than it could be without state interference. The state appropriates two types of effect: proceeds from the sale of fuel and the social utility of the control over inflation. This utility can be estimated as the budget expenditures that would be required to compensate the inflation growth of costs in the country's economy. The floor of these expenditures or social util-

---

[290]When estimating the capitalized revenue, only the actual monetary revenue obtained over the year before privatization is taken into account. For simplicity, we do not consider the issue of revenue discounting here, assuming that the discount period and the discount rate are known.

ity can be computed-based on the difference between the prices for petrol established by the law and those formed on the market.

Suppose one of the budget items includes revenues equal to 3,000 roubles per ton of fuel plus the marginal social utility of fuel equal to 2,000 roubles per ton. Then the total annual state revenue obtained from this concern amounts to 3.8 billion roubles = 1 million tons x (0.6 x 3,000 roubles + 2,000 roubles). Let us also assume that due to a lower level of income from petrol sale, the concern's shares are quoted on the exchange lower than it could be in the case of a removal of price restrictions. Let the value of the state share holding of *Petroller* (60%) be 18 billion roubles and the annual revenue 1.8 billion roubles.

Under such conditions the decision is made to privatize the concern, i.e. to sell the share holding owned by the state. As a result of this privatization deal, the state budget receives 18 billion roubles, a new owner is entitled to set selling prices for his petrol, the fuel loses its social utility, *Petroller* becomes a privately-owned concern, price of fuel increases from 3,000 to 5,000 roubles per ton, and quotations of *Petroller* stock grow (in particular, the value of the acquired 60% share holding increases from 18 billion to 30 billion roubles).

As a result of privatization, the new owner gained and the state lost 12 billion roubles = 30 billion roubles – 18 billion roubles. The annual loss of the state (the lost social utility) is 2 billion roubles = 1 million tons x 2,000 roubles, which transformed into an excessive income for the private owner equal to the 'privatized' social rent: 2 billion roubles = 1 million tons x (5,000 roubles – 3,000 roubles).

Example 7.8. *Privatization of a state television broadcast company.* Suppose 100% of shares of the company *TV-13* (with 250,000 air min. per year) is owned by the state, which, according to the cultural and information policy and respective social goals, restricts the commercial advertising on TV, thus ensuring a higher aesthetic level of programs. With advertisement being limited to 10,000 air minutes per year, the income of *TV-13* diminishes. But in addition to revenues from the sold air time, the state appropriates the social utility of the artistic and information product.

Keeping in mind the conditional character of the considered example, let us imagine that state revenues gained from *TV-13* consist of revenues from commercials (100,000 roubles per air minute) and the marginal social utility of TV programs, also equal to 100,000 roubles per air minute. Therefore, the total annual revenue of the state gained from *TV-13* is 25 billion roubles = 100,000 roubles/min. x (10,000 min. + 240,000 min.). Let us also assume that due to the restriction on advertisement, shares of *TV-13* are quoted on the exchange lower than it could be in the case of lifting this restriction. Let the exchange value of *TV-13* stock holding be the tenfold annual revenue from the sale of air time, i.e. 10 billion roubles.

After the privatization of the television broadcast company, the government receives 10 billion roubles, and a new owner of *TV-13* is entitled to decide on the amount of air time sold. This privatization leads to a threefold increase in commercial advertising on *TV-13*, which conditions a decrease in the social effect from the consumption of its artistic and information product from 24 billion to 22 billion roubles. Along with this, the company's annual revenues from advertising grow from 1 billion to 3 billion roubles, thus giving rise to an increase in the value of its stock from 10 billion to 30 billion roubles.

In this case privatization also results in an excessive income gained by its new owner and a total loss of the state in the amount of 20 billion roubles = 30 billion roubles − 10 billion roubles. The annual losses of the state, equal to the lost social utility (100,000 roubles/min. x (240,000 min. − 220,000 min.) turned into a social rent of the new owner: 100,000 roubles/min. x (30,000 min. − 10,000 min.) = 2 billion roubles.

Analyzing these examples, we want to emphasize that an increase in incomes and share quotations of privatized enterprises is not connected with production growth due to modernization or more efficient management. Excessive incomes gained by new owners after the restrictions on commercial advertising and petrol prices are lifted can hardly be called *entrepreneurial*. The only 'achievement' of these businessmen is that they managed to privatize a certain share of the state's revenue along with state property, having transformed the social utility of the goods produced by state companies into an individually appropriated social rent[291].

The experience of Russia, which underwent its second global redistribution of property in the 20th century, shows all the dramatic consequences of an infringement of the principle of correspondence. The loss of social utility of the 'people's property', including many types of natural resources and broadcasting that was transformed into a social rent of a small group of people as a result of incorrect privatization deprived the state of even those resources necessary for the performance of its minimum compulsory functions. Infringement on the principle of correspondence and emerging social rent gave rise not only to the chronic underfinancing of the social sphere and a dramatic increase in tax burden but also to a rise in business crime and social tension and instability.

---

[291]This view is shared by V. Polterovich, who uses the term 'transition rent'. Considering economic reforms, he writes, 'During the transition, private firms receive rent incomes rejected by the state, which can be high enough… to provide rapid fantastic enrichment of those who found themselves "in the proper place at the proper time" ' (Polterovich V.M. On the Way to a New Theory of Reforms // Economic Science of Contemporary Russia, 1999, No. 3, p. 37). Agreeing with this judgement, we still want to emphasize that the point is not the rejection by the state of a rent income but incorrect privatization and transformation of social utility of a good into a rent income of an individual who was lucky to privatize it 'in the proper place at the proper time' and, which is the most important, under proper conditions. For details, refer to: Grinberg R. Rubinstein A. Social Rent in the Context of Theory of Rational Behaviour of the State// Russian economic journal, 1998, No. 3, pp. 58-66.

In this situation, introduction of a rent tax aimed at withdrawal of the excessive revenue of new owners is absolutely within the rational behaviour of the state, ensuring efficient resource allocation. This governmental measure would also be an act of recovery of the social justice. We are not calling for the cancellation of privatization results or any other reallocation of property. Rather, excessive revenues of their new owners should be withdrawn.

We want to note that budget replenishment through a new rent tax on property would create real prerequisites not only for reduction of the total tax burden imposed on small and medium-size firms but also for resolution of the problem of non-payments and support for the social sphere. But other important problems are also waiting to be resolved. What actions should the state take regarding the use of additional budget revenues and the allocation of public resources in general? What characterizes the rational behaviour of the state? In other words, the question is how it should behave in the sphere of market exchange, i.e. in the area in which – being directly involved in market relations – the state exchanges its resources for social utility of different goods and services.

7.3 The State in Market Exchange

Economic sociodynamics gives rise to another important principle of rational state behaviour concerning its day-to-day activity regulating the market turnover of production factors. It can be called *'Polanyi principle'* after the famous Hungarian economist who was the first to give a detailed substantiation for specific interests of society regarding the use of labour, land and money[292].

Trying to realize the interests connected with society's need to ensure sustainable and safe development, the state establishes behavioural norms for market agents in general and special rules regarding labour remuneration, ground rent and interest rate in particular. We are going to show some opportunities for Pareto-improvements in every area where the 'Polanyi principle' is realized.

> Example 7.9. *Introduction of a minimum wage rate.* Realizing the irreducible public interest of 'equity', many states try to maintain or decrease the status gap between the top and bottom 10% of income earners. This is the reason for the legal introduction of a minimum wage rate. At first glance, this action leads to a worsening in the status of employers, since it causes labour cost growth without a corresponding increase in revenues. However, this measure can save entrepreneurial resources. It can be witnessed that a decrease in living standards of a considerable part of population leads to increased social tension that then necessitates additional budgetary expenditures. In this case an increase in tax burden usually exceeds employers' expenses relating to the

---

[292]'Polanyi K. The Self-Regulating Market and the Fictitious Commodities: Labor, Land and Money //K.Polanyi. The Great Transformation. – New York: Farrar & Rinehart, Inc., 1944.

establishment of a minimum wage rate. Therefore in this case, governmental regulation as an alternative to tax growth and respective budgetary expenditures, improves employees' well-being without worsening those of the state and employers. It is an obvious Pareto-improvement[293].

Example 7.10. *Regulation of the interest rate.* If the macroeconomic situation requires regulation of monetary circulation to decrease the inflation rate, the Central Bank makes credit resources, among other things, more expensive. At first glance, this measure worsens positions of all market players, except for the state. However, possible losses are usually offset by the gain in the form of prevented depreciation of money in general and financial assets of market agents in particular. If the threat of accelerated inflation is ignored (the interest rate is not raised), expenses of firms will increase not due to a rise in the price of credit resources, but due to a decrease in their real incomes caused by a sharp rise in prices of goods and services. Therefore, we can see a Pareto-improvement here; the state improves its situation without causing damage to other market agents.

Example 7.11. *Establishment of a ground rent.* Now we are going to show that a Pareto-improvement can be realized when ground rent and the price of land are regulated by the state. According to the social utility of plots, in the first case the rent is increased, and in the second case a certain rent tax is imposed on land owners (a social rent is withdrawn). If we assume that the state is indifferent to the price of land and does not take its social utility into account, then its buyers or lessees gain unreasonable additional benefits not connected with their business activities. This is evidently a case of Pareto-deterioration. By adjusting the market price of land, taking into consideration its social utility, the state improves its status. In this situation, positions of other parties to the deal – new land owners or lessees – are not worsened. The final (adjusted) market price or rent for plots simply equals the starting conditions for their business. In case the principle of correspondence is observed, reallocation of resources takes place, evidently ensuring a Pareto-improvement.

In addition to regulating the use of labour, land and money, the state also deals with other specific goods having both individual and social utility: culture, education, public health, social security, and environment protection – the whole social sphere. What distinguishes this sphere here is that the private demand, corresponding to individual utility, usually falls behind the supply, which takes into consideration the state's demand conditioned by the social utility of the mentioned goods. Therefore, in this case marginal costs are equal to a sum of marginal individual and social utilities. In other words, spending budget funds to support the social sphere is characteristic of any state's functioning.

---

[293]Of course, all this makes sense unless the principle of correspondence is violated, i.e. if the established minimum wage rate is adequate for the identified social utility.

The practice has proved the expediency of patronizing the social sphere. This is how another principle of the state's rational behaviour is realized. We called it the *'Baumol principle'*. It was William Baumol who theoretically substantiated the necessity of public support for some specific sectors of economy that we mentioned in the second chapter above. Introduction of this principle allows us to answer the question constantly under discussion: state funding of social expenses – is it a political compromise or a natural requirement of the market?

If every individual consumer pays for the individual utility of a good, its social utility can be exchanged only for adequate public resources. Taking this into account, it is impossible to agree with the economists who reject the necessity of state support for social and cultural spheres. According to these economists, this sector was overdeveloped in former socialist countries and in the process of market formation should have been reduced considerably to further develop in accordance with economic growth on a qualitatively new basis[294]. Rather we would state quite the opposite. Without public support for social sector, it is impossible to expect any economic achievements.

Actually, we doubt any succession like 'first economic growth, then satisfaction of other public needs'. The concept of growth in the context of economic sociodynamics integrates interaction of all market agents aimed at the realization of various interests of individuals, their groups and society as a whole. The nature and contents of the sociodynamic multiplier of economic growth testify to it. Failure to take into consideration irreducible social needs will make any equilibrium an imaginary one and cause social tension, which will destroy this fictitious equilibrium and eventually stop any economic growth. Support for the social sphere provided by the state is completely within its rational behaviour.

> Example 7.12. *Support for education.* Suppose the sum of marginal social and individual utilities does not offset the marginal costs of educational services. This situation, as it was shown above, threatens to cause a reduction in their supply and hence a partial loss of the social utility corresponding to the secondary benefits of education (development of culture, scientific and technological advance, strengthening the grounds for a constitutional state, etc.). Therefore, an increase in budgetary subsidies or an expansion of other forms of state support can be regarded as reasonable actions ensuring Pareto-improvements. The state's behavior is rational because an improvement in its status does not damage the well-being of other market agents, since their additional tax expenses are compensated by the secondary benefits of education.

One of the state's most important functions is the allocation of recourses possessed by the society. But it is this form of its participation in the market process that traditionally gives rise to misgivings of neoliberal economists. It is believed that the decisions by officials on the allocation of resources which are 'not their own' nearly always result in irrational use. Practice is the evidence of such 'state

---

[294]Friedman M. Four Steps to Freedom//National Review, 1990, May 14.

failures', and they are explained theoretically[295]. That is why it is so difficult to introduce the allocation processes in the context of the rational state behaviour, implying that every use of budgetary resources results in Pareto-improvement, including an improvement in the position of the state itself without causing damage to other market agents.

While the tax system, replenishing the budget, ensures the movement of financial resources bottom-up, the allocation of budgetary resources in the opposite direction – necessary for the realization of public interest – requires special mechanisms to be created. Taking into consideration the mentioned studies of the 'public choice' school, one should aim these mechanisms at neutralizing the 'specific interests' of bureaucrats, who should be kept as far as possible from the 'nobody's' resources. In the marginal case, market and quasi-market procedures should be used involving *only* individual market in the process of the allocation of public resources.

On the other hand reduction of state involvement and attempts to neutralize the interests of special groups through market and quasi-market procedures of public resource allocation may result in the loss of the initial social motivation. Individual preferences act as a refractive prism; in general, they do not aggregate into an autonomous interest of the state and cannot ensure an adequate allocation of public resources without distortion of the set social goals.

Thus, any allocation processes are affected by two main forces: first, interests of specific groups, and second, individual preferences of market agents. It is always a matter of compromise between them. Its achievement is complicated by another collision which can be represented in the form of the general thesis on the *incompatibility of irreducible public needs with market procedures of allocation of public resources required for satisfaction of these needs.*[296] Therefore in their pure form, market and quasi-market procedures cannot be included in the zone of compromise. This zone is limited to the sphere of the state institutions' functioning and depends considerably on the extent of the society's democratization.

In this context, we are going to consider the *principle of pragmatic democratism,* whose realization partially resolves the mentioned collision by establishing certain regulations for activities of the groups pursuing specific interests. This principle determines the zone of compromise and establishes a general rule of rational state behaviour. Accordingly, *the procedures servicing any allocation of public resources connected with the realization of the interests of a society as such*

---

[295]Besides the famous work by Anne Krueger, devoted to the theory of political rent (Krueger A.O. The Political Economy of the Rent-Seeking Society//American Economic Review, 1974, Vol. 64, pp. 291-301), numerous publications of a rather influential school of 'public choice' (J.Buchanan, A.Niskanen, M.Olson, G.Tullock) should be mentioned here. Currently, most of publications dealing with the issues of state function are overfilled with references to a 'rent-seeking class', 'political profit', 'bureaucratic rent', 'logrolling', etc.

[296]It is easy to prove that the thesis 'on incompatibility' arises directly from the definition of irreducible public needs, whose interrelation with individual needs is exclusively of an institutional nature.

should be as democratic as possible, considering that the more public resource allocation is left to the market, the higher the probability of missing their 'destination point'. Let us consider two examples from the zone of compromise.

> Example 7.13. *The arm's length principle.* An evident example of compromise resolution is public resource allocation according to the 'arm's length principle'. This principle implies the allocation of budgetary resources to intermediary organs independent from the government[297]. In this case the principle of pragmatic democratism allows for the use of tenders and public opinion when deciding on resource allocation, thus moving beneficiaries away from the representatives of the government. We wish to note that agencies involved in public resource allocation also have their 'specific interests'. As a rule, however, officials' egoism manifests itself more vividly than that of 'public electors', who depend more on public opinion. That is why the arm's length principle applied to the direct allocation of public resources results in Pareto-improvement; public interests get less distorted, and the well-being of other market agents remain unaltered.

> Example 7.14. *Tax protectionism.* Another illustration of the rational state behavior in the zone of compromise is the model of public resource allocation using tax protectionism. In this situation the state establishes only special 'rules of play', providing market agents with respective tax benefits. Giving up a portion of tax revenues, it actually allocates public resources bypassing the hands of officials. In this case, the groups with 'specific interests' also affect the process of public resource allocation, but their impact is limited by respective legislative acts regarding the implementation of tax protectionist policy. Here again we see a typical Pareto-improvement, making tax protectionism an instrument of rational state behavior.

Concluding the study of rational behaviour of the state in the market exchange area, we once again stress that like in all other spheres of its functioning, one thing is the most important, realizing society's specific interest not reflected in individual preferences, in combination with Pareto-improvement for all market agents. Our analysis has shown that in a market environment, in which a state exchanges its resources for social utility, the requirement that it behaves rationally transforms itself into three principles: the *Polanyi principle* which demands state regulation for the use of production factors; the *Baumol principle* which establishes the rationality of state support for the social sphere; and the *principle of democratic pragmatism,* which deals with the methods and procedures of allocating resources possessed by a state.

---

[297]For instance, the Russian Fund for Fundamental Research or Russian Humanitarian Scientific Fund.

8 Instead of a Conclusion...

We certainly do not assume that the reader of this book will immediately abandon the beaten track of the 'mainstream'. Stereotypes, even if not wholly consistent with the surrounding world, may sometimes be significantly stronger than reality. In cases of theoretical abstraction the situation is even more complex. The usual axioms are perceived as being so natural that any change in their initial assumptions may be seen at best as an eccentricity, and at worst as blasphemy and a total failure to comprehend the theoretical fundamentals as such. Although many researchers philosophize with obvious pleasure on topics related to Popper's 'falsificability principle' – as it applies to concrete scientific theories –, a 'conservatism spasm' in thinking binds their souls and limits their scientific perception.

However, the history of science shows that its principal developmental potential lies in the revision of initial statements. Euclid's fifth postulate or the second law of thermodynamics or a host of other examples that show that the repudiation of fundamental and seemingly absolutely stable fundamental principles alters the theoretical vision of the world are sufficient to prove this; eternal wisdoms do not exist in science. This is even less the case in the humanities, which deal with human perception of the world, which in itself is variable and highly temporal.

Attempts to canonize theoretical postulates have always been related not to science, but to ideology, which has tried to instrumentalize science in the service of current political goals. We see the popularity of Marxism in the end of the 19th century in this way, and so we treat the attempts to preserve the 'postulate of individualism' at the end of the 20th century. We hold that economic theory with its unjustifiably narrow notions of the state and society and its excessively broad assumptions as to the possibility of achieving a consensus among individuals, has fallen victim to the latest 'mainstream' ideologizing.

With this in mind, the only goal of our research is *to revise the postulate of individualism*. By denying the universal character of the reducibility hypothesis, we have formulated a more general statement on the aggregation of interests within the socium. Therefore, aside from personal needs and their aggregates, specific social needs do exist as such and fail to be reflected in individual preferences. A revision of the strictly guarded postulate of individualism requires a reconstruction of the entire edifice of modern economic theory and radically changes the relationship with the state, transforming the latter into an independent market player.

This statement not only helps to explain many of the realities of our times but also to formulate an important theoretical concept on the rationality of state behaviour by tying it to a generalized interpretation of the Pareto scheme. Nevertheless, we risk repeating that the entire concept of economic sociodynamics, the initial axioms, the notion of balance and the principles of the rational behaviour of the state proceed merely from the revised postulate of individualism.

After the book was published in Russian, we had a chance to take part in Jacob Marschak Interdisciplinary Colloquium on Mathematics in the Behavioral Sciences, University of California, Los-Angeles. Our paper presented at this colloquium actually relays the quintessence of our book; this is why we chose to insert it here instead of a summary.

9 Economic Sociodynamics: Variations on a Given Theme

Introduction. To begin with a few words simply about emotions. It seems that the vocabulary of economists today includes a number of closely related terms which despite of having a lot in common and even being connected with each other still are not identical. For example, externalities, collective forms of consumption (air flight or visiting opera house) and its specific conditions (non-excludability and non-rivalness) as well as public and merit goods. They are usually described with the help of almost the same terms.

We think that the modern theory has failed to define the clear boundaries of the usage of these terms. That is why economists have found themselves in a 'linguistic trap': they often mean different things pronouncing the same words. For example, for some researchers the term 'public' applied to goods turned from an illustrative adjective (not very correctly selected from the beginning) into a substantial characteristic. Then, non-excludability and non-rivalness in consumption as the principal characteristics of such specific goods became the sign of their social utility which in general they do not posses. The same happens with the so-called merit goods which are often referred to as public goods though; in fact, any good can be considered as merit including those divisible in consumption.

We suspect that such a mess of terms and notions covers the fundamental economic problem of complementarity of individual and social utility that reflects the basic conflict between an individual and society. Today the old recipe of Vicksel stating that if the utility for each citizen is zero then the aggregate utility for all members of society is also zero and nothing more than zero can hardly be considered sufficient.[298] The solution of this problem exclusively from the standpoint of an individual (the principle of methodological individualism) as well as the opposite perception of the world, viewing an individual only as an element of the public organism (organic concept), did not and could not bring positive results. As any one-sided approach these 'orthogenious' attempts were unable to appreciate the advantages of a 'vis-à-vis' alternative.

---

[298]Almost 100 hundred years later J. Buchanan being a passionate proponent of methodological individualism used these words of the great Swede as an epigraph to one of the sections of his Nobel Prize winner lecture (Buchanan J., 1997. Constitution of Economic Policy. In: Nobel Prize Winners in Economics. J. Buchanan. Moscow. p. 19 (Russian edition)).

Everything is seen by us in another light. And the words of Kovelman seem to reflect the real state of affairs best of all.[299] Changing them a little, it is possible to say that individual is 'another part' of society, as well as society is 'another part' of individual. Is there any point of view from which both can be seen? Our report is meant to answer this question within its economic boundaries and to find such methodological points of view. This is what we referred to as 'a given theme'.

Our final aim is to change the mainstream of the economic theory by removing the principle of universality of the methodological individualism from its foundation, at least, its version that does not allow for the existence of interests of socium as such and fails to consider the state as an independent market player which seeks to meet its interests. We are fully aware of the difficulty of this task and its challenge to the orthodox economic science that has canonized methodological individualism. We will try to present several aspects of this idea in the following variations on a given theme.

Variation One: *About irreducibility: three cases, five causes.* 'Men are not, when brought together, converted into another kind of substance'. [300] That was the way J.S.Mill saw the world in the XIX century. And almost a hundred years later, K. Popper insists that 'the "behavior" and "actions" of collectives, such as states or social groups, must be reduced to the behavior and to the actions of human individuals'[301]. Reducibility of any need of society to a need of individual is the milestone of the traditional economic theory. But it is this carefully guarded postulate that seems to be its Achilles' heel.

We would like to find out what the reasons for the postulate in question emerged, to go back to the starting point when reducibility was not yet a canon, when the attitude to the whole and its parts was not simplified thus enabling to see both streams of evolution. But we failed to find anything except the saying in Bible that 'I am in the Father and the Father in me'. It seems it was a theological view on the society, interpreted in the atheistic environment of the Enlightenment that determined the 'point of view' from which only a particular case of social dynamics was seen. As a result the universality of the principle of reducibility of needs to the needs of individuals and impossibility of the existence of autonomous interests of society were made indisputable truth. To leave such axioms unchanged means to come to an impasse.

It is not the fact that the conservative inclination to keep the customary point of view does not allow one to see the needs of society as a whole and state as a market player that is the only problem. This could have been ignored if the orthodox theory managed to provide an explanation of the reality and behaviour and actions

---

[299]Kovelman A.B. The Crowd and the Sages in Early Rabbinical Literature. Moscow: Evreiskij Universitet, 1996, p. 5.

[300]Mill J.S., A system of logic, ratiocinative and inductive; being a connected view of the principles of evidence, and the methods of scientific investigation. New York and London: Harper & Brothers, 1900 (Russian Edition – Moscow, 1914, p. 798).

[301]Popper K. Open Society and Its Enemies. V. 2. Princeton: Princeton University Press, 1971 (Russian Edition – Moscow, 1992, V. 2, p. 91).

of the state were incorporated into a traditional market model. However, such expectations have turned out to be too high. And only by neglecting the reality is it possible to insist that our world is wrong, that it would be much better if in accordance with the liberal doctrine state did not interfere at all or at least did not trespass the bounds of the powers of a 'night watchman' and everything was decided by a free choice of individuals. Inefficiency in such an approach does not require any proof.

The universality of the reducibility postulate has completely exhausted itself. It is necessary to admit the situation when there is an interest, on the one hand, not represented in any individual utility function and, on the other hand, there is no aggregate function of individual utilities reflecting this interest. We would like to stress the importance of the notion of irreducibility not only for our concept but for science in general. To prove this thesis let us look at three examples that demonstrate the use of this term in physics, biology and philosophy.

The notion of nonreducability is quite common in physics and mathematics in their various theories. In connection to this, let's pay attention to the concept of dynamics of Prigogine and Stengers. Studying the unstable dynamic systems and the chaotic systems as their main branch, they came to the conclusion that the study of the determined trajectories of movement was not enough and turned to the probabilistic description of dynamics. They stressed that 'probabilistic description introduced by us for the chaotic systems is *irreducible*. It cannot be applied to a single trajectory. This statement is a strict result, obtained as a result of the application of modern functional analysis to the analysis of chaos.' Defining the chaotic systems they also mentioned that 'we came to irreducible probabilistic description that could not be reduced to the study of single wave functions'[302]. It should be added that irreducibility plays the key role in the theory of Prigogine and Stengers.

'Biological irreducibility' can be traced to Darwin's theory of evolution. Switching in his studies from separate species to populations and discovering in the evolution of communities some specific features that differed qualitatively from characteristics of their selectively changing representatives, the famous biologist in fact also used the notion of irreducibility. Darwin described the mechanism of the emergence of irreducibility, showing that small variations in species could cause evolution at the collective level if present over a long period of time. That was how Darwin explained the origin of species and described life as an endless process of evolution.

Philosophical essence of irreducibility is more universal and of a structural nature. Applied to a multitude of objects it transforms into a well-known principle of holism or the "philosophy of integrity" introduced by J. Smuts, a South African politician of the first half of XX century, one of the creators of the Charter of the League of Nations. The statement that the whole can possess specific qualities

---

[302]Prigogine I., Stengers I., 2000. Time, Chaos, Quantum. Solving Paradox of Time. Moscow, pp. 8, 14.

which its parts do not have is the essence of this concept. Irreducibility of such characteristics of the whole to the characteristics of its parts is evident[303].

The recognition of the irreducibility phenomenon in economic theory, namely the legitimization of the interests of social groups and society that cannot be reduced to the preferences of individuals, requires a change from the postulate of individualism to the already-mentioned principle of complementarity of individual and social utility. Several reasons should be noted to justify the choice of this particular 'point of view'.

First, almost everyday and every moment we face situations when the market fails and the state has to correct its failures. Analyzing state interventions, we all the time come to the almost seditious thought that it is a rare case when individual interests can be clearly traced in an *a priori* motivation of such interventions. There are other reasons that induce the authorities to act independently by or even against the needs of individuals. These are the reasons falling beyond the 'visible' individual preferences that attract our attention stimulating a search for another 'point of view'.

Second, reviewing the expansions of the state involvement we have failed to find reasonable enough *post factum* explanations of how such interventions managed to correspond to the preferences of individuals[304]. All known attempts to provide individualistic explanations of state interventions despite sophisticated methods of analysis used (a free rider phenomenon, prisoner's dilemma, veil of ignorance, 'obedience paradox' etc.), have still failed to solve the problem.[305] Without any exaggeration we have the right to state that 'the paradox of state' is a fundamental contradiction between the principle of minimization of state activities dominant in the economic theory and the real role of the state in developed market economies. We think that this paradox covers a specific interest of society, that differs from any aggregate individual utility functions.

Third, previous attempts to define and incorporate this interest in a number of market models have obviously been insufficient. The social welfare function of Bergson-Samuelson[306] and even Margolis's[307] two utility functions are nothing

---

[303]Let's note a close link between holism and the theory of emergent evolutionary development. This philosophical concept of dynamics that states the spontaneous emergence of new qualities of the system, not noticed in the movement of objects it consists of also uses the notion of irreducibility.

[304]These doubts are strengthened by the famous Arrow's 'theorem on impossibility' (see K.J. Arrow, 1963. Social Choice and Individual Values. 2nd ed., New York)

[305]The constitutional theory of J. Buchanan with its contract paradigm and optimistic faith in a possibility of reaching a consensus seems to be the most integrative, though absolutely utopian. (Buchanan J.M. The Constitution of Economic Policy, American Economic Review, 1987, Vol. 77 (3) (Russian Edition – Nobel Prize Winners in Economics. James Buchanan. – Moscow, 1997, p. 25)).

[306]Bergson A. A Reformulation of Certain Aspects of Welfare Economics // Quarterly Journal of Economics, February 1938. See also: Samuelson P. Reaffirming the Existence of 'Reasonable' Bergson-Samuelson Social Welfare Functions. – Economics, 1978, No. 173. The inclusion of prices, capital, state services etc. into a function of public welfare

more than the study of social interest on the Procrustean bed of the postulate of individualism. The theoretical vision here is as before limited to the zone of 'universal reducibility' where any need is reduced to individual preferences which absorb any public interest. That is why the models mentioned above turned out to be inapplicable for the analysis of the needs of society.

Fourth, our acquaintance with Richard Musgrave's concept of 'merit goods' strengthens our wish to change the 'point of view'[308]. Merit goods are those whose demand on the part of individuals lags behind 'the desirable by society' and is stimulated by state. Researchers distinguish four types of merit needs that cannot be found among market-identified preferences of individuals. These are 'pathological' cases when society wants to protect poorly informed people from taking irrational actions; solving the famous paradox of the 'weak will of Odysseus', when the state corrects deliberately distorted preferences of individuals; need to redistribute goods in kind, aimed to help the needy citizens; collective needs inherent to society as a whole.

The debates on goods and services that should be supported by the state, that have been going on for more than 40 years, have clearly revealed two constantly repeating themes. On the one hand, the special needs of society (merit wants), in principal not coinciding with the interests of individuals are the object of analysis. On the other hand, endless attempts have been made to level such a peculiarity with the help of individualistic explanation of public needs. Acquaintance with the critique of meritorics[309] has strengthened our belief that it is impossible to solve this contradiction and to find a place for merit goods in the visible zone of 'the reducibility of all needs'. And in this case a change of the 'point of view' is necessary.

Fifth, after reading a number of books on economics and related disciplines we have come to the conclusion that the economic theory itself is unable to provide an answer to the question we are interested in. As Einstein noted 'the conceptual difficulties of his own science make a naturalist study philosophy'. Any attempt to prove an assumption that any public interest is reduced to individual preferences is

---

has given rise to a number of results which, however, failed to bring us nearer to revealing the interest of society as such.

[307]Margolis H. Selfishness, Altruism and Rationality: A Theory of Social Choice. Cambridge, 1982.

[308]Musgrave R.A. A Multiple Theory of Budget Determination. Finanzarchiv 17, 1957; Musgrave R.A. Finanztheorie. Tübingen, 1974; Musgrave R.A, Musgrave P.B, Kullmer L. Die öffentlichen Finanzen in Theorie und Praxis, Band 1, 6. Auflage, Tübingen, 1994.

[309]Andel N. Zum Konzept der meritorischen Güter, Finanzarchiv 42, 1984; Schmidt K. Mehr zur Meritorik. Kritisches und Alternatives zu der Lehre von den öffentlichen Gütern. // Zeitschrift für Wirtschafts – und Sozialwissenschaften, 108, 1988; Priddat B.P. Zur Ökonomie der Gemeinschaftsbedürfnisse: Neuere Versuche einer ethischen Begründung der Theorie meritorischer Güter. // Zeitschrift für Wirtschafts-und Sozialwissenschaften 112, 1992; Tietzel M., Müller C. Noch mehr zur Meritorik. // Zeitschrift für Wirtschafts – und Sozialwissenschaften. 118, 1998.

either right or wrong almost always ends in a discussion on the basic postulates, raising philosophical issues and crossing the boundaries of the economic theory.

We have in mind the basic notion of socium, the multitude of people, making up society and 'not turned into something else', the structure of social environment where economic entities act. There is a certain contradiction here between the modern understanding of socium and the postulate of individualism. Canonization of this postulate is similar to attempts to eliminate this contradiction by 'squeezing' a more complex and less determined 'public body' into a strictly limited individualistic space. In this sense the selection of another 'point of view' is associated with the step, which Einstein made in the general theory of relativity, declining Euclide geometry – the spatial cover of the classical Newton mechanics. This is of course only an association but nevertheless it urges on a discussion on some specific aspects of social space.

Variation Two. *Problem of interactions.* Pondering over socium, we seek to comprehend economic appropriateness in its dynamics and to determine the position of economic entities in the following moment of time.[310] At that the purely atomistic notion of society as an aggregation of individuals acting independently and the description of the trajectory of movement with the help of the 'invisible hand' *inevitably creating equilibrium* caused a gap between a theoretical image and reality. The subsequent discovery of game models and the registration of interaction of economies subjects the finding to possible advantages of corporate behaviour permitted to somewhat retrench that gap but did not solve the principal problem at all.[311] And reality as a well-known joke goes still remained a 'special case of theory'.

As Poincare once mentioned about the symmetry of time, 'any attempt to explain irreversibility in terms of reversible processes, however numerous they might be, is groundless even from the logical point of view'[312]. We have the right to say the same about the description of economic appropriateness of socium – *it is impossible in principal to discover the complete set of interactions of economic*

---

[310]Our view on these issues is expressed in a recently published monograph: Grinberg R., Rubinstein A., 2000. Economic Sociodynamics. Moscow: ISE-Press.

[311]Let's refer to the analysis of D.North. Speaking about the possibilities of the game model he argues that self-sustained corporate decisions exist only in very simplified conditions, namely in the case when the parties have complete information the game will be played for an indefinitely long period of time in the future and the composition of its players remains invariable all the time. North notes that these conditions are not only too strict but simply are rarely met in reality. (North D.C. Institutionen, institutioneller Wandel und Wirtschaftsleistungen, Tuebingen, 1992 (Russian Edition – Moscow, 1997, p. 79)).

[312]We cite these words of Henri Poincare from the following book by Prigogine and Stengers: Prigogine I., Stengers I., 2000. Time, Chaos, Quantum. Solving the Paradox of Time. Moscow, p. 26. It is this study that make us refer to the French mathematician works: Poincare H. La mecanique et l'experience // Revue de Metaphysique et de Morale. 1893, Vol. 1, pp. 534-537. The further acquaintance with this heritage and first of all the problem of 'non-integration' of dynamic systems has allowed us to define more precisely our notions of interactions in society and social dynamics as a whole.

entities in the zone of reducibility of all needs. In this sense models created and trajectories calculated according to them turned out at best to be only a rough approximation to social dynamics, while the problem of interactions remains unsolved.

The whole can have its specific properties distinct from those of its parts. This generally accepted postulate has been reflected in the terms of systematic and holism, which are used nowadays so habitually and easily as, say, the term 'gene' in biology. Elwin Toffler notes that fragmentariness and analytical approach without a general outlook of the whole do not allow for the explanation of too much.[313] Taking this into account, it is easy to understand that it is the same question concerning the theme raised at the beginning – about a search for a 'point of view' from which both separate parts and the whole are seen. In this sense the economic theory with its individualistic canon has found itself amongst those humanities where, as before, the spirit of reductionism reigns. Therefore, as a rule, economists see in any community its constituent parts only, collective interests being perceived exclusively from the individuals' positions. Remember Mill and Popper cited above – it is how our environment has found itself in the grip of the methodological individualism. And beyond the bounds of this narrow enough field the ever dreadful organic concept is being fancied. By this fact only the flat denial by the mainstream of the needs of the society as a whole can be explained.

We connect the main delusion here distorting the natural order of things with a simplification and even a wrong interpretation of the holistic version of the society's structure. It seems utterly clear that the examination of the aggregation of people as a whole does not yet mean its identification with a single organism which has the determined structure.[314] And even taking the position of Popper and Buchanan and a few other philosophers and economics rejecting the organic concept in principle, we cannot contend that any attitude toward society as a whole must be condemned.

If we turn our attention to the teleological principle which has been known to philosophers for a long time and is widely used in economic theories and which establishes a possibility of reaching a presupposed harmony the mere fact of the formulation of societal interests as such will be seen in another light.[315] Making start from the fact that in nature everything is arranged expediently, the existence

---

[313]Toffler A. The Third Wave. New York: Morrow, 1980 (Russian Edition – Moscow, 1999, p. 484).

[314]Let us remind that for K.Popper's oracles – Hegel and Marx – who recognised the organic concept of society nations and classes were the foundation of such a structure. Therefore, the collective interest according to Hegel is a 'national spirit' and public need according to Marx is the interest of a certain class.

[315]A good example of using the teleological approach in economy is market theory of A.Smith who succeeded to discern the potential of expediency in self-interest. Actually, the invisible hand which according to Adam Smith has to bring common prosperity is, in fact, the above mentioned teleological principle. It is this idea of Adam Smith that made it possible for Kant to construct the first model of the legal state. The Kant legal theory at that uses teleology as 'a secret plan of nature'.

of some social analogue to the laws of physics may be admitted. The question is about a peculiar social homeostasis or the *law of the self-preservation of socium*. In the context of this universal law, the words of Menger that any community of people has its own nature and therefore the necessity to preserve its essence"[316] should also be interpreted in the context of this universal law.

It should be stressed that we have in mind the modern interpretation of teleological principle, its philosophical filling in accordance with the postmodernist notions of the universe of Prigogine[317] and Toffler views[318]. Proceeding from them it may be stated that the growth of entropy and the inclination of socium for equilibrium is not the only possible plot.[319] The genuine intrigue of the dynamics of physical and social systems is carried on in the *counterpoint of necessity and chance*. Determinism in formation of equilibrium is followed by the stochastic non-equilibrium processes. The dominant of equilibrium is also only one of the restrictive assumptions of the orthodox economic theories.

Using the physical analogue let us imagine a multitude of individuals making up a society as a multitude of market players changing continuously, i.e. 'slightly trembling' and being influenced by all kinds of fluctuations which are connected with the dynamics of their positions and alterations of their personal preferences and possibilities. With the existence of the negative reverse connection – the mechanism of the invisible hand corresponds with it and only with it – entropy grows, the energy of disturbances falls, the fluctuation weakens and disappears: under the conditions of the competitive market and the reducibility of all needs the changing demand provokes the determined reaction of supply thus forming a new market equilibrium.

The choice of the 'point of view from which both of them are seen' leads to the formulation of the universal notion of society – in its association with a multitude of individuals acting independently and in various groups and where sociodynamic processes reflecting the negative and positive reverse connections – in a kind of the Prigogine's theorem analogue. In the event that obstacles arise in reaching equilibrium, the stationary condition of socium produces minimum entropy and the energy of disturbance is transformed into the irreducible interest of a social system converting the latter to a 'new level of complexity'.

---

[316]Menger. C. Grundsätze der Volkswirtschaftslehre, 2. Aufl., Wien, 1923. p. 8.

[317]The question is about studies concerning non-equilibrium processes and dynamics of chaotic systems full of abundant philosophic content (Prigogine I., Stengers I., 2000. Time, Chaos, Quantum; Prigogine I., Stengers I.,2000. Order from Chaos. A New Dialog of a Man with Nature.

[318]Toffler E. Op.cit., pp. 495-497.

[319]Following Prigogine let's pay attention on the theorem of H.Poincare who established in the last century that in the majority of dynamic systems the emerging resonance does not allow to exclude interactions and on the KAM (Kolmogorov, Arnold and Moser) theory that appeared sixty years later and has proved that resonances are fraught with two kinds of dynamics: trajectories with determined and casual behaviour. (Prigogine I., Stengers I. Op.cit. pp. 12-13).

To put it another way, any outer disturbance observed in any society every minute and everyday – the growing need in education, science, culture, the danger of a breach of ecological balance or the emergence of warthreat, the growing income differentiation or simply the appearance of a new product or technology – is fraught with two possible consequences.

In the first case when the external impetus 'dissolves' in the dynamics of individual preferences and a new equilibrium entropy grows, the social energy falls and fluctuation is suppressed. In the second case, the energy of fluctuation remains and even grows, ensuring the formation of a new interest of society as such. There is no need to say that the first situation is only a particular case. Therefore, we repeat once more that we proceed from more universal notions of society which in the course of evolution constantly encounters both situations.

In these circumstances external impulses and striving for self-preservation can give rise to such socium interests, which as it was noted by Menger 'should not, in fact, be taken for the needs of its individual members and even those of all members taken together'.[320] Therefore, the recognition of the phenomenon of irreducibility of social interest directly ensues from a solution of the problem of interactions as a result of applying the teleological mechanism to society in its holistic version.

The substitution of methodological individualism by the principle of complementarity of individual and social utility is the evident consequence of this fact. It is exactly how the problem of social interactions in holistic-teleological version of the given theme looks.

Variation Three: _Typologisation of goods and services._ While examining the economic dynamics of a social system and social space itself, the attention should be directed to another element, namely goods and services which are subjects of exchange between economic agents. Though in a different context, the complementarity problem has also displayed itself in this case now in relation with the object of market exchange.

A private good used as a universal item of exchange turned out to be only a _particular case_, a result of the same one-sided standpoint when 'both are not seen' in principle. Observed from this individualistic 'point of view' all other goods and services distinct from the universal specimen found itself in the same specific position as the moon with its invisible part.

In this way the genuine nature of many goods and services is in the shadow of theoretical knowledge and remains a secret phenomenon for economists. At the same time the clearly observed peculiarities distinguishing these goods and services from the aggregation of private goods caused the emergence of many exemptions to the general rule. So non-homogeneous public goods such as a lighthouse for example appeared, providing an equally useful service for many as well as nuclear and bacteriological weapons useless for everybody. This was the way marginal quasi-public services of education or theatre, useful not only for their di-

---

[320]Menger C. Op. cit., p. 8.

rect users but also for society as a whole, were born. 'Merit goods' have failed to correspond with the general rule of private goods, either.

In this constantly piling-up collection of such exceptions those already not entirely private or entirely non-private goods became difficult to distinguish from each other. Many authors simply ignore for example merit goods, not separating them from public goods. When they are divided into autonomous groups it is impossible in fact to draw any boundaries.[321] The existing inaccuracies of the translation of the key meritorics terms – *'merit goods'* and *'merit wants'* – completely obscure the problem.[322]

It is in no way possible to consider such a situation accidental. The matter is that in its understanding of both merit and public goods, modern theory proceeds from identical assumptions on the existence of some *genuine* preferences of individuals. It finds the principal distinction between the said groups of goods and services only in the motivation of users' behavior. In the case of merit goods users cannot *objectively* 'see' their genuine preferences and make only a false demand.[323] When public goods are discussed, individuals acting as free riders do not consciously demonstrate their preferences and do not make demand for the these goods at all.[324]

The very fact of introducing a 'double standard' legalizing the existence of some other individual utilities distinct from the actual preferences of the individual is a direct consequence of the choice of 'point of view' and corresponds with the attempts discussed above to reduce the thing which is impossible to reduce – the needs of society to the needs of individuals. Trying to solve this unsolved problem the traditional theory has designed yet another 'new historical community of people' who either do not see 'their happiness' pathologically or do not wish to confess it. Meanwhile the change in 'point of view' and the replacement of methodological individualism by the principle of complementarity of individual and

---

[321]Meritorics is not mentioned either in the standard textbooks on economics (P. A. Samuelson, W.D. Nordhaus, nor in a special monograph by J. Stiglitz on the state activities (Stiglitz J. Economics of the Public Sector. London, New York: WW Norton & Co., 1988 (Russian Edition – Moscow, 1997)).

[322]In the textbook of Fischer, Dornbusch and Schmalensee (Fischer S., Dornbusch R., Schmalensee R. Economics, 2nd Ed. New York: McGraw-Hill, 1988. (Russian Edition – Moscow, 1997) 'merit wants' are translated as 'vital goods' (p.67) and in the textbook by Atkinson and Stiglitz (Atkinson A., Stiglitz J.. Lectures in Public Economics. New York: McGraw-Hill, 1980 (Russian Edition – Moscow, 1995)) we encounter another poor translation: merit needs are referred to as *'worthy needs'* (p. 22). Along with them the textbook by Jakobson says: 'A peculiar intermediate position between private and public goods is taken by *goods which possess special merits.*' (Jakobson L.I. 2000. Public Sector of the Economy. Economic Theory and Policy. Moscow, p. 42).

[323]Musgrave R.A. Op. cit., p. 452.

[324]Many economists mention the interest of individuals to give false signals of the absence of demand for a public good (Samuelson P.A. The pure theory of public expenditure. Review of Economics and Statistics, 1954; J. Stiglitz. Op. cit. p. 121, McConnell C.R. Brue S.L. Economics: principles, problems, and policies. Op. cit., p. 64. Fischer S., Dornbusch R., Schmalensee R. Op. cit., p.64; McConnell, Brew Op. cit., p. 100).

social utility makes these pretentious novelties superfluous. Having restored their 'sight and conscience' people will not suffer bifurcation of personality and again find the sole and always genuine function of utility. And along with them, the state becomes a market player with its inherent function of social utility.

From this 'point of view' the distinction between public goods and merit goods becomes evident. The latter may also include usual goods in no way coinciding with public goods. The actual motivation for making goods merit is always caused by the interest of society as such which is the criterion indication of merit goods.[325] Let us say that goods and services have the property of *irreducibility* if public need for them is not reduced to the needs of individuals. The introduction of this property of goods and services, the equivalent of their social utility, allows us to make a very important conclusion concerning merit goods: if not every merit good is public then some merit goods have the property of irreducibility.

The connection between public goods and socium is of another nature.[326] A few definitions of these goods reflecting two specific characteristics are known. *Non-excludability* in consumption means that it is impossible to exclude anyone from consuming it; *non-rivalness* implies that their consumption by one person does not diminish the consumption opportunities of another. These fundamental characteristics distinguish public goods within the world of goods and services. However, the definition of public goods themselves has a rather vague meaning which follows from the absence of clear bounds between non-excludability and non-rivalness. This vagueness has given rise to such broad interpretations that the demarcation of boundaries which separate these goods from other ones becomes nearly unreal. Apart from public goods we often encounter 'pure public goods' and 'goods the consumption of which is useful for the society' as well as the above mentioned quasi-public goods that are only partially public and other mixed public goods that are defined still less clearly.[327]

---

[325]Grinberg R., Rubinstein A. Op.cit., pp. 175-186.

[326]In Samuelson's interpretation, for example, 'public is a good which in equal quantity comes into two or more individual functions of utility' (Samuelson P.A. The Pure Theory of Public expenditures and taxation. Public economics. J. Margolis and H. Guitton (eds.). London: Macmillan, 1969, p. 108). As to Blaug, 'the specific nature of public goods lies in the fact that their consumption can be only common and equal' (Blaug M. Economic Theory in Retrospect. Fifth English edition. Cambridge: Cambridge University Press, 1997 (Russian Edition – Moscow, 1994, p. 549)).

[327]In dividing public goods into social goods and *goods, the consumption of which is useful for society* L.G. Khodov defines the latter as goods 'which are somewhere in the middle between individual consumption goods and social goods'. (Khodov L.G., 1997. The Fundamentals of the State Economic Policy. Moscow, p. 37). Using the criterion properties of public goods such as non-excludability and non-rivalness, L. Jakobson writes that *mixed public goods* are those in which 'at least one of the properties is displayed moderately' (Jakobson L.I., 1996. Economics of the Public Sector. Fundamentals of the Theory of the State Finances. Moscow, p. 42.). In his fundamental study 'Economic Thought in Retrospective' Blaug speaks about *quasi-public goods* as goods which "at least partially have a public nature" (Blaug M. Op.cit., p. 550). It is clear that the strictness of these notions may be spoken about only in the terms 'at least', 'moderately' and 'partially'. Let's

In particular, we see no grounds to include all goods and services which are in the zone of state interests into public goods, for example, national defense and fundamental science. It seems to us that a real reason for their inclusion into this specific group was an absence of a respective niche in the market model. It is most likely that in such an 'unlawful' way special properties of public goods have also been attributed to the said products. It is quite commonplace now and the example of national defense has been used in all standard textbooks on economics.[328] Nevertheless, we see here an evident juggling of facts and an evident inaccuracy in using the well-known notions.

In this connection let's come back to the definition of public goods and direct our attention to the fact that we speak about the properties of *the consumption of goods by individuals,* about the impossibility to exclude anybody from the consumption of the goods in question and the absence of rivalry on the part of these individuals. The very fact of the consumption of the good by individuals has to be stressed in this definition once more. The above-mentioned definition by Samuelson, according to which a public good must by all means be included into individual utility function, says the same.

It is clear, for example, that the beam of a lighthouse is really consumed by seafarers. But an evident discrepancy has happened with national defense: such military products as poisonous gases, mortal viruses, nuclear warheads and other weapons are not directly consumed by any individual and they do not come into any individual function of utility.[329] The same is to be said about fundamental science. It is difficult to imagine for example that the Pontryagin-Kuratovsky theorem in the graph theory, Arrow-Debre and MacKensey models in mathematical

---

take note that five years later in a new textbook for undergraduates Jakobson repeated almost literally his rather vague definition: 'Goods which possess both properties in the high degree are called pure public goods. If at least one of the said properties are displayed only in a limited degree we have mixed public goods on hand' (Jakobson L.I. 2000. Public Sector of the Economy. Economic Theory and Policy. Moscow, p. 41). In the clash with reality which can in no way be incorporated into the existing theory apparently has given rise to these uttermost amazing definitions.

[328]Let's take extracts from the three popular books. 'The best example of a public goods is the system of national defense. When a country defends its freedom and way of life it does that also for its population irrespective of whether it wants it or not' (Samuelson P.A., Nordhaus W.D., 1997. Economics (Russian edition). Moscow, p. 76). 'Clear air is a public good exactly like national defense. If the army defends a country from a threat then the maintenance of your security does in no way impede its maintenance for somebody else' (Fischer S., Dornbusch R., Schmalensee P. Op.cit., p. 64). 'National defense is one of a few pure public goods meeting such conditions as impossibility and undesirability of excluding their consumption' (Stiglitz J. Op.cit., p. 124).

[329]In a private talk in July, 2000 in Moscow about our book on economic sociodynamics Michael Intrilligator acknowledged that goods and services which are not produced as a *choice of individuals* do exist. He agreed with the conclusion only on the basis of the following compromise: defense goods as a whole come into the individual utility function but an element of it, even the most important, may not be included into the individual utility function.

economics and even our own concept of economic sociodynamics can be items of individual consumption included in individual utility functions.

In the mess that crops up, we again face the consequences of the same not very successful starting choice of 'point of view' from which nothing else but normative individualism can be seen. In this particular case all needs including the interests of the state in the production of weapons must by all means be reduced to the needs of individuals. But once one changes 'point of view', irreducible public interests can be seen. It then becomes clear that other goods consumed only by the state also exist. These goods are not included in any individual utility functions and in principal are not meant for individual consumption. In our opinion the majority of products of national defense and fundamental science can be considered such goods.

As to non-excludability and non-rivalness they become apparent only as consequences of the consumption of these goods. Only the results of the consumption of military products or fundamental science products in fact have the said characteristics: they are available to all members of society and no one can be restricted during their appropriation. Bacteriological weapons themselves as well as scientific achievements do not possess such characteristics because they are not consumed by individuals at all. That is why they can be seen neither as public nor merit goods. However, though not having individual utility, the said goods and services are able to meet irreducible needs of society, i.e. they possess social utility. With this in mind, we shall call them *'social goods'* from here on.

Let us pay attention to another noteworthy fact. It is not difficult to notice that both merit and social goods are able to satisfy irreducible public needs. Both of them hold the fundamental property of irreducibility. In other words, both of them hold the fundamental property of irreducibility. But the existence of a similar social characteristic, however important, does not make the said goods identical. If a merit good has social utility, it does not mean that every good having social utility is a merit good. Let us stress that merit goods as well as public goods are to be consumed by individuals. Social goods are to be consumed solely by the state. On the whole, the above mentioned specific properties – irreducibility of needs, non-excludability and non-rivalness in consumption – allow us to construct a new typology embracing all the aggregation of goods and services which are produced and consumed with participation of all market players including the state.

To better expound on our theory, let us introduce a few additional definitions. Speaking about the properties of goods and services we have until now examined them from the standpoints, so to say, of 'negation' – irreducibility, non-excludability and non-rivalness. Now we mute two characteristics of public goods into one positive property of *communality*[330] meaning both non-excludability and

---

[330]While using the said term let's pay attention to its broader interpretation. S. Kiridina, for example, argues that 'communality means such a property of material and technological environment that presupposes its use as a single undivided system which parts cannot be isolated without a threat of the disintegration of the whole system... The communal environment can function only in a form of public good which cannot be divided into units of consumption and sold (consumed) by parts.' (S.G. Kiridina, 2000. Institutional Matrix

non-rivalness in consumption. And, on the contrary, we divide irreducibility of needs into two positive properties: *social utility* of goods, which have a property of irreducibility and *individual utility* of goods which does not reflect such a characteristic.

This change does not influence the content of social properties themselves but makes it possible to examine their more convenient analogues. These positive characteristics create necessary prerequisites for the construction of the sought typology. With this purpose, let us examine all possible combinations of the three above mentioned properties – individual utility, property of communality and social utility of goods. The results of their combinations – the aggregation of all *possible* combinations of the three properties – make the sought for typology presented in Table 9.1.

As a commentary on Table 9.1. let us stress once more that the property of communality of a good (non-excudability and non-rivalness in consumption) can exist only in a case in which this good has individual utility and is consumed by individuals. Taking this into account, it becomes clear that amongst all the aggregation of goods and services there are no goods displaying the property of communality if individual utility is absent (the second and fifth combinations). In other words the information given in Table 1 and the interpretation of the content of all admissible combinations of the analyzed social properties provide every reason to make the following conclusion. The five groups that do not overlap – private, mixed, communal, mixed communal and social – completely cover the whole world of goods and services, and at every given moment of time any good belongs exclusively to one of those groups.[331]

---

and Development of Russia. Moscow, p. 39). Agreeing with such understanding of the communality as a property we deem it more correct to call goods and services possessing such property the communal goods instead of a vague notion of public goods used nowadays.

[331]In a new forthcoming book of the authors of the 'General Theory of Social Economy' a detailed substantiation of this typology is given and the sociodynamic evolution model of the world of goods and services is constructed (SDEM). It shows the determined and stochastic interactions of market players carried out in the collision of individual and social interests of individuals, their groups and society as a whole and manifesting themselves in an endless evolution of goods consisting of three dynamic cycles of private, communal and social goods as well as two quasi-cycles of social and mixed goods.

Table 9.1. Combinations of Properties and Groups of Goods

	Groups	Individual utility	Communality in consumption	Social utility
		Combination of three by one		
1	**Private good**	Individual utility		
2	*None*		Communality in consumption	
3	**Social good**			Social utility
		Combinations of three by two		
4	**Communal good**	Individual utility	Communality in consumption	
5	*None*		Communality in consumption	Social utility
6	**Mixed good**	Individual utility		Social utility
		Combination of three by three		
7	**Mixed communal good**	Individual utility	Communality in consumption	Social utility

Thus, in this case a change of 'point of view' has allowed us to shed a new light on the three specific negations – irreducibility of needs, non-excludability and non-rivalry in consumption. These fundamental properties of goods make it possible to consider neoclassical models to be the ultimate truth and designate a boundary of the universality of normative individualism. Those parts of the market space where goods are not 'aggravated' with the above mentioned social properties conditions for market mechanism continue to work in accordance with the Procrustean views of the '*mainstream*'. But in parts where goods 'suffer' from those specific properties, another model of market mechanism with another composition of players are required.

Variation Four: *Solving the 'paradox of the state'*. Born together with the theory of Adam Smith, this paradox has survived all subsequent development in economic science. The teleological mechanism of the "invisible hand" discovered by Smith simply did not need the state and, on the contrary, demanded to free the energy of self-interest of individuals, restricted by Fetters feudal power.[332] After Smith, the hostility towards market interventions therefore became a kind of theoretical norm and the majority of researchers persistently tried to find ways to eliminate the state from the economic space.[333] It is surprising that at present when the state, with its powerful and systemic intervention, is firmly built into a reproductive process of any developed market economy, mainstream economic theory is still dominated by the total critique the state activities. The ideological invocation 'the less state, the better for economy' is still appealing.[334]

The centrally planned economy that establishes the priority of state needs over the needs of individuals regardless of the degree of rigidity of different variations of this system is at the other end of the spectrum. Whether the Stalinist thesis on 'the priority of the higher profitability' dominates or a more attractive 'system of optimal functioning of economy' is implemented in any case such method of solving 'the paradox of state' bears a danger of elimination of the market as a means of organizing economic life. The experience of the former socialist countries, including attempts to imitate the market by building various systems of management of the national economy should leave no space for such illusions.

A more balanced view on state participation in economic life belongs to the neo-liberal doctrine and, in particular, to ordoliberalism and the concept of 'social market economy' which even incorporates a notion of complementarity of the 'social' and the 'market'. Euken, the founder of ordoliberalism only mentions the subsidiarity principle in accordance with which 'state should intervene only when its interventions cannot by any means be avoided'.[335] Mueller-Armak, the creator of the concept of 'social market economy', allowing for state intervention into the

---

[332]Smith agreed that the state should have only three functions and as it is well known placed the state out of the market model.

[333]This situation reminds a story of the famous paradox of physics – a 'paradox of time'. From the beginning nobody seemed to notice this paradox and physicists lived in the two parallel worlds. The laws of classical mechanics in accordance with which time was reversible and the past did not differ from the future acted in the one world. In the other world – the real world – there was no symmetry of time and time was hopelessly irreversible. Attempts to combine these worlds in the XIX century led to the denial of the 'arrow of time'. Bolzman and later Einstein in the theory of relativity stated that the time is reversible explaining the realities of our world by the subjectivity of its observer. Only in the second half of XX century the time in its real meaning was introduced into physics and "paradox of time" was close to solution. (See for details: Prigogine I., Stengers I., 2000. Time, Chaos, Quantum; Prigogine I., Stengers I., 2000. Order from Chaos.). It seems that the 'paradox of state' has the same history. Here as well the ambivalent attitude towards state should be al last replaced by building it into the general economic theory.

[334]Hayek, Friedman, Buchanan and Washington Consensus.

[335]Euken W. Grundsätze der Wirtschaftspolitik, 1959, p. 348.

free play of market forces does not in fact go further than demanding separate 'market-comfort and market-not-comfort interventions'[336]. It can be stated, therefore, that neoliberal doctrine failed to solve the 'paradox of the state,' because *it has left the state beyond the boundaries of market.*

Only by fully rejecting one-sided approaches is possible to find the 'point of view' which gives the possibility of understanding the real essence of the modern state which is organically built into market rather than existing somewhere out of market or above it. The change in ideology and the adoption of the principle of complementarity of utilities allow us to position the state as an autonomous player responsible for the implementation of the interests of society. That is the way complementarity of utilities is transformed into complementarity of individual market participants and the state, thus determining a new composition of participants of a generalized market model.

Assigning the function of 'bearer' of public interest to the state is not something absolutely new or extraordinary. There were many situations in economic theory in which the state and public interest were treated almost synonymously. Categorically rejecting such views, we stress once more that in our case it is another story and, what is more important, the story about *one more player*, that has *equal* rights with other players in market. From this point of view defending state and turning it into a 'directing economic finger' is as ineffective as ignoring it altogether.

The above-mentioned planned economy model is one such example. The state was considered the absolute authority, subjugating all private and corporate interests of the citizens and their various groups into compliance with the main criterion. Here even assuming reducibility of any public needs traditional for the alternative theory unexpectedly provoked a search for a way to aggregate individual preferences, which would enable the selection of one criterion for the national economy. When any public interest can be presented as a function of individual utilities then constructing a global optimum criterion does not seem to be something absolutely unrealistic.[337]

It should be mentioned that numerous attempts to define such a supercriterion, though being more a search for 'Saint Graal'[338], have not caused much irrita-

---

[336]Müller-Armack, A. Wirtschaftslenkung und Marktwirtschaft. Hamburg: Verlag für Wirtschaft und Sozialpolitik, 1996, p. 19.

[337]In this context even the outstanding findings of L. Kantorovitch - the theory of optimal planning, its mathematic apparatus and the content interpretation of the results of double task, that led to the development of objective estimates – 'supported' an illusion that it was expedient to construct one criterion for the national economy.

[338]We owe such an emotional comparison to J. Buchanan (Buchanan J., Tullock G. The Calculus of Consent: Logical Foundations of Constitutional Democracy. Ann Arbor Paperbacks, 1962 (Russian Edition: Nobel Prize Winners in Economics. James Buchanan. – Moscow, 1997, p. 48)). A critique of the global optimum criterion by the Russian researches should also be mentioned (Makarov V.L., Rubinov A.M., 1973. Mathematic Theory of Economic Dynamics and Equilibrium. Moscow, pp. 12-13; Pol-

tion.[339] However, the change of the initial position leads to the conclusion that an assumption on the existence of the global optimum criterion subordinating individual preferences is as unrealistic as a demand to reduce any public need to the interests of individuals. It should once again be stressed that allotting the state functions as the bearer of public interests – we have in mind the principle of complementarity of utilities –, which demands the consideration all economic entities, individuals, their groups and state as equal market players.

The change in the composition of market participants due to the introduction of the state should be reflected in the standard economic description. Put another way, it is necessary to include state activities under market transactions. Thus, a new 'point of view' requires a correction of the well known condition of equilibrium – equilibrium of marginal costs and marginal utility. Taking into account complementarity of utilities and the fact that the state contributes to demand together with individuals, the following conclusion can be drawn. The conditions of equilibrium are only met when marginal costs are equated with *marginal individual and marginal social utility*. However, a serious methodological difficulty arises, which is here and after referred to as a 'problem of summarizing'.

The problem involves including the state as a market player, while the thesis on equality of all market players does not eliminate the principal differences between the needs of society and needs of its individual members. As a result, irreducibility of public interest to individual preferences is transformed into *incomensurability* of individual and social utility. If individual utilities joining the market stream are brought to the same level for the multitude of individuals, social utility by definition (having a meaning of their aggregation as a whole) does not involve a process of reduction. These are qualitatively different types of utilities each defined in its own metrics and therefore to sum them up in any way, including the usage of weight functions, is evidently not correct.[340] That is how solving the 'paradox of state' is related to the 'problem of summarizing' individual and social utility.

We think that this methodological dead lock can be overcome with the help of one of the key mechanisms of economic sociodynamics — sociodynamic multiplier which ensures the removal of 'metrics damnation'.[341] A new 'point of view' and the analysis of the consequences of the implementation of irreducible interests

---

terovitch V. M., 1990. Economic Equilibrium and Economic mechanism. Moscow, p. 8, etc.).

[339]Let us mention the Soviet theory known as the System of Optimal Functioning of Economy. It aknowledges the existence of one criterion for the national economy. (Problems of Optimal Planning and Management of the Socialist Economy / ed. by N.P. Fedorenko).

[340]This is exactly, in our opinion, what the principal mistake of Margolis is. Accepting a possibility of the existence of an autonomous public interest he made an attempt to sum up this interest with the interests of individual members of society using the weights. Therefore, though assuming the existence of an irreducible need of the multitude of individuals he in fact tried to reduce this need to the interests of individuals.

[341]For a more detailed description of the sociodynamic multiplier and the analysis of the mechanism of its functioning see: Grinberg R., Rubinstein A. Op.cit., pp. 137-158.

allowed us to discover an important fact. We have already mentioned that raw products of military production or fundamental science – for example bacteriological weapons and mathematical theories – that *initially do not have any individual utility* in the end having gone through state consumption are transformed into *individual benefits,* reflected in the improvement of the public environment (defense and scientific potential of the country). Moreover, it can be stated that the implementation of irreducible interests of society creates a specific consumption effect, displaying the properties of public goods and thus affecting all members of society.

The sociodynamic multiplier, characterized by the interaction of the three components – social effect as a result of the implementation of irreducible public interest, the creative propensity of individuals and institutions of society –, is used in this process.[342] The availability of all three elements allows for the initiation of the mechanism of the sociodynamic multiplier when the implementation of the interests of society is transformed into individual benefits. That is what we mean when we speak of the multiplier as a mechanism of overcoming initial differences in the measurement of individual and social utilities.

The difference between the sociodynamic multiplier and the weight function explains the difference between our concept and the mentioned above Margolis model. It is also clear that the latter can be considered a particular case of sociodynamics for a situation when public interest is reduced to individual ones. In these circumstances all utility functions initially exist in one metrics, and the sociodynamic multiplier becomes an ordinary constant, reflecting the weight of social interest.

It should be stressed that the 'problem of summarizing' is left out of the traditional theory because if the reducibility of any needs is assumed, then consumption effects are always comparable. Inability to rightly evaluate the social effects is the reverse side of such 'narrow-minded' philosophy. Systematic underestimation of many state activities, aimed to serve its specific interests, is a consequence of such a situation.[343]

Meanwhile taking into account the transformation of social effects into individual benefits, secured by the multiplier, enables us to not only correctly evaluate the outcomes of the implementation of public interests but to look from another point of view at the standard economic description.

In this connection, the inaccuracy of summing up qualitatively different utilities forces to reject the classical means of analysis of state demand should be stressed. What is considered acceptable for the *determined* functions of individual utility (the law of diminishing utility) is not always right for the *stochastically deter-*

---

[342]Op. cit.

[343]It is prominently displayed in the evaluations of activities connected with merit goods. Using traditional mathematic models a number of authors demonstrate that the growth of the aggregate consumption income as a result of the implementation of a merit interest is less than the sum of state subsidies to producers of merit goods necessary to satisfy this public need (See, for example, Tietzel M., Müller C. Op.cit., p. 91). There is nothing unexpected here. Such a verdict directly follows from the fundamental theorems of welfare.

mined social utility. For this reason, the above-mentioned equilibrium condition should be modified. The following general statement is possible here: *marginal costs at the equilibrium point are equated by the marginal individual utility and state money demand* [344]

Now a very important definition of Pareto-improvement can be used for the part of the market space where the traditional assumption on reducibility of all needs is not true. In general, one should speak of the Pareto-improvement if the increase of well being of some market players (including state) does not worsen the well being of other players (including state). Then many actions of the state aimed at implementing irreducible public interest should be considered as Pareto improvements because they directly cause improvement in the position of state, while improvement in the position of individual market players can be secured by the mechanism of the socio-dynamic multiplier, transforming social effect into individual benefits. This conclusion enables us to adequately evaluate the real role of the state in various spheres in which it operates as well as to formulate one more rather important proposition, concerning criteria of state activities in compliance with the Pareto scheme. *The behavior of the state can be considered rational if it maximizes social utility, simultaneously implementing Pareto-improvement.*

Finishing this variation, we would like to quote a famous American culturologist and economist P. Di Maggio. Speaking about one of the social sectors, he mentions that 'the government needs courage and wisdom to support those spheres of culture that can count on neither commercial success nor the help of private philanthropists'.[345] In fact, such a seemingly benevolent attitude toward culture and emotional words conceals a typology for orthodox economic science's lack of understanding of the real state of affairs and the underestimation of the true value of goods and services capable of satisfying interests of society as such. Social utility of these goods simply demands the rational behaviour of government as an economic entity rather than courage or even wisdom.

---

[344]Mathematic analysis of the state money demand requires modelling of two processes, namely stochastic process of generating irreducible social interest and the reverse process of individualization of social effect, or mechanism of sociodynamic multiplier. We think that the construction of these models though being quite a difficult task is nevertheless possible especially with the help of the modern relativity theory tools and mathematic methods of chaotic systems analysis.

[345]Will the Culture Survive in Market Conditions? Saint-Petersburg, 1996, p. 63.

References

Andel N. Zum Konzept der meritorischen Güter, Finanzarchiv 42, 1984.

Arrow K.J. Social Choice and Individual Values. 2nd Ed. New York: Wiley, 1963.

Arrow K.J. The Potentials and Limits of the Market in Resource Allocation, in Feiwel, ed., Issues in Contemporary Microeconomics and Welfare, 1985 (Russian Edition: THESIS: Theory and History of Economic and Social Institutions. – Moscow, 1993, V. 1, No. 2).

Arrow K.J. Values and Collective Decision-Making. Philosophy and Economic Theory. Oxford, 1979.

Atkinson A.B., Stiglitz J.E. Lectures on public economics. New York: McGraw-Hill, 1980 (Russian Edition – Moscow, 1995)

Baumol W.J., Bowen W.G. Performing Arts: The Economic Dilemma. The Twentieth Century Fund. New York, 1966.

Baumol's Cost Disease: The Arts and other Victims. Ed. Ruth Towse. University of Exeter, London, 1997.

Bergson A. A Reformulation of Certain Aspects of Welfare Economics. In: Quarterly Journal of Economics, February 1938.

Blaug M. Economic Theory in Retrospect. Fifth English edition. Cambridge: Cambridge University Press, 1997 (Russian Edition – Moscow, 1994)

Bonus H. Verzauberte Dörfer, oder: Solidarität, Ungleichheit und Zwang. ORDO 29, 1978.

Boyd R., Richardson P.J. Culture and the Evolutionary Process. Chicago: University of Chicago Press, 1985.

Brennan G., Lomasky L. Institutional Aspects of 'Merit Goods' Analysis, Finanzarchiv 41, 1983, S. 183-206.

Buchanan J. The Limits of Liberty: Between Anarchy and Leviathan. Chicago: The University of Chicago Press, 1975 (Russian Edition: Nobel Prize Winners in Economics. James Buchanan. – Moscow, 1997)

Buchanan J., Tullock G. The Calculus of Consent: Logical Foundations of Constitutional Democracy. Ann Arbor Paperbacks, 1962 (Russian Edition: Nobel Prize Winners in Economics. James Buchanan. – Moscow, 1997)

Buchanan J.M. Liberty, Market and State, Brighton, 1986.

Buchanan J.M. The Constitution of Economic Policy, in: Buchanan J.M. Noble Prize Winners in Economics (Russian Edition, Moscow: Taurus Alfa, 1997).

Buchanan J.M. The Domain of Constitutional Economics. Constitutional Political Economy 1, 1990, pp. 1-18.

Coase R.H. The Firm, the Market and the Law. Chicago, IL: University of Chicago Press, 1988.

Coase R.H. The Problem of Social Cost. In: Journal of Law and Economics 3, 1960, pp. 1-44.

Cuhel F. Zur Lehre von den Bedürfnissen, Innsbruck, 1907.

De Viti de Marco A. Grundlehren der Finanzwirtschaft, Tübingen, 1932.

Elster J. Ulysses and Sirens, Cambridge, 1979.

Eucken W. Grundsätze der Wirtschaftspolitik, 6. Auflage, 1990, Tübingen.

Fichte J. Einige Vorlesungen über die Bestimmung des Gelehrten. — 1794, p. 306. Cited in: Michel H. L'idée de l'état. Essai critiquesur l'histoire des theories sociales eu politiques en France depuis la révolution. – Moscow: Tipografia Tovarishestva Sytina, 1909 – p. 68.

Fischer S., Dornbusch R., Schmalensee R. Economics, 2nd Ed. New York: McGraw-Hill, 1988. (Russian Edition – Moscow, 1997)

Friedman M. Four Steps to Freedom. «National Review», 1990, May 14.

Golitsyn G.A. From Collectivism to Individualism (In Russian). In: Kulturologhicheskiye zapiski (Culturological Notes), No. 2, 1997.

Grinberg R., Rubinstein A. Difficulties in Market Adjustment: Prices, Incomes, Social Security (In Russian). In: Obshestvennye Nauki i Sovremennost (Social Sciences and the Present) No.5, 1995, p.43-44.

Grinberg R., Rubinstein A. Ökonomische Soziodynamik und rationales Verhalten des Staates. Köln, 1999.

Grinberg R., Rubinstein A. On the General Theory of Social Economy (In Russian). In: Ekonomicheskaya Nauka Sovremennoy Rossii, 1998, No.2.

Grinberg R., Rubinstein A. Social Economy: a New System of Economic Axioms (In Russian). In: Rossiysky Ekonomichesky Zhurnal. – 1997, No.1.

Grinberg R., Rubinstein A. Social Rent in the Theory of Rational Behavior of the State (In Russian). In: Rossiysky Ekonomichesky Zhurnal (Russian Economic Journal). No. 3, 1998, pp. 58-66.

Habermas J. Legitimationsprobleme im Spätkapitalismus. – Frankfurt a. M., 1973.

Habermas J. Zur Logik der theoretischen und praktischen Diskurses. In: Riedel M. (Hrsg.) Rehabilitierung der praktischen Philosophie. Bd. 2. – Freiburg, 1974.

Hansmeyer K.-H., Caesar R., Koths D., Siedenberg A. Steuern auf spezielle Güter. In: Andel N., Haller H., Neumark F. (Hrsg.), Handbuch der Finanzwissenschaft, Band 2,3. Auflage, Tübingen, 1980, S.734.

Hayek A.F. The political order of a free people, Chicago, Ill.: Univ. of Chicago Press, 1979 (Russian Edition – Society of Free People. Overseas Publ. Interchange, London, 1990).

Hayek F.A. Freiburger Studien. Tübingen, 1969.

Hayek F.A. Scientism and the Study of Society. Part II, Section VII. In: Economica, 1943.

Hayek F.A. The Road to Serfdom. Chicago: The University of Chicago Press, 1994 (Russian Edition – Moscow, 1992)

Head J.G. On Merit Goods, Finanzarchiv 25, 1966.

Head J.G. On Merit Wants, Finanzarchiv 46, 1988.

Hegel G.W.F. Vorlesungen über die Philosophie der Geschichte, in Hegel G.W.F. Werke, Bd.12. Frankfurt/Main: 1969-1971 (Russian Edition: Collected Works. – Moscow, 1932, V.X).

Herman F.B.W. Staatswirtschaftliche Untersuchungen, 2. Aufl., München, 1870.

Hobbes T. Leviathan. Hamburg: Meiner, 1996 (Russian Edition – Moscow, 1991, V.2).

Hofecker F.-O. Current Trends in the Financing of Culture in Europe. European Task Force on Culture & Development. Circle-Round-Table. Barcelona, 1995.

Howard K., Zhuravlyova G. Principles of Economics of Free Market System. — Moscow: Zlatoust, 1995.

Jakobson L.I. Economics of Public Sector. Foundations of the Theory of Public Finances (In Russian) – Moscow, 1996.

Jakobson L.I. ublic Sector of the Economy. Economic Theory and Policy. Moscow: SU-HSE, 2000.

Jecht H. Wesen und Formen der Finanzwirtschaft, Jena, 1928.

Johansson S. The Computer Paradigm and the Role of Cultural Information in Social Systems. Historical Methods, N 21, 1988.

Kaizl. J. Finanzwissenschaft, 1.Teil, Wien, 1900.

Kant I. Foundations of the Metaphysics of Morals. Chicago: University of Chicago Press, 1950 (Russian Edition: Collected Works. – Moscow, 1965, V. 4(2)).

Keynes J..M. The General Theory of Employment, Interest and Money. London, Macmillan, 1936 (Russian Edition – Moscow, 1993).

Khodov L.G. Grounds of State Economic Policy (In Russian). – Moscow: Verlag C.H. Beck, 1997.

Koboldt C. Ökonomie der Versuchung; Drogenverbot und Sozialvertragstheorie, Tübingen, 1995.

Koslowski P. Gesellschaft und Staat. Ein unvermeidlicher Dualismus. Stuttgart: Klett-Cotta Verlag, 1982 (Russian Edition – Moscow, 1998).

Kovelman A.B. The Crowd and the Sages in Early Rabbinical Literature. Moscow: Evreiskij Universitet, 1996.

Krueger A.O. The Political Economy of the Rent-Seeking Society. In: American Economic Review, 1974, vol. 64, p. 291-301.

Lindahl E. Die Gerechtigekeit der Besteuerung, Lund, 1919.

Locke J. Two Treatises on Government, 3 Vols. – Moscow: Mysl, 1988, V. 3.

Macpherson C.B. Die politischen Theorie des Besitzindividualismus. Von Hobbes zu Loocke, Frankfurt a.M., 1973.

Makarov V.L. Why is Russian Economy Inefficient? (In Russian) In: Vlast. – 1998, No.6.

Makarov V.L., Rubinov A.M. Mathematic Theory of Economic Dynamics and Equilibrium. Moscow, 1973.

Mandeville B. The Fable of the Bees. (Harmondsworth, Penguin, 1970 (Russian Edition – Moscow, 1974)

Margolis H. Selfishness, Altruism and Rationality: A Theory of Social Choice. Cambridge: Cambridge University Press, 1982.

McConnell C.R. Brue S.L. Economics: principles, problems, and policies. Boston, Mass.: McGraw-Hill, 2002.

McLure C.E. Merit Wants: a Normatively Empty Box, Finanzarchiv 27, 1968.

Menger C. Grundsätze der Volkswirtschaftslehre, 2. Aufl., Wien-Leipzig, 1923.

Michel H. L'idée de l'état. Essai critiquesur l'histoire des theories sociales eu politiques en France depuis la révolution. – Moscow: Tipografia Tovarishestva Sytina, 1909.

Milchakova N. Evolution of the Neoclassical Theory in Works by Kenneth Arrow (In Russian). In: Voprosy Ekonomiki (Economic Issues), No.5, 1995, pp. 108-113.

Mill J.S. A system of logic, ratiocinative and inductive; being a connected view of the principles of evidence, and the methods of scientific investigation. New York and London: Harper & Brothers, 1900 (Russian Edition – Moscow, 1914)

Mises L. von, Liberalism in the Classical Tradition. – Irvington on Hudson, New York, 1985.

Moll A. Sociodynamics of Culture (Russian Edition). – Moscow, 1973.

Müller-Armack, A. Wirtschaftslenkung und Marktwirtschaft. Hamburg: Verlag für Wirtschaft und Sozialpolitik, 1996.

Musgrave R.A, Musgrave P.B, Kullmer L. Die öffentlichen Finanzen in Theorie und Praxis, Band 1, 6. Auflage, Tübingen, 1994.

Musgrave R.A. A Multiple Theory of Budget Determination. Finanzarchiv 17, 1957, p. 333-343.

Musgrave R.A. Finanztheorie. Tübingen, 1974.

Musgrave R.A. Fiscal Systems. New Haven, 1969.

Musgrave R.A. Merit Goods. In: Eatwell J., Milgate M., Newman P. (Hrsg.). The New Palgrave, London-Basingstoke, 1987, S.452-453.

Musgrave R.A. Principles of Budget Determination. In: Joint Economic Committee, Federal Expenditure Policy for Economic Growth and Stability, Washington, 1957, pp. 108-115.

Musgrave R.A. Provision for Social Goods. In: J Margolis, H.Guitton (eds.). Public Economics. London-Basingstoke, 1969.

Musgrave R.A. The Theory of Public Finance. N.Y.-London, 1959.

Nekipelov A.D. Essays on the Economics of Postcommunism (In Russian). – Moscow: IIEPS/RAS, 1996.

Nesterenko A.N. Current State and Basic Problems of Institutionalism (In Russian). In: Voprosy Ekonomiki (Economic Issues), No. 3, 1997.

North D.C. Institutionen, institutioneller Wandel und Wirtschaftsleistungen, Tuebingen, 1992 (Russian Edition – Moscow, 1997).

Olson M. Toward a More Theory of Governmental Structure. Budget Reform and of Theory of Fiscal Federalism. AEA Papers and Proceedings, May 1986, Vol. 76, No. 2, pp. 120-125.

Pareto V. Manual of Political Economy. Augustus M. Kelley, New York, 1971.

Pigou A.C. The Economics of Welfare. London: Macmillan, 1962 (Russian Edition – Moscow, 1985).

Plato. Der Staat. Zürich: Artemis-Verl., 1950 (Russian Edition – Moscow, 1971, V. 3(2))

Plato. Laws. Amherst, N.Y.: Prometheus Books, 2000 (Russian Edition – Moscow, 1971, V. 3(1))

Plato. Protagoras, Philebus, and Gorgia. Amherst, N.Y.: Prometheus Books, 1996 (Russian Edition – Moscow, 1968, Vol. 1).

Polanyi K. The Self-Regulating Market and the Fictitious Commodities: Labor, Land and Money. In: K.Polanyi. The Great Transformation. N.Y.: Farrar & Rinehart, Inc., 1944.

Polterovich V.M. Crisis of the Economic Theory (In Russian). In: Ekonomicheskaya Nauka Sovremennoy Rossii (Economics in Russia Today), No. 1, 1998, p.54.

Polterovich V.M. On the Way to a New Theory of Reforms (In Russian). In: Ekonomicheskaya Nauka Sovremennoy Rossii. – 1999, No. 3.

Pommerehne W.W., Hart A. Drogenpolitik aus ökonomischer Sicht. In: G. Grozinger (Hrsg.), Recht auf Sucht, Berlin, 1991, S.66-96.

Popper K. Open Society and Its Enemies. V.2. Princeton: Princeton University Press, 1971 (Russian Edition – Moscow, 1992, V.2)

Priddat B.P. Zur Ökonomie der Gemeinschaftsbedürfnisse: Neuere Versuche einer ethischen Begründung der Theorie meritorischer Güter, Zeitschrift für Wirtschafts-und Sozialwissenschaften 112, 1992, S. 239-259.

Prigogine I. Stengers I. Time, Chaos, Quantum. Towards Solving the Paradox of Time. Moscow: Editorial URSS, 2000.

Prigogine, I. Order out of chaos: man's dialogue with nature. London: Heinemann, 1984.

Ramo S. Cure for Chaos: Fresh Solutions to Social Problems Through the Systems Approach. – N.Y., 1969.

Rawls J. A Theory of Justice. Oxford: Oxford University Press, 1980. (Russian Edition – Novosibirsk, 1995).

Ritschl H. Theorie der Staatswirtschaft und Besteuerung, Bonn und Leipzig, 1925.

Rubinstein A. (Ed.). Artistic Life of Contemporary Society. Arts in the Context of Social Economy (In Russian). – Moscow, 1998, T. 3.

Rubinstein A. Introduction into Economics of Performing Art (In Russian). – Moscow: Teatron, 1991, pp. 18-22, 188-190.

Rubinstein A. On the Theory of Prices, Subsidies and Rent (In Russian). In.: Economics of Culture: Intensification Issues. – Moscow, 1986, p. 39-41.

Samuelson P. Reaffirming the Existence of «Reasonable» Bergson-Samuelson Social Welfare Functions. - Economics, 1978, N 173.

Samuelson P.A. Economics (Russian Edition). – Moscow, 1992, T. 1, T. 2.

Samuelson P.A. The pure theory of public expenditure. Review of Economics and Statistics, 1954;

Samuelson P.A. The pure theory of public expenditures and taxation. Public Economics, J.Margolis and H.Guitton (Eds), Macmillan, London, 1969.

Samuelson P.A., Nordhaus W.D. Economics. New York: McGraw-Hill, 1992 (Russian Edition – Moscow, 1997)

Sax E. Grundlegung der theoretischen Staatswirtschaft, Wien, 1987.

Schaffle A.E.F. Das gesellschaftliche System der menschlichen Wirtschaft, 3. Aufl., 1. Band, Tubingen, 1873.

Schelling T.C. Ethics, Law and the Exercise of Self-Command. In: ders., Choice and Consequence, Cambridge-London, 1984.

Schlesinger A.M. The Cycles of American History. Boston: Mifflin, 1986. (Russian Edition – Moscow, 1992)

Schmidt K. Mehr zur Meritorik. Kritisches und Alternatives zu der Lehre von den öffentlichen Gütern. In: Zeitschrift für Wirtschafts – und Sozialwissenschaften. 108. Jahrgang 1988 Heft 3.

Schmidt K. Zur Geschichte der Lehre von den Kollektivbedürfnissen. In: Kloten N. u.a. (Hrsg.). Systeme und Methoden in den Wirtschafts-und Sizialwissenschaften, Erwin von Beckerath zum 75. Geburtstag, Tübingen, 1964.

Seligman E.R.A. Die gesellschaftliche Theorie der Finanzwirtschaft. In: Die Wirtschaftstheorie der Gegenwart, 4 Band, Wien, 1928.

Seligmen B. Basic Trends of Contemporary Economic Thought (In Russian). Moscow, 1968.

Silvestrov S.N. Politics as Business (In Russian). In: Rossiysky Ekonomichesky Zhurnal, 1995, No. 2.

Smith A. An Inquiry into the Nature and Causes of the Wealth of Nations. London: Dent, 1981 (Russian Edition – Moscow, 1962)

Smith A. The Theory of Moral Sentiments. Cambridge: Cambridge University Press, 2002 (Russian Edition – Moscow, 1997)

Society on Research of Jewish Communities. Brief Jewish Encyclopaedia. Jerusalem, 1988, V. 4.

Stiglitz J. Economics of the Public Sector. London, New York: WW Norton & Co., 1988 (Russian Edition – Moscow, 1997)

Sugden R. The Economics of Rights, Co-operation, and Welfare. Oxford: Blackwell, 1986, p. 173.

Taylor M. Community, Anarchy and Liberty. Cambridge: Cambridge University Press, 1982.

Taylor M. The Possibility of Co-operation. Cambridge: Cambridge University Press, 1987.

Thaler R.H., Shefrin H.M. An Economic Theory of Self-Control. In: Journal of Political Economy 89, 1981, pp. 392-406.

Tietzel M. Zur Theorie der Präferenzen. Jahrbuch für Neue Politische Ökonomie, 1988, pp. 38-71.

Tietzel M., Müller C. Noch mehr zur Meritorik. In: Zeitschrift für Wirtschafts – und Sozialwissenschaften. 118. Jahrgang 1998 Heft 1, Duncker & Humblot, Berlin.

Toffler A. The Third Wave. New York: Morrow, 1980 (Russian Edition – Moscow, 1999)

Veblen T. The Place of Science in Modern Civilisation and Other Essays. New York: Huebsch, 1919.

Von Neumann J., Morgenstern O. Theory of Games and Economic Behavior. Princeton: Princeton University Press, 1944 (Russian Edition – Moscow, 1970).

Wagner A. Grundlegung der politischen Ökonomie, 3. Aufl., 1. Theil, 2. Halbband, Leipzig, 1893.

Weizsaecker E.U. von, Lovins A.B., Lovins L.H. Factor Four: Doubling Wealth — Halving Resource Use. The New Report to the Club of Rome. London: Earthscan Publ., 1998 (Russian Edition – Moscow, 2000).

About the Authors

Prof. Dr. Ruslan S. Grinberg (1946) is Director of the Institute for International Economic and Political Studies, Russian Academy of Sciences. He graduated from the Moscow State University and received doctor's degree in economy from the Russian Academy of Sciences. Grinberg holds the professor's chair at the Moscow School of Economics, Moscow State University. He published over 150 papers and books both in Russia and abroad on international monetary policy and macroeconomic issues, and is lecturing a lot in the USA and Europe. He is a consultant to the Russian State Duma and Ministry of the Russian Federation for Economic Development and Trade and chairs the CIS  Committee of the National Investment Council. Grinberg is Vice-Chair of the Russian ECAAR (Economists allied for Arms Reduction), co-founder and member of the Russian-American Economic Transition Group (ETG), Editor-in- Chief of the international journal *The World of Changes*.

Prof. Dr. Alexander J. Rubinstein (1947) is Director of the Institute for Social Economy, Russian Academy of Sciences, professor at the Moscow School of Economics, Moscow State University; and heads the chair at the Higher School of the Chekhov Art Theater, Moscow. He received MS in math from the Moscow State University, doctor's degrees in economy and philosophy from the Russian Academy of Sciences. Rubinstein lectured on cultural economics at Yale University (USA), Heriott-Watt University (Scotland), and Hamburg High School for Arts (Germany). He is a member of ERICArts (European Institute for Comparative Cultural Research) and Association for Cul-  tural Economics International (ACEI). Rubinstein published over 200 books and papers both in Russia and abroad on the issues of theoretical and applied cultural economics, general economic theory and social economics.

Further Publications by R. Grinberg

Regional Dimension of the Market Transformation in Russia, in: Real and Financial Economic Dynamics in Russia and Eastern Europe (T.Lane, N.Oding, P.J.J.Welfens (Eds.)), Berlin, Springer-Verlag, 2003.

Integration und Desintegration im postsowjetischen Wirtschaftsraum, in: Regionale Integration und Osterweiterung der Europäischen Union. Lucius & Lucius, Stuttgart, 2003.

Ergebnisse der Wirtschaftstransformation in Osteuropa. Allgemeine Merkmale und russische Spezifika, in: Oekonomie – Kultur – Politik. Transformationsprozesse in Osteuropa. Bremen, Edition Temmen, 2003.

Russia in the Post-Soviet Space: Is the Rebirth of the Soviet Union Possible? In: Between the Past and the Future: Russia in the Transatlantic Context, Moscow, 2001.

Trade Within the Commonwealth of Independent States, in: The New Russia: Transition Gone Awry. Stanford, California, Stanford University Press, 2001.

The Deceptive Recovery of the Russian Economy: Alternatives to Economic Policies in Russia, in: Beyond Transition: Ten Years after the Fall of the Berlin Wall. New York, UNDP, 2000.

Zur Zwischenbilanz der Wirtschaftsreform in Rußland, in: Die Staaten des östlichen Europa auf dem Weg in die europäische Integration: Analysen und Perspektiven. Bonn 1999.

Towards Competition in Network Industries (P.J.J.Welfens, G.Yarrow, R.Grinberg, C.Graack (Eds.)), Berlin, Springer-Verlag, 1999.

CMEA History: the Rise and Fall of Socialist Economic Integration, in: Eastern Europe: Joining the World Market, 1998.

Russland und die GUS: Auf der Suche nach einem neuen Modell wirtschaftlicher Zusammenarbeit (mit L.Kosikova), BIOST, Nr. 50, 1997.

Further Publications by A. J. Rubinstein

Рубинштейн А.Я. Структура и эволюция социального интереса. – Moskau, 2003.

Экономические аспекты культурной деятельности. Индивидуальные предпочтения и общественный интерес. В 3 томах (Под общей редакцией Рубинштейна А.Я.) - СПб., 2002.

Художественная жизнь современного общества. В 4 томах (Гл. ред. Рубинштейн А.Я.). – СПб., 1995-2001.

Rubinstein A. Finanzierung der Kultur in Russland: Analyse und Mechanismus der Staatlichen Unterstützung, BIOST, Köln, 1997.

Rubinstein A., Baumol W., Baumol H. On the Economics of the Performing Arts in the USSR and the USA: A Preliminary Comparison of the Data. in «Cultural Economics». New York London Paris, Springer-Verlag, 1992.

Рубинштейн А.Я. Введение в экономику исполнительского искусства. – Moskau, 1991.

Rubinstein A.J. Issues of Price and Subsidy in the Arts in The U.S.S.R. Akron, USA, Journal of Cultural Economics, Volume 11, N2, 1987.